Title Page

The Astrological Foundation Of The Christ
Myth, Book Four ... Second Edition

By Malik H. Jabbar

Published By

Rare Books Distributor

PO Box 3224

Dayton, Oh 45401

http://www.malikjabbarbooks.com

Copyright

Library Of Congress Catalog Card Number

LCCN: 2019907647

ISBN 10: 1-57154-012-1

ISBN 13: 978-1-57154-012-6

Contents

Books In Print 2019

BOOKS AUTHORED BY MALIK H. JABBAR

The Biggest Lie Ever Told 4th Edition — $9.95

The Astrological Foundation Of The Christ Myth Book One — $9.95

The Astrological Foundation Of The Christ Myth Book Two — $14.95

The Astrological Foundation Of The Christ Myth Book Three — $14.95

The Astrological Foundation Of The Christ Myth Book Four — $14.95

Lifting The Gnostic Veil — $14.95

Secret Origins Of Judaism — $14.95

WWW.MALIKJABBARBOOKS.COM

PREFACE TO THE SECOND EDITION

Preface

This is the fourth book of a 4-book series of books on the subject of Astro-theology. Astro-Theology is defined as religious theology structured in reflection of ancient star lore. The premise being, that the ancients of various cultures, including the cultures of the Near East region, formed much of their tribal and cultural mythologies based on the anthropomorphizing of the risings, transits, settings, and occultations of the cosmic lights. The cosmic lights were fashioned by the ancient ones as deities, warriors, demons, and other various appellations. The risings of the heavenly lights were recorded as births in the ancient star lore, the transits signified the life-span of the personified star-characters, the settings of the stars signified the death and/or imprisonment of these mythic cosmic figures. The occultations were, at times, an indication of battle or defeat or triumph of one starry light (personified mythical figure) over its rival. As the cultures advanced over the millennia, and religion slowly evolved from within, the mythological star-stories became the basis for the evolving religious lore of these cultures, and thus many of the signs and symbols of ancient star-lore remain today as fundamental components within the theology of our modern religions. This book deals with the unveiling of the astro-theological symbolisms and myths yet current within modern religion.

This is the 2nd Edition of the book. All of the essential information of the 1st edition remains, with much improved clarity I believe. Astro-theology, being that it is based on the science of astronomy, can, at times, be a very intricate study. This is why I have written the book in a series of four books which incrementally delves into this interesting and sometimes challenging arena.

I have added much information to this 2nd edition that is not found in the 1st edition. I am confident that this edition will serve to rise the reader to a much more advanced understanding of this subject.

Malik H Jabbar

INTRODUCTION

Introduction

A Guide to The Purposes And Focus Of This Book

This is the fourth and final book of the series of books titled *The Astrological Foundation Of The Christ Myth*. Books *One, Two* and *Three* have served to lay the foundation for the extensive interpretations that are offered in this volume.

Our search is for Truth - throughout the three previously published volumes of this four-part series of books, we have focused on proving that religion, as we know it, is actually the symbolic rendering of natural phenomena. That is to say that the mythical stories embodied within religious text, in truth, actually describe cosmic interactions recorded over the millennia (by the Priesthood) whereas the celestial entities (planets, stars, sun, moon, cycles, constellations) are labeled as personified deities and the courses and cycles of these heavenly objects are likened to the intrigues, wars, conflicts, marriages, etc. of human types, royal and common. We have traced the origin of religious culture from its root as astronomy, evolved into myth and finally into modern religion. We have shown that ancient primordial man, in his never-ending struggle to survive amidst the sometimes devastating forces of nature, found it incumbent to *study* and *record* the cycles of the seasons, the planets, sun, moon and stars and their associations with the earthly environment. This was necessary so as to take a cue from the cosmic and other cycles as indicators of regular cyclical environmental changes. And by observing and heeding the warnings and forecasts indicated by various cosmic cycles, humanity was more or less able to safely sidestep and/or adjust to the vicissitudes of the natural environment.

Humanity's survival is dependent, (and has always depended) on our ability to cope with and profit from our ecological environment. Mankind's earliest supplications to the deities, which prayers were often instigated by fear and superstition, were indeed desperate efforts toward gaining supernatural assistance to withstand the

INTRODUCTION

sometimes-hostile forces of nature, as well as earnest solicitations for divine aid in harnessing the seemingly fickle forces of Mother Earth in the never-ending quest for food, shelter, and clothing. The primary focus of the aboriginal inhabitants of this planet was survival, period.

The spiritual concept of god, as maintained by our ancient ancestors, was engendered by superstition and animism on one hand; and on the other hand, by a perceived cultural need to invoke the assistance and/or mercy of the supernatural divine spirits that (they perceived) controlled the forces of nature. They yearned for god's help in harnessing, contending, and withstanding the various pestering, combative and hostile natural forces within their ecological environment. Our *spiritual path* to god in this era (era of modern religion) is, in fact, *a continuation of the primitive and superstitious path pursued by our ancient primeval ancestors* of the ageless past; hence, in our effort to correctly and clearly define this enigma called religion, we must go back in history and attempt to *reevaluate our concepts of the earliest cultural forces that launched us upon the puzzling theological path* that we now tread.

The truth of religious symbolism lies in correctly understanding the history of its evolution – from primordial times to the present. The fundamentals for crafting these symbolisms were established long ago in prehistoric eras, that is to say before the establishment of writing, at a time when humanity did not express their ideas in books or journals, but rather through oral traditions. They had not the ability to write or read and their grunting languages consisted of only a few hundred general and ambiguous words and/or gestures that related to their limited knowledge and understanding of their ecological surroundings. They supplemented and augmented their languages by incorporating signs (pictures) and symbols as means of expressing and/or preserving ideas and information. They often drew or imitated the images of animals, birds, insects and natural objects to express and preserve their thoughts and ideas. For instance, a lion may have symbolized strength, bulls fertility, rabbits procreation. Migratory animals that appeared during certain seasons may have been used pictorially or in gestures to indicate the coming or arrival of that

INTRODUCTION

season with which they were associated. Likewise with cosmic configurations that accompanied certain seasons or natural activities such as floods or rains and sowing and harvesting etc. – these starry configurations may have been exhibited pictorially (drawn on natural rock formations, cave walls etc.) or in gesture or dance so as to indicate the coming seasons with which particular constellations were associated. The *declinations* of the sun and *phases* of the moon were, of course, prominent indicators of environmental changes and seasons as well as measurers of time.

These old primitive customs *and more* are the foundations from which our modern religious cultures have evolved - the major focus of this Chapter (Introduction) is pursuant to proving that fact. In this book, we bring final, or at the least, enhanced clarity to many theological or scriptural mysteries of the ages, such as the book of Revelations and various other enigmatic portions of the bible. We have successfully interpreted the mystical signs and symbols of our modern religious doctrines by deductively tracing them to their origins. Within this book we shall explore the evolution of religion from a more precise perspective than perhaps we have heretofore endeavored. Our premise and focus is clear, that is to say that by accurately defining and interpreting the mysteries of the past *with precise correlations to the present* we have successfully and accurately unveiled the truth in a way and manner that no rational mind can reasonably doubt.

Evolution Of Religion

In order to properly evaluate and trace the evolution of religion and its impact on our modern religious culture, we must go far back in time to the *earliest anthropological and archeological indications of the ascendancy of man* from roving bands of scattered families, foraging and hunting for foodstuffs wherever possible, to nascent establishments of settled tribal communities.

The history of ancient mans emergence from the *nomadic state* into *settled communities* with organizational structure, agriculture, animal husbandry, and the partitioning of permanent hereditary duties to

INTRODUCTION

families and/or members of the community, the nascent formations of Military, Royal, Ecclesiastical and Artisan Class structures with centralized authority and rules of conduct is *Key* to pinpointing the embryonic cultural and social traditions that over the millennia would eventually evolve into the social force popularly known today as *revealed religion*, inclusive of its social creeds and spiritual concepts. In fact all forms of religion practiced in this (our) era can be traced to this same type source or origin. Our religious doctrines are an evolutionary and symbolical reflection of mankind's historical interaction with nature, shielded in myth and fable. *These myths and fables of the distant past have evolved into our modern religious concepts.* There is no truth to the concept of Revealed Religion (Revelation From a god (supernatural spirit) to a messenger (prophet)) – all religious beliefs are the result of mankind's cultural evolution, and the Key to interpreting the myths and symbols embodied therein is found when we accurately separate *actual* history from *mythical* history, and then *evaluate* the actual history *dispassionately* – and this task is not easily accomplished when and if we are *emotionally attached* to any particular religious persuasion. I *must* re-emphasize that the *Key* to unlocking the veiled theological mysteries of the distant past and thereby shedding great and illuminating light upon the religious enigmas of the present, lay in *uncovering* and *analyzing* the early social structures of the *first settled agricultural communities* emerging from pre-history. That is *not* to say that mankind did not possess potent god concepts in his nomadic phases – most certainly he did, especially if we accept the widely held assumption that *belief* in a great-unknown *first cause* or *emanating spirit* is the natural outgrowth of an advancing human intellect - the intellectual human most often espouses a natural curiosity of the unknown. Natural history and Time have no beginning, no origin that we can point to, no year one (or 0) so to speak; and herein lays the eternal unfulfilled quest of the *enlightened* of mankind – to find this Source (First Cause) of our beginnings with the hope that such knowledge will help unveil our ultimate purpose and destiny as a species. Of course there are some that assert that life or nature holds no teleological secrets; I do *not* share that attitude.

INTRODUCTION

Evolution Of The Priesthood

The evolution of religious thought from primitive times to the present is explainable but entails a dispassionate study of history and some common unbiased logic. The first step in this long process of religious evolution started with the emergence of the Priesthood. They evolved from a class of *Star Gazers* and *Naturalist* whose appointed hereditary duty, within ancient society, was the recording and forecasting of seasonal transitions. They (the Stargazers) signaled the planting of seeds and the harvesting of the crops. They studied and measured the cycles of time and the seasons by observing and recording the comings and goings of the celestial entities i.e. star groups and constellations – and noting the terrestrial associations (rainfall, flooding, drought, animal migration, etc.) that accompanied the arrival and departure of these cosmic entities (stars, planets, asterisms, etc.) to and from specified coordinates. They were the first astronomers and meteorologists and masters of mathematics, which was a required skill within their ranks.

These early societies were stratified – whatever caste or class that an individual was born of determined his destiny throughout life, that is to say the obligation of the child to his society and rank or position within the society was inherited from the parents. This worked fine for the stargazers, in that the academic skills developed within their pivotal profession as prognosticators, and recorders of Time Cycles and Seasonal Transitions blossomed intellectually far, far beyond the scope of the masses. Their abilities became prodigious over time, to the amazement of the common classes. They not only predicted the coming of the seasons in their order, but they forecasted the rains, the floods, solar and lunar eclipses, the phases of the moon and declinations of the sun and the Impact of their transits upon the land and its inhabitants. They charted the heavens, grouped the stars and named them. These stargazers garnered this phenomenal knowledge and ability at a time when the general public was overwhelmingly illiterate – they became a lordly class unto themselves. They cherished their supreme position and it was, of course, preserved within the caste system that prevailed. But the security afforded by Class distinction was not enough for these elitists who through

INTRODUCTION

superior knowledge had de facto control of the ancient emerging world which over time would evolve from community farms into city-states and into empires. Overtime they encoded their knowledge into cryptic (symbolical) form – they invented the language of esoteric mythology, symbolism and allegory –an arcane mystical code that could only be correctly interpreted by those of the same or similar status who would have normally undergone similar tutelage as to that which prevailed among those of their elite class.

THIS ANCIENT MYSTICAL CODE that was incorporated to *preserve* and *enshroud* the wisdom and knowledge of the emerging sacerdotal class of antiquity is the archetypical mythology that has confounded common society spiritually and interpretatively down to this day. This mythology at the *exoteric* level is literal *nonsense* but within its esoteric folds resides the supreme wisdom of the ages.

When Primitive man began to settle in agricultural communities, it became necessary that they regulate their farming and animal husbandry within the constraints of the seasonal changes. It therefore was necessary for the tribes to assign some individuals (stargazers) to devote themselves to the study and tracking of the coming seasons and of course to financially support these appointees who worked for the common good. The offices or positions of these appointees (stargazers) were hereditary and their scientific knowledge increased exponentially and was kept strictly secret, not shared with the other levels of society. Their cosmic prognostications took on the aspect of secret wisdom; and of course it was to their advantage to conceal their methods and knowledge so as to secure their privileged position in society. So as society evolved religiously (over thousands of years), these astronomers and mathematicians (calculators of the seasons) became the primary ministers of religious thought, thus the sacerdotal class was begun.

In order to clearly understand the seminal evolution of religion as emanating from the science of astronomy, we must recognize that this process of religious evolution covered many thousands of years. The actual birth of the process is forever lost in antiquity, and the motivations of those who engineered and in later times diverted (or modified) the *focus* of the process (in terms of the mythical and/or

INTRODUCTION

religious illustrations of cosmic and other physical realities in encoded symbolic forms) were varied. I am sure that the *original focus or purpose* of the sacerdotal class in communicating their astronomical knowledge in an encrypted (mythological) form *was secrecy*; but as the exoteric fiction (Mythology) morphed and merged into religious doctrine and ritualism, then also *a societal function emerged* wherein the mores, customs, and rituals derived from mythologically based religions became the mechanisms by which the effected societies were guided and controlled by the elite classes. ORIGINALLY, the primitive stargazers (astronomers) of primordial times were certainly dedicated to the common good of their tribes. But as the centuries passed and their intellectual advances so greatly exceeded those of the general population, they succumbed to the inevitable temptations of avarice and lust for power. They applied their superior knowledge in a way that enhanced and secured their privileged status. First of all their positions as Timekeepers were hereditary, so this served to keep their advanced knowledge of mathematics, astronomy and meteorology confined within close ranks. But this did not satisfy them – they also established secret codes and symbols so that their knowledge was elevated to another language that was incomprehensible to the uninitiated. They covered the possibilities of dissension within their families also so as to prevent the unworthy or untrustworthy access to this esoteric wisdom; they established secret and closed societies for those that were chosen as candidates to be trained in the mysteries of their esoteric wisdom. The candidates had to pass certain arduous test, which served to gauge their loyalty and dedication to the inner circle. They also had to swear life and death oaths - that they would never reveal the secrets of their closed society. Even when the candidates were accepted, all the doors of the esoteric wisdom were not opened to them. The ancient Priests established a tier system for the gradual advancement of the potential hierophants – knowledge was unveiled to the candidates in degrees and each advancement required tasks of qualification.

The ancient Priesthood of primordial times and early civilization possessed an environmental knowledge that rivals our understanding

INTRODUCTION

of the environment here in the 21st century. They possessed this knowledge (higher mathematics, astronomy, geography, meteorology) at a time when a significant percentage of the population was, undoubtedly, illiterate. The ignorant masses were superstitious and uneducated with little or no understanding of the cycles of nature and the causes of the seasons. And this ignorance suited the tactics of the Priesthood just fine. The esoteric wisdom was maintained and controlled by the priesthood and shared somewhat with the Royalty. As religion evolved from astronomy, that is to say, the *symbolic illustration of the science* of astronomy, the Priesthood used their advanced scientific knowledge to mesmerize and astonish the masses.

So as the Priesthood (this sacerdotal society that over hundreds and thousands of years had evolved from a class of Timekeepers, star gazers, weather forecasters) began to proselytize the public and formulate the religious tenets of the various societies, they touted themselves as the vicars of the gods, as gods' emissaries to the populations of earth. The Priesthood had the Power (knowledge) within their domain to actuate and perpetuate this chicanery- they would astound the people, for example, by declaring that at a certain time and location at their command, the moon shall blot out the light of the sun, or perhaps they would predict a Lunar Eclipse or the onslaught of turbulent weather or drought. All this they could predict by means of their scientific knowledge, but in the minds of the ignorant masses these Priest, Soothsayers and Witchdoctors were visualized as true emissaries of the gods. How else could they possess such powers was the thought of the benighted.

Star and Nature Worship

I would add that the special dates that were established for harvesting or planting or whatever, may have at first only been secular notations on the calendar, but over time these special days became sacred days and eventually deities were attached to these sacred days as well as religious ceremonies which served to offer sacrifice or obeisance to the deities so designated. It also follows that the priesthood became very adept at the science of architecture and that religious buildings

INTRODUCTION

and monuments were therefore designed to help aid in the effort of tracking time. The orientation of the structures were laid so as to measure the movements of the sun, moon and stars and thereby give notice to the initiated of various cosmic cycles, as well as notices of the entrances and exits of the seasons.

ORIGINALLY, THE TASKS ASSIGNED to the ancient Time Keepers (Stargazers) of these fledgling agricultural communities was to track the seasons and notify the public of the appropriate time to sow their seeds and of the appropriate time to harvest the crops. This agricultural information was vital to the survival of these newly settled hamlets of antiquity, making their first attempts at transition from the hand to mouth existence of nomadism. And as these ancient Timekeepers recorded their observations by the customary methods of oral traditions or markings on natural landmarks etc. they had in fact entered the embryonic stages of the science of astronomy, and concurrently (and I think unknowingly) laid the foundation upon which the world's religions would be fashioned in the millennia that followed.

Of course the system of tracking the seasons by using stars as *signpost* to announce their (seasons) comings and goings worked fine, just as it does to this very day. But anciently, as the system of using stars to mark the skies and announce the entrances and exits of the seasons became customary and second nature to the peoples, the original purposes (or understanding of how and why the system was initiated) became lost or clouded in the minds of the masses. As the years rolled by, the custom of searching the heavens for particular asterisms or constellations to signal various agricultural and related activities became *ritualized*. AFTER A WHILE, in the public mind, it was not enough spiritually or psychologically to just run into the fields and sow or harvest when the appropriate heavenly signpost appeared on the horizon. They fashioned that celebrations (Holidays or *Holy Days*) were in order, and Festivals (*Feast Days*) and the like. As more years rolled by, just celebrating the arrival of the starry signpost became spiritually insufficient and psychologically non-fulfilling – *so much depended upon the arrival of the stars* that announced not only the agricultural activities, but marked the seasons

INTRODUCTION

for rain and sprouting fields and forest and spawning fish, animal migration and so forth. The masses began to look to the starry signposts not only as markers of the seasons but also, and perhaps more importantly as divinely connected *Bringers* of the seasons and/or life-saving rains, floods, animal migrations, warm weather or what have you . They imagined that their *rituals of celebration* that greeted the annual arrivals of various stars or star groups (constellations) did not carry enough glory (significance) for these momentous occasions. Now praise and supplication were in order – the starry signpost at this point took on aspects of divine deities, in the minds of the superstitious masses, deities worthy of praise and laudable beyond limits. The stars were no longer viewed as only heavenly lights but also as temples of the gods – these stars were imagined to house the spirits of the divinities and were not only worthy of praise but praise was required. The stars were the first celestial entities to be ranked as deities, according to the scholars that have researched these matters, then came Lunar deities, followed by the Solar deities – they (the stars) were imagined as residents of heaven and the bringers of fair weather and bounty and rain and blessings to their human subjects.

THE ABOVE WRITTEN expresses the early stages of human *cultural* development and also of human *religious* development – and all is innately connected with the cosmos, the heavenly vault of the skies. The link between all is the element of Time, that is the tracking and measurement of Time, and Time tracking is the basis on which much of our symbolic mythologically based religious scripture is formulated. The scriptures are, in fact, registries of astronomical phenomena written in a mythological format, plain and simple.

IT IS LOGICALLY EVIDENT that Star Worship evolved from the *ritualizing* of the system of using stars and asterisms (groups of stars) as markers so as to track time. The stars were used to signal the comings and goings of the seasons, and to locate the position of the sun on its annual journey. These stars, asterisms, common constellations and zodiacal constellations enabled early man to identify the cardinal points and use other assorted stars and constellations as signpost for measuring the span in between cardinal

INTRODUCTION

points and tracking the sun as it traveled throughout the year. This was of obvious importance so that early civilization could successfully plant and harvest crops as well as for other reasons such as migration, animal husbandry, food storage and export and so on and so on.

It is very easy to understand that by making these *signal* days[1] of the stars into holidays and festivals their remembrance was assured. And it follows that as society became more and more religious that these *signal* days (that were a matter of life and death in terms of their importance to agriculture) – that these *signal* days would over time evolve into religious or sacred days dedicated to certain deities (stars) that were now not just *signals* of the seasons but actually viewed as the bringers and generators of the seasons. After humanity deified the stars, it of course followed in natural progression that the deities became deserving of worship and sacrifices. And in this we have the evolution of religious rituals based on primitive astronomical observations that were geared to tracking time in order to assure propitious agricultural and related enterprises.

The first stellar deities were depicted as animals, some malevolent and some benevolent. They chose animals names for the various constellations, animals whose presence or activity was somehow associated with the season of the stars heliacal appearance on the eastern horizon, such as the heliacal rising of the Dog-Star *Sirius*, barking its announcement of the dog days of summer. A stars heliacal descent on the western horizon was also a reference indicator and the stars that transited the midnight meridian served as another reference coordinate for tracking time. The characteristics of the animals would in some way be associated with the concurrent activity or season that the stars arrival on the horizon was found to indicate. For example, the bull deity was associated with fertility – hence a Spring constellation indicating new birth. The lion was in some instances associated with ferocious heat – hence it was a summer constellation. The Virgin with a stalk of Wheat may have been

---

[1] Of course the *signal days* were the days marked by the appearance of certain stars that *signaled* that the time/season had arrived for some agricultural or other related activity to take place

INTRODUCTION

associated with harvesting and so forth. The deities were not limited to just one symbolic indication. As time passed the deities became humanized in form but maintained animal attributes as part of their guise, perhaps in the attire of the deity or some ornament. And in many cases human and animal anatomies were fused so as to create a mythically symbolic portrayal that was part animal and part human in visual appearance. I'm thinking mainly of ancient Egyptian symbolism as I write this.

Of course some stars (deities) were indicators of propitious events (seasons) while other stars (deities) were witnessed with foreboding. The benevolent stars (deities) were greeted with great offerings of flowers, foodstuffs, dancing and various tangible demonstrations of gratitude and welcoming. But the ominous stars (deities) were served with blood sacrifices, fasting, self-mutilation and various rituals that were designed to appease and placate the wrathful deities. Our religious rituals of today have sprung from the sources that I have just described.

Theology Of Time

Hence, this is the true and accurate account of the evolution of religion – it started as astronomy that evolved into cryptic Myth, for reasons that I have explained above – and out of this mix has emerged our present day religious creeds. The biblical stories that we call religious history are, in truth, *works of literature* - not history; these stories are fables derived in great part from primitive oral traditions. THE EVOLUTION of our modern Religious Concepts began with Astronomy, and evolved through Mythology and Astrology into modern religion. Jesus Christ, Moses, Abraham and all of the other so-called prophets of the Quran, Bible and Torah are cosmic myths – they never existed in actual history. They are the personifications of cosmic entities and their tales, in truth, are no less than a registry of astronomical phenomena written in a mythological format.

INTRODUCTION

The best term that I have ever heard as a description of religion is *Theology Of time* – that's exactly what religion is and has always been. Religious myth was born out of a system of Time-Keeping, its originators were primitive stargazers whose history goes back more thousands of years than I would like to count, in fact I could say millions of years, but I won't stress the point since that time-frame covers cycles that we haven't covered to this point, in my previous books on this subject. The largest cycle that we have discussed is the precession cycle that spans 25,920 years, and this is where our focus should remain for the moment, but the ancients actually measured time in excess of that cycle.

Subjects Reviewed In Book Four

Within this Book, we shall also bring greater clarity to the important book of Genesis. Witness this quote from Book Three: Chapter One

"Genesis One contains a Lot more Symbolism. The First chapter and more of Genesis is actually Bursting At The Seams with Stellar Symbolism, but that is not our Focus, at this Time. Furthermore the Interpretations are much more involved and tedious, so we will move on"

In Chapter two I have included much of the Stellar and Circumpolar symbolism that was omitted from the previous volumes i.e. Books 1, 2, and 3. The inclusion of the stellar symbolism and its interpretations will give the reader a much broader comprehension of biblical allegory. I have found astronomical correlations going back over 8,000 years in the Book Of Genesis. The interpretations are very vivid and jolting.

We have attacked and explained many of the most enigmatic portions of the bible within Book Four, and that includes the Book Of Revelations – that mystery of the Ages. We have included many interpretations relating to Environmental (Agricultural) symbolism within this Volume, as it is very pertinent to the New Testament and to Revelations as well.

We have included an extensive explanation of the cycles of Time in Chapter One. It is fundamentally important that the reader delves intensely into that chapter, as it is Key to many interpretations that

INTRODUCTION

follow. And furthermore I have written this book with the assumption that the reader is familiar with the information contained in my previous books on this subject, which serves as a sort of stepping-stone to the more intricate matters that are reviewed within this Volume.

MALIK H JABBAR

A Note in Regards to Chapter One

Chapter One contains a variety of mathematical formulas dealing with Calendar reconciliation, and also a good deal of data enumerating the spans of cosmic cycles. This information, though *very* important, is mainly for reference as well as the exemplification of various methods of Time-Cycle reconciliation.

If perchance you find *Chapter One* somewhat pedantic or frustrating because of the plethora of numerical citations, I suggest that you go from here directly to **Chapter Two (page 45)** as a start for reading the remainder of the book. You can always refer back to *Chapter One* as needed.

CHAPTER ONE

Chapter One

Chapter One

Definitions and Detailed Information on Cycles, Formulas and Terms

Cycles Of Time, Types And Purposes

Ancient systems Of Time Tracking

The number one premise of this book is that the Bible, Quran, Torah and other religious scriptures are, in fact, *Registries of Astronomical Phenomena written in a Mythological Format*. This is the crux and focus of our presentation, and all else surrounds and is supported by this one overriding fundamental fact. I have explained, I believe conclusively, in the Introduction the basics of how and why all religions were founded - that is as a result of the observation and *recording* of astronomical phenomena or at the least (theology/religion) tended to evolve from and reflect the scientific and empirical astronomical study of the heavens by the ancients, as they *recorded* their findings. We explained that this empirical observation and *recording* commenced before the advent of writing, far back into prehistory, when mankind first evolved from nomadism into settled agricultural communities, and hence *recorded their information for posterity in the forms of oral tales and myths* – in rudimentary languages that were colorful and graphic (imaginative), but not technically precise in terms of modern languages. They did not give technical scientific names to the elements of the cosmos because they did not possess such terms back in those early days many millennia ago. But rather they named the stars and planets etc. after (in duplication of) the animals and things in their earthly environment. THEY PERSONIFIED THE ELEMENTS of the cosmos with human names and royal titles and with titles of benevolent spirits as well as malevolent spirits. So as society evolved intellectually, philosophically and religiously over many thousands of years and formulated their religious beliefs, the elements of their *physical* heaven (cosmos) were duplicated in kind as the elements (titles) of

CHAPTER ONE

their *spiritual* heaven. The *transits* and *occultations* of the planets within the *physical* heaven (cosmos) became the *quests* and *intrigues* of their gods within their *spiritual* heaven. It was a natural and logical progression that really, I think, could not have gone any other way – this is vivid.

THE ORIGINAL FUNDAMENTAL CAUSE, purpose and function of those ancients who composed the theological scriptures of all the various ancient religions was *Time Tracking*. Time Tracking was the primary or underlying objective of the ancient Priesthood, as it still is today. All of your ancient calendars can be traced to the Priesthood. They (Priesthood) are the *spiritual progeny* (i.e. maintainers and preservers of the esoteric system) of the stargazers of antiquity that we discussed in the Introduction.

The importance of cosmic Time Tracking has not diminished – it is just as important today as it was in antiquity for various *ominous* reasons as well as immediately practical ones. There are major cycles of great foreboding that had been calculated by the ancients is the indication, cycles that extend in excess of the precession cycle of 25,920 years, and measure cyclical events of severe adverse environmental impact on our planet. However we are not focused on those larger cycles within this work, but *may* cover that aspect in another effort. This system of Time Tracking (veiled under the symbolism of mythology) was started anciently for very important reasons connected with food production, harvesting and so forth – and has worked well in fulfilling those basic needs. The *physics* of the system also had the ripple effect of providing us with a *model* by which we (chiefly the Priesthood) were able to fashion our cultural theological notions. As I wrote before, our religions are in truth *Spirits* based on *Physics* i.e. the concepts of our imagined spiritual world are really an idealized reflection of this material world to a great extent. The beginnings of the system (of observing and charting the cosmos) were very basic and rudimentary. But what started out as mere observation of the stars so as to obtain cues for planting and harvesting has evolved into one of the most complicated, perplexing, enigmatic and intriguing of all scientific endeavors attempted or

CHAPTER ONE

encountered by mankind. The study of this incomprehensible, endless, ever expanding universe is mind boggling, but so, so necessary for our very survival.

AND ON TOP of the prodigious intellectual challenges encountered in our attempts to unravel and navigate the endless mazes of the physical universe, we are also entangled in a philosophical maze of our own making, that being this theological quagmire that we have fashioned in (spiritual) imitation of the physical cosmos. This *spiritual labyrinth* that we have developed concurrently with our advances in the sciences of the physical universe has now reached the point of its own self-destruction. It (our modern religious concepts) cannot stand of its own weight – it is decaying and rotting from within. THIS IS because the ever widening gap between faith and reason has expanded to the point that no rational leap of faith can span the breach. The Fairy Tales of old that mesmerized the benighted masses of ages gone by do not work in this advanced technological age. Too many of yesteryears mysteries are common knowledge today – we know that heaven is not situated above the clouds and some of us have experienced more hell on earth than we could ever rationally conceive as being within it. People say that they believe in god out of habit and tradition but seldom on the basis of genuine conviction, because they are skeptical of our religious tenets and have grave doubts about theology in general, is my take. The hocus pocus religions that worked 3000, 2000 and 1400 years ago (and before) cannot cut it today and need to be *updated* i.e. intellectually expanded and enhanced to match the intellect of the present technologically enlightened era.

BUT THE CLERGY (Priesthood) is caught in a quagmire as well as a Catch-22 of their own making, because if they attempt to update or modify their dogmas, such action would have the affect of belying the alleged divinity of these outdated and vacuous religious concepts that they steadfastly propound, which certainly and indeed urgently need to be adjusted or rationally revised so as to intellectually fit into the modern world. ACTUALLY what they need is another so-called prophet to come on the scene with a new *21st century message* from

CHAPTER ONE

the deity, but I doubt they could pull that one off nowadays - but who knows! I'VE SEEN people on TV who believe they are in communication with the dead and such related nonsense, so who knows what's next. But I digress – the subject of this chapter concerns the various *cycles of time* tracked by the ancients that are recorded (although shielded) within the symbolism of religious scripture.

THE UNTANGLING of the web of falsehood and misunderstanding that prevails in modern scripture is not an easy task, especially when we are contending with irrational and superstitious human minds that find it extremely difficult to accept this one basic and fundamental truth – that religion was not bestowed upon us by some omnipotent deity but rather is the product of our own minds. Religion like all other social systems designed or fashioned by man is simply another unit within our social structure, representing our best attempts (howbeit so inadequate) to communicate or relate to our creator. So the age-old question again rears its head – *did god create man or did man create god?*

AT THIS JUNCTURE we need to review the major categories of cycles that were tracked and charted by the ancients, and are symbolically rendered in biblical scripture. First we shall define those cycles generally and then give detailed explanations with some examples of their applications. Some of these explanations are intricate but I suggest that we all hang in there and re-read certain portions if necessary. An understanding or perhaps I should say a familiarity with these cycles that I shall introduce is essential to a proper comprehension of the intriguing allegorical explanations that shall follow within ensuing chapters of this book.

There are several categories of Time cycles that were of primary interest to the ancient stargazers and their spiritual progeny (succeeding generations of the Priesthood) throughout the Ages. We shall focus on four of those categories within this chapter. The other primary cycles are listed in the Appendix of Book Three. The cycles that we shall review in this chapter are three annual cycles, namely the *Lunar Year*, the *Tropical Year* and the *Sidereal Year*. We shall

CHAPTER ONE

also review what the ancient Egyptians called the *Great Year*, consisting of 25,920 tropical years. These are not the only Time cycles that were used but rather are the ones on which we shall focus for the time being.

A major problem that confronted the ancient astronomers (Priesthood) was how to reconcile these three annual cycles with each other and also with the Great Year. We shall explain some of the methods by which that reconciliation was or may have been accomplished. The methods that I shall explain are related to biblical methods of symbolism – this will manifest itself more clearly in later chapters of the book when we get into the actual task of deciphering the symbolism. Of course, in order to explain how these cycles were reconciled or calibrated, it will be necessary that I introduce and explain several other minor and major cycles.

But I want the reader to keep in mind that all the cycles introduced play a role in explaining the major objective of the ancient Timekeepers, which was to reconcile the fractional differences between minor cycles by calculating a future date when the appearance of the cycles would coincide, that is intersect or conjunct. For example, lets suppose that we have two minor cycles (scheduled events) of different lengths commencing *from the same date* and we want to know on what date in the future will these events occur on the same date again. Lets say that one cycle spans 15 years and the other spans 20 years and each cycle (event) starts out on the same date - now at what date in the future will these two different cycles again appear on the same date is the question. The answer for this question is pretty easy – we simply multiple the cycles i.e. 20 times 15 and the result is 300 years. This means that the two minor cycles (of 15 and 20 years) will intersect each other at intervals of 300 years, thus 300 years becomes the major cycle of the two minor cycles of 15 and 20 years. And thus 300 years becomes a step by which we can measure even larger cycles, if desired.

This little formula is very basic to the methods of the ancient stargazers – they would note the conjunctions of various heavenly bodies, they would calculate the elapsed time (duration) of the varied

CHAPTER ONE

cycles and compute a date into the future when the celestial bodies would meet (intersect, conjunct) again - and the computed future date would represent a major cycle by which they could measure time[1]. Also, in order to keep this future date in the minds or remembrance of their community and its descendents, they would schedule a festival that had to be observed on that future date, when the designated celestial bodies again intersected each other, thus completing a major cycle[2]. It is important to remember that, for the priesthood and their cohorts, the original purpose, and the continuing underlying purpose of Religious Festivals and Holidays (Holy Days) was to mark the calendar for some eventful cosmic or ecological event. The most prominent of these events so designated revolved around *planting*, *harvesting*, and *seasonal transitions*.

The problem that generated the need for the ancient agricultural communities to develop a system of Timekeeping based on cosmic observations was the need to track the seasons so that crops could be planted and harvested within the natural constraints of the seasons. This seemingly simple task led to complications and intricacies that I'm sure the first primitive stargazers never imagined. That's because time must be measured by observation, that is the observation of the cycles of the heavenly bodies such as the sun, moon and stars. But neither the sun, moon or stars alone and independently can provide sufficient data for accurate prolonged timekeeping. This, the ancients discovered, once they got into the actual workings of their systems and encountered false readings as the millennia rolled by. An interesting side note is that within the biblical symbolism, a *false reading resulting from errors in calculation* may be described as a *False Prophet* (some one (Calculation) that leads people astray). But back to our point – the cycles of the sun, moon and stars are not in natural harmony, that is their cycles do not fit neatly or evenly into

---

[1] Of course they also fashioned monuments, portholes, floor and wall markings that would capture or reflect the light of some cosmic entity as its rays intersected a particular latitude and longitude thus indicating a cycle of time. Please note - they captured the rays of lights from bright stars and planets as well as the sun and moon.

[2] A major cycle is created when two or more cycles intersect., Thus a major cycle may also be a minor cycle if used in combination to create larger cycles

CHAPTER ONE

each other. So THE ANCIENTS had to develop mathematical formulas and calendars and artificial cycles (such as the **week**, **Metonic cycle**, **Saros** cycle etc.) so as to harmonize (in terms of calculation) the various time spans evolved, into a convenient system of measurement. This is the subject that your bible and other mythologies deal with, in a mythical format.

Of course the shortest natural cosmic cycle that fits our needs is the 24-hour day – they calculated 365 ¼ days to the tropical year, which is approximately correct. They measured their months by the revolutions of the moon, which orbits the earth (synodical month) in approximately 29 ½ days. Now 29 ½ days *to a lunar month* will not fit evenly into 365 ¼ days *to a tropical solar year* – so this was one of the first problems that they (the ancients) had to solve. They had to find a mathematical way to calibrate the natural monthly cycles of the moon to the natural annual cycles of the sun in order to accurately measure the tropical year. This was important because without an accurate measurement of the year, they would over time lose track of the seasons, and thereby not be able to plant and harvest at the appropriate time.

ANOTHER PROBLEM that they encountered was the DIFFERENCE between the length of the *Tropical year* and the *Sidereal year* – this discrepancy amounts to **20 minutes 24.04 seconds** each year. This accumulates to a loss of a whole day in **72 years.** This discrepancy had to be rectified because since they were observing the stars in order to gauge the yearly cycle, this difference between the sidereal year and the tropical year would over time skew their calculations.

NOW THIS LEADS into the matter of the *Precession Cycle* or the Great Year, as the Egyptians called it – the precession cycle covers **25,920 years**. This cycle is caused by the slow wobble of the earth, according to the astronomers of today. The result of the cycle of precession is that the *axis point of the celestial pole tends to shift* in a pattern that describes an ellipse in the starry skies of the *Circumpolar Constellations* over the period of 25,920 years. A complete revolution of 360 degrees is completed in the span of 25,920 years, and then renews at the point of its commencement. IN CONSEQUENCE

CHAPTER ONE

of the *elliptical orbit of the earth polar axis*, the point of the *vernal equinox[1]* (and all other cardinal points) also shift westward at the rate of *one degree* every **72** years i.e. *30 degrees* every **2160** years, along the path of the zodiac, making a complete revolution *360 degrees* in **25,920** years. THE CELESTIAL polar axis and the vernal equinox move in sync but describe ellipses of different sizes. The *polar axis* passes through about *six circumpolar constellations* (namely Draconis, Ursa Minor, Cepheus, Cygnus, Lyra, Hercules) in its revolution of 25,920 years while the *vernal equinox* passes through the *twelve zodiacal constellations* in its revolution of 25,920 years. This information is very pertinent to the interpretation of biblical symbolism.

Of course the vernal equinox marks the beginning of Spring, about March 21. The fact that the stars serving as signpost for the vernal equinox, were not stable or fixed, as the ancient stargazers thought originally, presented them with some perplexing problems. In order for them to accurately note the beginning of Spring and thereby schedule when to plant and harvest their crops, they had to solve the problem of the shifting equinoxes, that is they had to somehow calculate the rate of the westward migration of the equinoxes. By calculating the rate of migration of the vernal equinox (and other *signal stars*) along the path of the zodiac, they then could designate stars along that path that in turn would take up the position as signpost for the vernal equinox, the gateway to the salvation of Spring and the New Year. It was also necessary for them to track other signal stars for various times of the year that, of course, were precessing westward at the same rate of one degree every 72 years. Well, they successfully calculated the rate of precession at one degree every seventy-two years, as I have already indicated. Next they divided the *ecliptic path* of precession into twelve parts called the *twelve signs* (kings, tribes, stations, etc.) of the *zodiac*. They measured the distances and named the stars of the twelve signs of the zodiac and designated the appropriate stars that would serve as signpost in turn as the equinoxes migrated through the years.

---

[1] The Vernal Equinox is the intersection of the *Celestial Equator* and *Ecliptic* in the East

CHAPTER ONE

So NOW the ancient stargazers had developed a system by which to accurately track the shifting equinoxes; but, in due course, they had to assure that this information was passed on to posterity, to the future generations of their community. The information as to when to abandon the old starry signposts and when to transfer their sights to new starry signposts had to be passed on to their descendants. They accomplished this task in the same way they had always done throughout their history from primordial times till then. They incorporated the message of the calculations into their folk tales and fables in the form of mythology. Of course they did not use scientific astronomical terms in the tales. They used the names and titles of things, and animals and peoples (royal and common) that existed in their environment. When they referred to the time spans between signpost they spoke of generations and the like – when they issued directions to abandon a signpost they spoke of the failure of a prophet or king to perform faithfully, or perhaps of a wicked person or prince or deity being overthrown. When they spoke of a newly designated sign post, they would possibly mention a savior that was predicted to come to save the people from despair or waywardness or they might speak of the newly designated signpost as a son that usurps the position of his royal father or brother or uncle, what have you. In some cases they might refer to the joining of the signpost to the equinox as a marriage or a joining of kingdoms or the conquering of a kingdom or crowning and the like. And in some cases they might refer to a great death or destruction or perhaps positively to a great birth or redemption to signify a transition of the starry signpost. THE SYMBOLISMS are varied and intriguing and we will expose major biblical symbolisms as we go along in the following chapters, but for now our focus must remain on the important explanations of cycles.

WE ARE FOCUSED on the following *Time Cycles* within this Chapter:

Lunar Year of 354.36708 days, that is 354 days 8 hours 48 minutes 36 seconds

Tropical Year of 365.2422 days, that is 365 days 5 hours 48 minutes 45.51 seconds

CHAPTER ONE

Sidereal Year of 365.2564 days, that is 365 days 6 hours 9 minutes 9.54 seconds
Precession (Great Year) of 25,920 years

Examples Of Cosmic Cycles

At this point we shall review some of the cycles that we may encounter in biblical symbolism. First off we shall examine some cycles that focus on reconciling the discrepancy between the *tropical* year of 365.2422 days and the *sidereal* year of 365.2564 days. Next we shall review cycles that reconcile the discrepancy between the tropical year of 365.2422 days and the Calendar year of 365 days. The Metonic cycle is used to reconcile the discrepancy between the Lunar year and the Tropical year – since we reviewed the Metonic cycle in Book Three, we will not review it in this Volume. We have already explained above that this discrepancy or difference in the two cycles (tropical and sidereal) amounts to 20 minutes 24.04 seconds a year. And if a means were not found to reconcile this discrepancy of 20 minutes 24.04 seconds a year, the two yearly cycles would diverge from each other at the rate of one whole day in every seventy-two years. That means that in a period of 2160 years the seasons would be out of sync (as indicated by a starry signpost) by 30 whole days, which, of course, is unacceptable. Under such divergence the ancient farmers would not have been able to plant and harvest within the constraints of the seasons and the populations would have starved to death as a result.

Symbolic Years

The interpretation of biblical symbolism is based on Symbolic years of 360 days. This is important information and the basis of much mythological allegory. The Symbolic year is a Convenient year of 360 days – it does not replace the actual 365 day year but rather it is an adaptation that is used for mathematical purposes. The Symbolic year of 360 days is the year that is used in biblical symbolism. The use of the Symbolic year as a means of tracking and computing the annual and larger cycles originated in Egypt, as far as I can tell. The

CHAPTER ONE

actual year is not reduced to 360 days – the year remains at 365 days or 366 days during Leap Years. But the last 5 or 6 days on the calendar are left blank and are not counted (included in the computation) but *the days are observed* as uncounted holidays. Under this system the New Year does not recycle until a full term of 365-66 days has passed, but the ancients stopped the counting at 360 days. The reasons for this will become obvious as we review the following formulas on cycles of time. Also this matter (of the uncounted days) is reviewed in Book Two in the Chapter titled *The Egyptians*.

A S A REMINDER, let me repeat! - religion, *at its root*, is, in fact, the *Theology of Time*. The tracking of time, that is to say, the tracking of the cycles of time,and the seasons was the foundation upon which ancient mythological tales were composed, in allegorical formats. Our modern religions have evolved from the mythologies of the distant past, and are underpinned by the same chronological symbolisms as the mythical tales of old; hence the major purpose of this book is to prove and expose the numerous allegorical connections between *biblical symbolisms* and the *tracking of Time Cycles* - we shall accomplish this goal or purpose by means of an *Astro-Theological* methodology. Our procedure is to first introduce some of the Time Cycles that were problematic for our ancestors, and secondly we will connect various biblical passages directly to selected cycles and seasonal transitions, and prove through exegetical analysis the astro-theological relationships. You will find that the elucidations, although carved out from very puzzling and arcane scriptural settings, are very, very vivid.

Cycles of Reconciliation 20 Minutes 24.04 Seconds

Cycles Focused on reconciling the discrepancy (20 minutes 24.04 seconds) between the sidereal year and the tropical year

Cycles of Time, Types, and Purposes   34

CHAPTER ONE

Cycle of 1440 years

The purpose of this cycle is to reconcile the discrepancy between the sidereal year and the tropical year at 20 minutes 24.04 seconds each year. I have made the following calculations based on the *cycle* of 1440-years. This cycle (1440 years) is optimized or matures in 2,160,000 years, that is to say, the *tropical year* is brought into reconciliation to the *sidereal year* after that period of time to the *fraction of a second*[1]. The Great Year of 25,920 years contains 18 divisions of the 1440-year cycle. The time difference between the tropical year of 365 days 5 hours 48 minutes 45.51 seconds and the sidereal year of 365 days 6 hours 9 minutes 9.54 seconds is 20 minutes 24.04 seconds. IT IS USEFUL to remember that units of *Days and Degrees are equivalent in the measurement* of the cycles of precession (that is 360 degrees are equivalent to 360 days (a Symbolic Year)). *One day of time is equivalent to one degree of arc* in the measurement of the discrepancy or difference (20 minutes 24.04 seconds per year) in Time between the two annual cycles (sidereal and tropical) - and when the discrepancy between the two annual cycles expands to 360 Degrees/Days, then at that time the cycle of precession has completed itself and is back at its starting point. IT TAKES 25,920 YEARS for the *discrepancy of 20 minutes 24.04 seconds* between the two annual cycles to expand to 360 Degrees/Days. The net result of this aforementioned discrepancy is that the stars (signposts by which we chart the cosmos) are changing their position by precessing westward by one degree every 72 years. Since a complete revolution, whereas the stars return to their starting point, is accomplished at 360 degrees, we find that by multiplying 72-years times 360 the result is 25,920 years to complete one cycle of precession.

THE RATE OF PRECESSION is measurable as the Time-span discrepancy between the two annual cycles (sidereal and tropical years). In order to calculate the rate of precession (at 20 minutes

---

[1] The time-span of the tropical year is determined by the successive transits of the vernal equinox by the sun as seen from Earth; while the time-span of the sidereal year is determined by using a star for a reference point. The sidereal year is 20 minutes 24.04 seconds longer than the tropical year due to precession.

CHAPTER ONE

24.04 seconds each year) and also the completion of the cycle the precession (at 25,920 years) - let us consider the following system - we shall sequentially reconcile the discrepancy of *minutes*, then *seconds*, then *fractions of seconds*:

THE FIRST STEP is to reconcile the minutes at 20 minutes a year. Since there are exactly *1440 minutes in one day*, we divide the 1440 minutes by 20 (the precessional discrepancy in minutes for one year) and the result is 72 years. This result tells us that it takes 72 years for the precession discrepancy to accumulate to one full day i.e. 1440 minutes. That means that vernal equinox will shift by One Whole Day (which also equals one degree of arc) in 72 years *relative to minutes of time*. In other words 20 minutes of time is equivalent to 1/72 degree of arc in the elliptical path of precession, so 72 years makes one degree of precession. Now, in order to find out how many years it will take the equinox to make a *complete revolution of 360 days and/or degrees* (one calendar year) along the elliptical arc of precession, *with regards to the minutes of discrepancy*, we multiply 72 times 360 (a symbolic year) and the result is 25,920 years for a complete precession of the equinoxes *refined to the nearest minute;* that is to say, by adding one day every 72 years which amounts to 360 days/degrees, that tropical (solar) time and sidereal (star) time are synchronized in 25,920 years resulting in the elimination of the 20-minute annual discrepancy.

THE SECOND STEP is to reconcile the discrepancy of the *whole seconds at 24 seconds a year* so that we may find how many years it takes for the discrepancy in seconds to amount to *one whole day*, thereby signaling the adjustment of the calendar with the addition of one day so as to bring *solar time* and *star time* into sync. Since there are exactly *86,400 seconds in a day*, we must divide the 86,400 by the *24-second discrepancy* that occurs annually due to precession, and the result is 3600. THIS MEANS THAT IN 3600 YEARS, WE CAN RECONCILE THE DISCREPANCY between the *tropical year* and the *sidereal year* with an adjustment of exactly *one whole day*, to the nearest second. For the period of 25,920 years (The Great Year) the adjustments for seconds would accumulate to 7.2 days. This was

CHAPTER ONE

derived by dividing 25,920 by 3600, resulting in the number 7.2; but since 7.2 is not a number of whole days, it stands that the discrepancy in seconds cannot be reconciled in sync with the precessional cycle of 25,920 years.[1]

THE THIRD STEP is to reconcile *the fractions of seconds* at .04 seconds to the year so that we may find how many years it takes for *the fractions of seconds* to amount to One Whole Day. Again, since there are 86,400 seconds to the day we must divide 86,400 (seconds to the day) by the yearly discrepancy (between the sidereal year and tropical year) *in fractions of a second* and that amount is .04. The result of dividing 86,400 by .04 is 2,160,000 years. This means that it will take two million one hundred sixty thousand years for the discrepancy between the sidereal year and solar year *in fractions of seconds* to accumulate to One Whole Day. If we desired to correlate the discrepancy in *fractions of a second*, to the Great Year of 25,920 years, we could do the following:

Since we know that the discrepancy in fractions of seconds will accumulate to One Whole Day (86,400 seconds) after 2,160,000 years, we may compare the ratio of 86,400/2,160,000 to X/25,920 and thereby discover the discrepancy in *fractions of a second* as applied to the Great Year (25,920 years) – being 1036.8 seconds or 17 minutes 16.8 seconds. *However* this is not the way the ancients did it in terms of the mythical symbolism, rather they stuck to whole numbers in the symbolism for the most part. Consequently the mythology probably would not have addressed the issue of *fractions of a second* being applied to the Great Year but rather a *festival* or coming *Avatar* would be designated to come after 2,160,000 years as a signal to the Priesthood of that generation that the time had arrived for an adjustment to the calendar of One Whole Day relevant to *fractions of a second.*

SO THIS IS WAY the mythology was formed in terms of predictions of the future advents of eras and saviors; once the math was completed they recorded it in coded mythical language and thus preserved the

---

[1] It is noteworthy, I think, that the discrepancy in seconds can be reconciled at 25,200 years with the addition of exactly 7 whole days to the calendar -7 times 3600 = 25,200 years.

CHAPTER ONE

gnosis for future generations. So we can see from the aforementioned data that I have supplied, that a festival for instance, spaced at intervals of 72 years may serve to signal shifts in the equinox position of one Degree/Day to the nearest minute. And also various multiples of 72 could be used to signal larger shifts in the position of the equinox, for instance 360 years would indicate a shift of 5 Degrees/Days to the nearest minute. And so a festival or advent spaced at 3600 years would signal an adjustment in the calendar of One Whole Day/Degree bringing accuracy to the nearest second and of course an adjustment of One Whole Day made after 2,160,000 years would bring accuracy to the nearest fraction of a second.

It is interesting to note that 72 years times 360 days (symbolic years) = 25,920 days. This shows that a shift of one degree in the equinox, which occurs after 72 years, is a microcosm (in days) of the larger Great Year cycle of 25,920 years. I am truly amazed at how the basic numbers, when linked to the cycles of the cosmos, are maintained throughout the various levels of the symbolism i.e. the base of 9, which is the key divisor of all cycles tracking the *Precession Cycle* at 25,920 years. This uncanny synchronization (that we shall encounter more as we go along) and recycling of the same base number (9) which serves to *Proof* our calculations makes me think that possibly the number system (Hindu-Arabic) may have originated from the charting of the cosmos, or at the least was refined anciently so as to harmonize with the cosmic cycles.

1000 Year Cycle

The purpose of the One Thousand Year cycle is to reconcile the discrepancy between the sidereal year and the tropical year at 20 minutes 24.04 seconds each year over a period of six thousand years. The Cycle of Precession moves westward at the rate of 20 minutes plus 24 seconds a year. This is the Time difference between the Tropical year and the Sidereal year.

I have successfully decoded the 1000-year cycle as a minor cycle within the major cycle of 6000 years. Over a period of 1000 years the difference of 20 min 24 sec accumulates to 14.16666667 days.

CHAPTER ONE

So by inserting 14 days into the calendar (calculations) at 1000 yr intervals, the calendar (registry) will remain reliable. In the 6000th year the remainder (.16666667 partial days) will accumulate to one whole day. So 15 days must be added (6 times .16666667 = 1) and the two cycles (sidereal and tropical) are completely reconciled at 0 discrepancy.

This clearly shows that the world coming to its end after 6000 years may actually be a reference to the completion of the major cycle of 6000 years.

1260-day cycle (3 ½ yr cycle, 42-month cycle)

The purpose of the One Thousand Two Hundred And Sixty Day cycle is to reconcile the discrepancy between the sidereal year and the tropical year at 20 minutes 24 seconds each year over a period of Twenty-Five Thousand And Two Hundred years

This 1260-day cycle is a favorite of the Dooms - day crowd. Actually the cycle is just another means of tracking time. I did have difficulty in decoding it, but once I adjusted the major cycle to 25,200 years instead of 25,920 years, all the figures fell right into place.

The purpose of this cycle is to reconcile the discrepancy between the sidereal year and the tropical year (at 20 minutes 24 seconds) over a period of 25,200 years. The Cycle of Precession moves westward at the rate of 20 minutes plus 24 seconds a year. This is the Time difference between the Tropical year and the Sidereal year.

This *1260-day cycle* is the base of a three-part cycle. The second part is the *504-year cycle* and this *evolves into a major cycle of 25,200 years*. The purpose of this 3-phase cycle is to reconcile the tropical year to the sidereal year with accuracy to the seconds. The annual difference between the tropical and sidereal year is 20 minutes plus 24 seconds. The 1260-day cycle reconciles this difference to zero over a period of 25,200 years. For these purposes the year is measured at 360 days a year not 365 days. The Ancients used the number 360 in order to facilitate computations. The disparity between the sidereal and tropical year is 20 minutes plus 24 seconds and this difference is based on the actual 365 day yearly cycle The use of a 360 day year for computation is for mathematical expediency; the

CHAPTER ONE

years were not actually reduced from 365 to 360 days. All calculations reflect the actual 365-day year. Three hundred and sixty five days were observed but not counted. This stems from the Egyptian originators of this system who included five Epagomenal days (uncounted days) at the end of each of their 365-day years. This will become clearer as we go along. We shall call the *360-day* years *Symbolic Years*.

The base of the major cycle of 25,200 years is 1260 days (42 months or 3 ½ years) and the second phase spans 504 symbolic years. Five hundred and four symbolic years contains 181,440 days. When we divide the 181,440 days by the base cycle of 1260 days the result is 144. This means that 144 *1260-day cycles* are contained within 504 symbolic years. The first stage of the reconciliation process starts at this point.

The purpose of the first step in the reconciliation process is to eliminate the discrepancy in minutes that exist between the two annual cycles i.e. the sidereal year of 365 days 6 hours 9 minutes 9.54 seconds and the tropical year of 365 days 5 hours 48 minutes 45.51 seconds, which discrepancy is 20 minutes plus 24 seconds. First we must determine the total disparity that has accumulated over 504 years. This is done by multiplying 504 years times (20 minutes + 24 seconds) which equals (10,080 minutes + 12,096 seconds). There are 1440 minutes in one 24 hour day. The next step is to divide the 10,080 minutes by 1440 minutes and the result is 7 days exactly. This means that if we intercalate (insert) 7 days into the calendar in the 504th year we will have reconciled the differences in the sidereal year and the tropical year to zero minutes. In other words by adding a Leap Week of 7 days every 504 years, the Ancients were able to reconcile the disparity between the sidereal and tropical years to the nearest minute. There is a remainder of 12,096 seconds (504 times 24 seconds) that is not dealt with at this phase of the computations but rather is carried forward to the final phase of computations.

The major cycle contains 25,200 years. When we divide 25,200 by 504 the result is 50 exactly. This means that the major cycle of 25,200 years contains 50 sub-cycles of 504 years. Each sub-cycle of 504

CHAPTER ONE

years contains a remainder of 12,096 seconds carried forward from the reconciliation process in minutes. In the last year of the 50th sub-cycle i.e. the 25,200th year, end of the major cycle, we must finally reconcile the sidereal and tropical year to the nearest second. Now we shall multiply 50 times 12,096 seconds and the result is 604,800 seconds. There are 86,400 seconds in one 24-hour day. Next we must divide the 604,800 by 86,400 and the result is 7 days exactly. So now at the completion of the last of the 50 *504 year cycles* which is the *completion of the 25,200 year cycle* we must add an *additional* leap week of 7 days and this completely reconciles the tropical year to the sidereal year to the nearest second of time.

So here we have it, the prophecy in the bible concerning 1260 days or 42 months or 3 ½ years may actually be coded language to the initiated to enact the reconciliation cycle that I have explained in the forgoing.

Actually, the discrepancy between the sidereal year and tropical year is 20 minutes 24 seconds and *.04 seconds*. I did not address the *fraction of a second (.04 seconds)* in this explanation of the symbolism, because this formula does not work efficiently when carried forward to fractions of a second. The 1440-year cycle is the most efficient formula for reconciling the fractions of a second and that reconciliation stretches out to 2,160,000 years.

CHAPTER ONE

Calendar Reconciliation Cycles 365.2421 Days

Cycles focused on reconciling the discrepancy between the tropical year of 365.2421 days and the Calendar year of 365, 366, or 360 days

120 Year Cycle

This cycle is used to reconcile a Calendar of 365 days to the year to the tropical year of 365.2422 days.

This (120-year cycle) is the Minor cycle for a *Major cycle of 3840 years* after which the calendar is reconciled to the tropical year to a tiny fraction of a second. THE PURPOSE OF THIS CYCLE is to *reconcile the 365-day calendar year* with the tropical (solar) *year of 365.2422 days*. FIRST, at 120 years intercalate a 30-day month[1] into the calendar and this will average the days of the year to 365.25 days. That's (120 times 365) + 30 = 43,830 days at the end of 120 years. NEXT divide the 43,830 days by the 120 years and the result is 365.25 days average to the year.

NEXT, COMPLETE 32 SUCH CYCLES i.e. 32 times 120 = 3840 years. Also 32 times 43,830 days (120 year cycle) = 1,402,560 days. *But since this marks the End of the Major cycle of 3840 years, the 30-day month is not added (intercalated).* So consequently we will subtract the 30 days from the aggregate amount of 1,402,560 days (which includes 30 added days) and the remainder is *1,402,530 days to a cycle of 3840 years.* Now divide the 1,402,530 days by 3840 years and the result is 365.2422 (365.2421875) days – and thusly the calendar is reconciled to the tropical (solar) year over a cycle of 3,840 years. This is marvelous. So the ancients may have used this or a similar cycle to reconcile their calendar of 365-day years to the tropical year of 365.2422 days and thereby keep their calendar synchronized to the seasons of the year. THE NUMBER *One hundred*

---

[1] Of course these days could be inserted incrementally at shorter intervals such as 1 day every 4 years, however the primary cycle we are focused on at this stage is the 120 year cycle

CHAPTER ONE

twenty is widely used in the bible and may have other indications also.

40 Year Cycle

This cycle is used to reconcile a Calendar of 365 days to the year to the tropical year of 365.2425 days

This (40 year cycle) is the minor cycle for a Major cycle of 4000 years. The purpose of this cycle is to reconcile the 365-day calendar to the tropical year of 365.2425 days[1]. First, in the 40th year of the cycle intercalate 10 days into the calendar. That's 40 times 365 + 10 = 14,610 days to a 40-year cycle. Now divide the 14,610 days by the 40 years and the result is 365.25 days average to the year. This minor cycle (40-years) completes to the Major cycle after 100 turns, so 100 times 14,610 days (40-years) = 1,461,000 days and that is 4000 years. Now subtract 30 days from the aggregate of 1,461,000 days and the result is 1,460,970 days. Next divide the 1,460,970 days by the 4000 years and the average days to the year at the end of the calendar cycle comes to 365.2425 days. This is the same accuracy that is obtained by the Gregorian calendar. The 30-day adjustment that I enacted in the last year of the Major cycle (4000 years) could have been accomplished by *not* intercalating 10-days into the last 3 minor (40 year) cycles. I don't know exactly how the ancients manipulated their calendar in detail, but the example that I have supplied here achieves the net result of the system; and thereby may explain the symbolism of the biblical scriptures in relation to the 40-year cycles, in some instances.

IN SUMMATION, my goal thus far has been to supply the reader with a working knowledge of cosmic and artificial time cycles. I have attempted to inform the reader of the origin and evolution of cycles and explain how and why, in its infancy, that the science of astronomy was merged with mythology. The process covers many,

---

[1] This is the length of a solar year based on lunar-solar calculations such as the Hebrew system produces

CHAPTER ONE

many thousands of years – I suspect hundreds of thousands of years, at least. I know this observation may be shocking to those who are of the impression that civilization is less than 15,000 or so years old. We yet have much to cover in this book but I believe that we are now ready to attempt some of our first basic biblical interpretations that unveil the astronomical symbolism within biblical scripture.

CHAPTER TWO

Chapter Two

Time Begins With Creation

Perspectives On Biblical Creation Myth

A major Key and source to the unveiling of the symbolisms of biblical scriptures lay in the *Mystery and Religious Systems of ancient Egypt*. Egyptologists such as *Gerald Massey* have relayed to us that, for the ancient Egyptians, the astronomy of the heavens was *reflective*, in many instances, of their earthly *governmental districts* which were called *Nomes*. The Egyptians divided their nation into 42 Administrative Districts (Nomes) and likewise as they charted the starry cosmos they sectioned the night sky into *star districts* (*astro-nomes*) hence forming an etymological genesis for the term *astronomy* see Greek *Astronomos*. IT IS INTERESTING that when we take note of the names of the ancient Egyptian administrative districts or Nomes, we find various names that are similar in tone to our current names for constellations; designations such as Fish, Crocodile, Cobra, Thigh, Shrine, Southern Shield, and so forth. Other correlations have been noted also, such as the long and winding cosmic river *Eridanus*, seemingly symbolic of the great *Nile*. The celestial Eridanus winds its way up from the southern regions of the sky and terminates at the base of the Orion constellation thus forming the image of the magnificent *Orion* emerging from the great celestial river Eridanus in mythical parallel to the Egyptian Osiris likewise emerging from the great Nile as the Savior of ancient Egypt.

The ancient Egyptians divided their country into districts called *Nomes* - and as Astronomy evolved within that society the heavenly asterisms were named in reflection of the earthly counterparts of that region. The indication is that ancient Egypt was a primary source for the system of astronomy (astro + nomes) and that this cosmic science was symbolized in the ancient theology and occult rituals of that mysterious culture, not only from its recorded history but also going

CHAPTER TWO

back into Egyptian pre-history. In our effort to trace our modern religion back to its astronomical source, we have, in the preceding pages of this book, presented reasonable apriori evidence that logically explains how and why the evolution of astronomy into mythology was accomplished; and going forward, our goal is to supply substantial hard evidence of the seminal connections between astronomy, mythology, and modern religion as exemplified within the annals of astro-theology as expressed through select allegorical scriptures within the bible.

We further set forth, as have many erudite scholars such as *Massey, Volney, Higgins, Frazer, Kuhn, Churchward*, et al, that our modern religious systems are an outgrowth of various ancient occult, religious, and *Mystery Systems*, of which Egypt stands as, arguably, the most prominent source. The Judaic or Abrahamic religions, namely Judaism, Christianity, and Islam were all spawned out of the nexus of *ancient Near Eastern culture*. It cannot be rationally denied that the ancient cultures *native to that region* such as **Egypt,Sumer, Babylon, Canaan,**and **Persia**, (these being most prominent among others), must have had significant influence on early Judaic culture. The Hebrew plagiaristic entanglement is clear and definitive; and their postulant association with both **Egypt** and **Babylon** should not be disputed. History clearly shows that many of the *formulators of nascent Christian doctrine* were Egyptians, or they may be described if you prefer, as Greeks and Hebrews of Egyptian birth, cultural affiliation and education. Large portions of our bible were edited in Alexandria Egypt. The *Septuagint* i.e. Greek translation of the Old Testament, was translated at **Alexandria Egypt**, we are told. The *Naj Hammadi Library*, containing embryonic aspects of the so-called Christian/Gnostic doctrine were discovered in 1945 at *Naj Hammadi,* likewise located in **Egypt**. The apposing leaders in the early church's theological conflict (i.e. Arianism verses Orthodox Christianity circa 4th Century A.D.) concerning the nature of Christ etc. were **Egyptians** or strongly affiliated to Egypt – they were *Arius* (a priest at Alexandria Egypt, after whom the doctrine of Arianism is named) and *Athanasius* (Bishop at **Alexandria Egypt**) . The so-called *Cult*

CHAPTER TWO

Of Isis as well as the so-called *Cult Of Serapis* were very popular in ancient Rome according to our historians - both of these *Mystery Systems* were imported from **Egypt**. The theological battle between the early orthodox Christians and the *Gnostics* reflected an attempt to deflect **Egyptian** (a la Alexandria, Egypt) influence on the early church. The **Egyptian** theological influence on the early church is well documented – this is not hidden knowledge; our encyclopedias are saturated with information on this subject.

OUR RELIGIOUS SYSTEMS (Judaism, Christianity, Islam), were bequeathed to us by the Hebrews – the *Bibles* of the Christians and the *Qurans* of the Muslims are replete with Hebrew religious mythology. Both the bible and Quran refer to the Israelites as god's chosen people. Just as various civilizations were built upon the ruins of their predecessors, so also, in parallel, have the Hebrews formulated their religious precepts, traditions, and rituals based on the *Religious* and *Mystery Systems* of the surrounding Near East cultural environment in which they lived. Significant elements of Egyptian and Babylonian culture can be found in Hebrew culture - this is a given. So HEREIN LAY THE KEYS to the correct decipherment of biblical astrotheological allegories, that is to say, within the heart of the Egyptian and Babylonian mythological sources.

THIS IS THE METHOD that we shall use throughout the book – we shall compare various biblical scriptures to their ancient Egyptian and Babylonian mythical counterparts and successively to the astronomical and/or environmental origins *that served as a basis* for the mythological symbolisms found within the Bible. So AS WE COMMENCE our decipherment of the stellar symbolism embodied within the *biblical Hebrew concept* of the *beginning of time* as found in Genesis of the bible, we shall start by exposing and unveiling the Egyptian counterparts to the Jewish mythos – show their correlations and unveil their true astronomical/environmental origins - as mythical renditions of astronomical phenomena.

I have already expressed in my previous books that astronomical symbolism exist at various parallels of interpretation, namely Solar, Lunar, Environmental and Stellar as well as some some other

CHAPTER TWO

obscure, mystical and spiritual parallels. We shall also encounter subcategories of some classifications as we explore the symbolisms in more minute details – subcategories such as *Circumpolar,* within Stellar symbolism and *Agricultural* within Environmental symbolism. Let us now explore the stellar symbolism of the Creation as rendered in Genesis One of the bible.

Creation From The Biblical Perspective
In Genesis of the bible the creation is rendered thus:
Genesis: I: 2-4

2And the earth was without form, and void; and darkness was upon the face of the deep. And the Spirit of God moved upon the face of the waters.

3And God said, Let there be light: and there was light. 4And God saw the light, that it was good: and God divided the light from the darkness

Genesis: I: 6-8

6And God said, Let there be a firmament in the midst of the waters, and let it divide the waters from the waters. 7And God made the firmament, and divided the waters which were under the firmament from the waters which were above the firmament: and it was so. 8And God called the firmament Heaven. And the evening and the morning were the second day.

Genesis: 2: 8-10

8And the LORD God planted a garden eastward in Eden; and there he put the man whom he had formed. 9And out of the ground made the LORD God to grow every tree that is pleasant to the sight, and good for food; the tree of life also in the midst of the garden, and the tree of knowledge of good and evil. 10And a river went out of Eden to water the garden; and from thence it was parted, and became into four heads.

Genesis: 3: 14-15

14And the LORD God said unto the serpent, Because thou hast done this, thou art cursed above all cattle, and above every beast of the field; upon thy belly shalt thou go, and dust shalt thou eat all the days of thy life: 15And I will put enmity between thee and the woman, and between thy seed and her seed; it shall bruise thy head, and thou shalt bruise *his* heel.

CHAPTER TWO

Genesis: I: 27-28, 2: 7, 2: 22-23

So God created man in his *own* image, in the image of God created he him; male and female created he them. [28]And God blessed them, and God said unto them, Be fruitful, and multiply, and replenish the earth, and subdue it: and have dominion over the fish of the sea, and over the fowl of the air, and over every living thing that moveth upon the earth.

And the LORD God formed man *of* the dust of the ground, and breathed into his nostrils the breath of life; and man became a living soul.

And the rib, which the LORD God had taken from man, made he a woman, and brought her unto the man. [23]And Adam said, This *is* now bone of my bones, and flesh of my flesh: she shall be called Woman, because she was taken out of Man

IT MUST BE OBVIOUS to any rational mind that the biblical verses concerning Creation are not literally true, that the passages are expressing a Tale, a fable. But the tales of the scriptures have great merit when properly understood – the symbolisms of mythology serve to restrict the access to superior knowledge (esoteric wisdom) to only those that have been correctly initiated. We won't spend a lot of time attempting to debunk a tale that even a smart child would have trouble accepting literally, BUT WITNESS THIS QUOTE from my book, *The Biggest Lie Ever Told*, wherein this matter of the biblical mythical creation was touched upon.

Quote from The Biggest Lie Ever Told

"But, I seriously doubt that you are able to make intelligent sense out of the biblical verses herein quoted, in a literal sense. Lets take a quick look at what is described in this yarn (a yarn when taken literally). --The earth is described as being *without form* and *void.* Now, for the sake of clarity, let us imagine that we are holding a baseball in the palm of our hand, stretched out before us. Let us imagine further that this ball is the planet earth.

CHAPTER TWO

Now, keeping in mind that this ball is our model, let us analyze the bible verses that we have quoted above. A partial quote says *"And the earth was without form and void"*.   Okay--now let us imagine that our ball has lost all form and not only that--it's void too, empty as a hollow ball. Can you do it; can you make sense out of this nonsense? Well, lets go further. The quote continues "and darkness was open the face of the deep, and the spirit of God moved upon the face of the waters - Okay, don't take your eyes off the ball. The ball, in your hand, has no form and it's empty. Now! You must imagine that darkness is somehow on the face of the deep, of this shapeless empty ball. And not only that! But also, God's spirit has started moving on the face of the waters, located Somewhere in or on this formless, empty, and deep ball (earth) that you are holding in your hand.

"And God said, let there be a Firmament in the midst of the waters, and let it divide the Waters from the Waters. And God made the Firmament and divided the Waters which were under the Firmament from the Waters where above the Firmament"

Can you do it! Is your imagination still working? Remember you must keep your eye on the ball in your hand that represents the earth. So now the sky (firmament) is created; it slides in between the waters that are situated in or on the ball in your hand that has no shape, is empty, with deepness and a floating God traveling over or perhaps on the waters, which (waters) are situated in or on the ball (earth) that has no form and nothing in it. Is that clear enough for you? Do you understand it? Or is it time for faith to arrive. Good old faith solves any and all questions. Because whether you understand a thing or not, - with faith, all things are possible, so they say"

I THINK THAT THAT IS ENOUGH mentioned on the matter of the *literal* acceptance of the story of creation as depicted in Genesis of the bible; but nevertheless, in spite of the playful ridicule I exhibited in the quote above, *the Tale is absolutely true* or *accurate in terms of symbolism.* WE WILL BRING COMPLETE CLARITY to the Creation saga

CHAPTER TWO

of *Genesis One* within this chapter, *but first we need to review the Egyptian Tale from which the Hebrews derived their mythical concept* – which they have conveyed to the world as actual history. PLEASE WITNESS THIS QUOTE which tends to affirm our view concerning <u>Jewish plagiarism</u> written by the renowned scholar *Dr. Albert Churchward* in his book *The Origin And Evolution Of Religion* published in 1924.

"Modern research discovers in the <u>Hebrew writings</u> a composite work, not as the autogram of the Hebrew legislator, but as the editorial patchwork of mingling Semitic legends with <u>cosmopolitan myths</u>, which were <u>copied from the Egyptians</u>, either directly or indirectly, but without the gnosis"

Creation From The Ancient Egyptian Perspective

According to the ancient Egyptians, Creation began after this fashion: IN THE BEGINNING there was complete *darkness* and *void* and no visible life whatsoever - this circumstance was described as a *watery abyss* of darkness, chaos and void - it was called the *Nu (Nun)*. Out of this abyss of blackness and inactivity arose the original form of god as a self-created entity. This god, named *Ra* (the sun) and symbolized as a *Beetle* commenced the creation of himself in the watery *Nu*. Once *Ra* (also called *Khepera* and symbolized as a beetle) formed himself he *arose from the abyss as a form of light*. After *Ra* had completed his self-creation he commenced to create others (sub-gods). In that *Ra* was of an androgynous nature he produced his offspring by masturbation and consuming the seed of life within his mouth and subsequently spitting the formulated life forms into existence – his first creation was the pair named *Shu* and *Tefnut*. Egyptian ancient text describes *Shu* and *Tefnut* as representing Air (wind) and mist (moisture) respectively. *Shu* and *Tefnut* cohabitated and produced a pair of offspring named *Geb* and *Nut* – according to ancient Egyptian script Geb represented Earth and *Nut* represented the Sky. *Geb* and *Nut* cohabitated and produced the deities known as *Osiris, Set, Isis* and *Nepthys*. This story of the *Egyptian concept of Creation* (and other similar concepts) is widely known and can be

CHAPTER TWO

found in any of several books about Egyptian history. One source is *From Fetish To God In Ancient Egypt* by E. A. Wallis Budge.

Of course the Egyptian tale is just as ridiculous as the biblical Tale, *if taken literally* – both tales are masks (allegories)that shield great underlying natural and cultural truths, and both the Egyptian and the biblical tales are based on identical astronomical phenomena centered on solar time-cycles. As I have written so many times before, the underlying purpose of many allegorical scriptures is the tracking and recording of time – the bible is a Registry of Astronomical phenomena written in a Mythological format. WE SHALL first bring clarity to the Egyptian Fable and thereafter to the Biblical Fable and we will prove that both are reflective of *natural phenomena* reported in a mythological format. And we shall prove also that the Hebrew biblical rendition is a plagiarized version of the Egyptian mythos, as was suggested to us by the late erudite scholar, Albert Churchward - again, see quote from his book, The Origin and Evolution of Religion:

"Modern research discovers in the Hebrew writings a composite work, not as the autogram of the Hebrew legislator, but as the editorial patchwork of mingling Semitic legends with cosmopolitan myths, which were copied from the Egyptians, either directly or indirectly, but without the gnosis"

Interpretation Of The Egyptian perspective

We are focused on the Creation myth of Genesis ; however the actual underlying and *esoteric purpose* of the Eden allegory is *time-tracking*, most specifically, *The beginning of time-tracking* as measured by the transits of the sun. Actually the *universe is eternal* according to the ancients. There never was a time when the universe was not in existence. The universe is a mirrored reflection of god in this sense; in other words, just as the unseen God is eternal without beginning or end, so likewise is God's handiwork, that is, this unfathomable universe is likewise without beginning or end.

So the universe was not created ex nihilo, that is to say, magically from out of nothing and boom the world appears. THERE NEVER WAS A TIME WHEN THE WORLD WAS NOT - this is a difficult concept for the human brain to handle, but in reality it is no more difficult to conceive

CHAPTER TWO

than the concept of the world popping into existence from out of nowhere by reason of deified proclamation. Truthfully, *not* even the bible declares that the universe was created ex nihilo - the bible presupposes the preexistence of Matter, how be it, this Matter was unformed and seemingly ungoverned. see bible verses:

Genesis 1:1-2 *In the beginning God created the heaven and the earth. And the earth was without form, and void; and darkness was upon the face of the deep. And the Spirit of God moved upon the face of the waters.* Note, that according to the biblical verses just cited, water was primordial, or even preexistent; it was concomitant with God's first cycle of creation. The bible states that the Earth was without form and void, thus indicating that the act of creation actually brought form and essence to an assemblage of matter that was already present in the cosmic milieu, but present in a *state of chaos or disorder*. So if we think deeply we can see that creation is more akin to *bringing form* to matter rather than the act of magically creating or conjuring matter into existence. We should note also that *Beginning does not necessarily indicate the Beginning of all things*, but beginning also indicates, the *first in an order of events*. You will find, as our analysis proceeds, the the most accurate concept for the *biblical description of creation or beginning* is the marking of the *first* of a series of events or perhaps *formulations*, would be a better way of putting it. So this *first* in the order of things, according to the bible, was a matrix of *darkness, void or disorder, water, and God's spirit*; and from this primordial mix emanated the *Sky and the Earth* - THIS IS RIGHT IN ACCORD WITH THE ANCIENT EGYPTIAN STORY OF CREATION. According to Egyptian creation mythology, after Ra (the Sun) ascended from the *uncharted depths of the watery abyss, chaos and darkness,* the *first* in order of creation brought forth by Ra was Shu (Wind) Tefnut (mist, humidity) - then came *Nut* and *Geb*, that is to say the <u>Sky</u> and the <u>Earth.</u> And lo and behold the bible likewise states that the first in creation was the Heavens (sky) and the Earth, and the spirit of god moved upon the <u>watery abyss</u> (face of Waters) - this represents a complete 100% agreement or concurrence between

CHAPTER TWO

the essentials of the Egyptian and Biblical creation stories in this, the first phase of the creation allegory.

TIME BEGINS WITH CREATION and in reflection, *creation* begins with the evolution of *activity* and divine order from out of chaos, the abyss; that's the message conveyed in the Egyptian myth, that is that Ra (sun) *commenced activity* by which Time *could be measured* and the advent of measuring time marked creation, which is *synonymous to the beginning of Time*. So *that* which the mythology is actually describing is not creation ex nihilo (of something out of nothing) but *rather* that which is synonymous to creation; in other words the beginning of time or more correctly the beginning of *Time* Measurement. THIS IS A VERY IMPORTANT POINT, that is to say, that before the so-called Creation, *Time did not exist because it was not measured.* Time comes into existence *with* the dynamics of Creation, so *the commencement of one denotes the beginning of the other*. The ancients were describing the beginning of Time *measurement* under the type of Creation is the salient idea that must be understood.

But in order to accurately measure cosmic Time, we must have coordinates that serve as markers and we must have movement between those cosmic markers (starry signpost, points of conjunction, pivoting, etc.), so as to properly calculate time based on the movement of celestial entities. The ancient Egyptians gave us vague definitions of the symbolized elements of creation – that *Ra* was the sun, *Shu* was wind, *Tefnut* was mist, *Geb* was earth and *Nut* was sky. They revealed this in text and pictorially. Take note of the graphic (artists reproductions of Egyptian graphic reliefs) on the next page that depicts Shu (wind) raising the sky (Nut) from the embrace of earth (Geb), thus producing daytime. When Nut (the sky) is embraced by Geb (earth) we experience the evening, nighttime but when the sun rises in the morning the wind of Shu blows the night away and *this* they illustrated by the deity Shu, with arms upraised, pushing Nut (sky) from the embrace of Geb (earth).

CHAPTER TWO

Graphic of Shu, Nut, and Seb

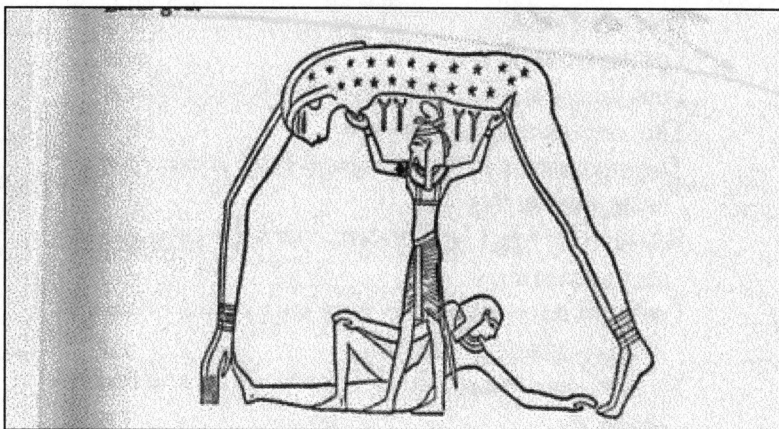

Figure A. Graphic depicts Shu, Nut and Seb . The night sky (Nut) is always above the earth (Seb) but in the daytime Shu as an agent of the sun intervenes and raises the sky from the embrace of earth

CHAPTER TWO

This Egyptian myth (of Creation) is describing the beginning of cosmic *time* measurement, and the *deities of Creation* are actually the *coordinates* and *physical factors* by which cosmic cycles are calculated. The first god of Creation was the sun (Ra). The sun is our primary and indispensable means of measuring time-cycles – the sun gives us our seconds, minutes, hours, days, seasons, years and cycles that run into infinity. They made the sun (Ra) first in creation because the sun is primary to the measurement of our most basic cycles i.e. hours, days, seasons, years. THE FIRST PAIR CREATED after the sun was *Shu* and *Tefnut*, described as Air and mist. Actually Shu and Tefnut represent the atmosphere that envelopes (surrounds and encloses) the earth and separates us from outer space. The atmosphere captures and contains the light of the sun thereby giving us daytime in its turn and also protects us from the hostile frigid elements of the cosmos. The earth is surrounded by layers of atmosphere (air, Shu), that shield the earth and capture the light of the sun – and all this is mated with the vital moisture, water (mist, Tefnut) of life that in combination sustains us.

SHU AND TEFNUT GAVE BIRTH to *Geb* and *Nut* – the Egyptians told us in their text and graphics that Geb was the earth and that Nut was the sky – and they noted that Shu intervened between Geb and Nut. The intervention of Shu was to raise the sky from the embrace of the earth, thereby giving us alternating day and night. THIS CLEARLY SHOWS that the Egyptians used the symbolism of Geb and Nut *separated* by Shu to denote the alternating night and day caused by rotation of the earth on its axis. The symbolic embraces and lovemaking of Geb and Nut, in the evening under the veil of darkness, was interrupted by the return of the sun (Ra) each morning. The sun (Ra) returned like a jealous or wronged husband returning to his abode and he dispatched (with the light of his coming), his servant (Shu), the winds of daylight (or the capturer of the suns rays) to separate the lovers from their embrace. So by this symbolism the ancient Egyptians symbolized the physics of our solar system inclusive of the ruling sun and the enlivened earth spinning on its axis in a regular daily cycle of 24 hours – and this alternating between

CHAPTER TWO

night and day was depicted as the conjoining of lovers (earth and sky) in darkness and their *forced separation*, caused by the earth's rotation, which let in the light of day.

THEIR (EGYPTIANS) NEXT STEP was to expand their timekeeping into the seasons, and they depicted that as follows: The embraces of Geb and Nut brought forth four children, namely Osiris, Set, Isis and Nepthys. Osiris and Set were twin brothers that were in eternal conflict with each other – this clearly shows them as representative of the apposing equinoctial points. *Osiris* was the vernal equinox *and gatekeeper* of the upper cosmic regions. *Set* was the autumnal equinox and *gatekeeper* of the lower cosmic regions, he that laid in wait in the lower regions and assassinated his brother *Osiris*. *Isis* as the wife of Osiris was the arc (space) of the upper regions, the northern hemisphere and *Nepthys* as the wife of *Set* was the arc (space) of the Lower regions. These four deities were used, *in this early phase* of the gnosis, to represent the four cardinal points, by which the seasons are measured, *namely the vernal equinox, the summer solstice, the autumnal equinox and the winter solstice.*

THIS ENNEAD composed of Ra, Shu, Tefnut, Geb, Nut, Osiris, Set, Isis and Nepthys served as symbols in the early phase of Egyptian mythology, which when properly interpreted, established a scientific astronomical bases for tracking cosmic time cycles. The evolution of these mythical deities was such that their symbolisms were (over time) migrated and adjusted in various phases of the symbolisms in-keeping with the focuses of the allegories. Our task at this point is to connect the biblical version of Creation with the Egyptian – to illustrate with a preponderance of evidence that the Jewish version is derived from the Egyptian version, and that both are, of course, reflective of astronomical phenomena.

The biblical version is a patchwork affair, as was noted by Churchward in the quote that I inserted from his book. The editing of the bible is such that the works of various authors of varying focuses and of even different centuries are brought together and presented as a force of one, within one timeframe, as if originally intended as one comprehensive composition – which was not the

CHAPTER TWO

case. There are contradictions throughout the bible because of this as well as just plain human error. For instance the bible speaks of two separate creations of Man in the first and second chapter of Genesis, in a very matter of fact manner:

Genesis I: 27-28 [27]So <u>God created man in his *own* image</u>, in the image of God created he him; <u>male</u> and <u>female</u> created he them. [28]And God blessed them, and God said unto them, Be fruitful, and multiply, and replenish the earth, and subdue it: and have dominion over the fish of the sea, and over the fowl of the air, and over every living thing that moveth upon the earth.

Genesis 2: 5-7 [5]And every plant of the field before it was in the earth, and every herb of the field before it grew: for the LORD God had not caused it to rain upon the earth, and *there was* not a man to till the ground. [6]But there went up a mist from the earth, and watered the whole face of the ground. [7]And the LORD <u>God formed man *of* the dust of the ground,</u> and breathed into his nostrils the breath of life; and man became a living soul.

THIS IS A CLEAR contradiction at the *literal level of interpretation.* In terms of symbolism, this is *not* a contradiction, because allegorically within those <u>two</u> <u>creations</u> of Man (mind) we have therein revealed a Gnostic aspect, <u>Dualism</u> – one Man or Force was created from *numinous* spirit (in <u>gods</u> <u>image</u>, ethereal) and the other *force, a blind, natural instinctive force of this lower world*, was created or embedded (from its beginnings) with a *geotic* psyche, from <u>lowly mud</u> (from matter) – and some think that it is the inherent conflict between spiritualism and materialism that has the world marching toward its own social, theological annihilation (i.e. the breakdown of our Value Systems and Social Guidelines). But I digress – we will cover this element of predestined conflict between the *numinous* and the *geotic* forces, and the expected consequences concomitant with our entrance into the Age of Aquarius, at a later time.

CHAPTER TWO

Interpretation Of The Biblical Perspective

Genesis: I: 2-4

2And the <u>earth</u> was without form, and <u>void</u>; and <u>darkness</u> *was* upon the face of the <u>deep</u>. And the *Spirit of God moved* upon the face of the <u>waters</u>.

3And God said, Let there be <u>light</u>: and there was light. 4And God saw the light, that *it was* good: and God <u>divided</u> the <u>light</u> from the <u>darkness</u>

THESE BIBLICAL VERSES come clearly into focus, after our review of the Egyptian myth of Creation that describes the *first* act of creation as the gods own *self-creation* out of darkness as a force of light – *the living sun titled as the god Ra.* THE HEBREWS ASSERT that the first creation by their *god* was *light* – THE EGYPTIANS ASSERT that the first creation of their god was light and that *god* was the *light.* Sound familiar? I think that the association between the two fables is vivid. SUBSEQUENT TO THE CREATION of light, god *divided* the *light* from the *darkness* according to the biblical verses. This is exactly in line with the activities of the sun-god Ra. After his self-creation in darkness, he stirred and arose, emerged from the watery darkness of Nu as the new-born god, alone without any companions. BOTH the Egyptian and the Hebrew tales of Creation begin with pre-existent water and darkness, followed by the emergence of light, and subsequently the division or alternating of light and darkness.

Genesis: I: 6-8

6And God said, Let there be a <u>firmament</u> [sky]*in the midst of the waters, and let it <u>divide</u> the <u>waters</u> from the waters.* 7And God made the firmament, and divided the waters which *were* under the firmament from the waters which *were* above the firmament: and it was so. 8And *God called the firmament Heaven.* And the evening and the morning were the second day.

ACCORDING TO THE BIBLE, after the creation of light, god created the firmament and slid it between the waters. This sounds so weird *until* we expand on the ancient symbolistic definition of water – the ancients referred to the skies as *celestial waters* – they even imaged their god or other deities sailing through the heavens (skies) with his companions in a mythical celestial boat. In some cases the ancient deities were fashioned as part fish and part man, because they

CHAPTER TWO

imagined that the deities needed fish attributes in order to navigate through the waters in the early phases of the symbolism, for instances the fish gods known as Oaanes or Dagon. So, in truth, the firmament that was slid between the *waters* referred to the *cosmic waters* of space that were divided by the sky (atmosphere that completely enshrouds the planet Earth). This was the occult message of the ancient Egyptians and also the esoteric message of the Hebrews in their fantastic biblical version that they have promoted as historical. I find it extremely difficult to understand how any reasonable person could accept the Eden saga as anything but a mystery, a mystery that begs to be unveiled. Judaic biblical theology does not represent genuine and true literal accounts of god's handiwork or god's interactions with humans in those bygone days. This Eden (Creation) tale was actually the symbolic rendering of cosmic phenomena written in a mythological format. The *underlying occult* truth of much of Genesis reflects an abyss of seemingly chaotic *cosmic disorder* or *lack* in *human psychic perception* that stunned and prevailed before the birth or evolution of intellectual Man (Mind), a disorder or chaos that was *transformed* into psychic order or form by the *emergence* of human *consciousness*, into the abstract, emerged from out of the depths of the unknown or unconscious, the symbolic Nu of the psyche - but I digress, we shall explore this higher aspect later. THE FIRMAMENT refers to the atmosphere (Shu and Tefnut), the blanket of air and moisture that separates the earth from the celestial waters of outer space – and divides the cosmos into two hemispheres, the *upper northern hemisphere* (waters above the firmament) and the *lower southern hemisphere* (waters below the firmament). The firmament is the atmospheric mass of gases that encases and surrounds the planet Earth. Our planet is the solid core of the firmament and our equator is the line, expanded into the heavens, that divides the cosmos into upper and lower halves.

Genesis: 2: 8-10

8And the LORD God planted a garden eastward in Eden; and there he put the man whom he had formed. 9And out of the ground made the LORD God to grow every tree that is pleasant to the sight, and good for food; the

CHAPTER TWO

tree of life also in the midst of the garden, and the tree of knowledge of good and evil. ¹⁰And a river went out of Eden to water the garden; and from thence it was parted, and became into four heads.

THESE VERSES in chapter Two of Genesis are actually next in the process of creation, that is to say, the mythic *symbolism* of the process of creation. We are told by the Hebrews, that god planted a garden eastward in Eden, plopped Adam and Eve into that Setting. The garden is described as having a tree in the midst (center) of it, called the *tree of life* and another tree thereabouts called the *tree of the knowledge of good and evil*. Also a river flows from the garden that branches into four heads.

The key terms within these verses are *Garden, Eastward, Eden, Tree, Midst, Four Heads.* It is through the proper interpretations of these words, in terms of their astronomical symbolisms, etymologies and biblical meanings, that the truth is revealed.

IMPORTANT DEFINITIONS ARE AS FOLLOWS: The term garden does *not* refer to a farmer's paradise (where the earth yields its bounty free of human toil) as we have been led to believe by teary-eyed sentimentalists and dreamers. The word *Garden* as used in the biblical context referred to an *enclosure, a fenced in area, an area surrounded or bordered by some object or objects[1].* This is confirmed by perusing many the biblical dictionaries and encyclopedias available on the market. The term garden, as used biblically was derived from the Hebrew G*an* or G*annah* which means to surround – and this is on the mark as to the correct mythological interpretation that I shall render presently. The term *Eden* means *Wilderness*, traceable to the Sumerian-Akkadian root of *Edinu,* which means a wilderness area, plain uncharted place. And the term *Tree,* as used biblically in Genesis refers to Firmness – see Strong's concordance of biblical terms #H6095.

---

[1] The celestial Garden of Eden as defined in the *stellar symbolism* is demarcated by the circumpolar constellations

CHAPTER TWO

Now WITH THESE DEFINITIONS and more in mind, we can get on with the task of correctly deciphering the biblical symbolism of this portion of Genesis.

First the bible states that god planted a garden eastward in Eden – now we know that the term garden means a enclosed area, and this definition of enclosure goes to the core of the astronomical symbolism – the editors were describing, *in the stellar phase of the symbolism,* the enclosed area of the northern celestial pole. The circumpolar stars of the *North Celestial Pole* surround the garden referred to in the stellar phase of the biblical mythology. This celestial garden of the non-setting stars *enclosed within the perimeter of the circumpolar constellations* is the *stellar Garden Of Eden.* The Eastward direction of Eden refers, in essence, to the e*astward rotation* of the earth on its axis. The term *Eden* (which means Wilderness) probably refers to the *wilderness or abyss of outer space.* The Tree at the center (midst) of the garden refers to the point of the celestial polar axis itself i.e. the *Firm* and *stable* pivot about which the circumpolar constellations revolve, which is terrestrially identical to the planetary axis about which earth rotates. The river that branches into *four heads* refers to the *four cardinal points* – the four compass directions, celestial and/or terrestrial.

THE STELLAR SYMBOLISM ALSO EXTENDS into the allegory of the serpent that deceived Eve and caused the so-called fall or expulsion of Adam and Eve from paradise.

Genesis 3:1 through Genesis 3:7

[1]Now the serpent was more subtle than any beast of the field which the LORD God had made. And he said unto the woman, Yea, hath God said, Ye shall not eat of every tree of the garden? [2]And the woman said unto the serpent, We may eat of the fruit of the trees of the garden: [3]But of the fruit of the tree which *is* in the midst of the garden, God hath said, Ye shall not eat of it, neither shall ye touch it, lest ye die. [4]And the serpent said unto the woman, Ye shall not surely die: [5]For God doth know that in the day ye eat thereof, then your eyes shall be opened, and ye shall be as gods, knowing good and evil.

CHAPTER TWO

⁶And when the woman saw that the tree *was* good for food, and that it *was* pleasant to the eyes, and a tree to be desired to make *one* wise, she took of the fruit thereof, and did eat, and gave also unto her husband with her; and he did eat. ⁷And the eyes of them both were opened, and they knew that they *were* naked; and they sewed fig leaves together, and made themselves aprons.

WE HAVE already established that the *tree* in the midst (center) of the garden was the *Celestial Pole*; so defining the serpent that lurks about the tree is rather simple. The *stellar* serpent was the constellation of Draconis. This is the constellation that occupied the celestial polar region at the time, apparently, of the original writing of this particular symbolism of the deceitful, talking serpent i.e. the opponent deity of the Eden saga. This was during the equinoctial or astrological era of Gemini that commenced circa 6606 BC. Within the time-frame that Gemini came into the position at the vernal equinox, the constellation of Draconis, in tandem, took position on the throne of the celestial pole. See pictograph on the following page (Heading: *Egyptian Planisphere*) - it depicts the Egyptian representation of the circumpolar constellations and asterisms, with the constellation of Draconis at the center of the celestial pole. Next, take note of the second following pictograph titled, *Circle of Perpetual Apparition,* which shows the celestial circumpolar region and notes the locations of the *Celestial Pole* and the *Pole of the Ecliptic* which represent respectively the *Tree of Life* and the *Tree of the Knowledge of Good and Evil* as referenced in the biblical Eden saga.

CHAPTER TWO

Egyptian Planisphere, Draconis encircling the Pole

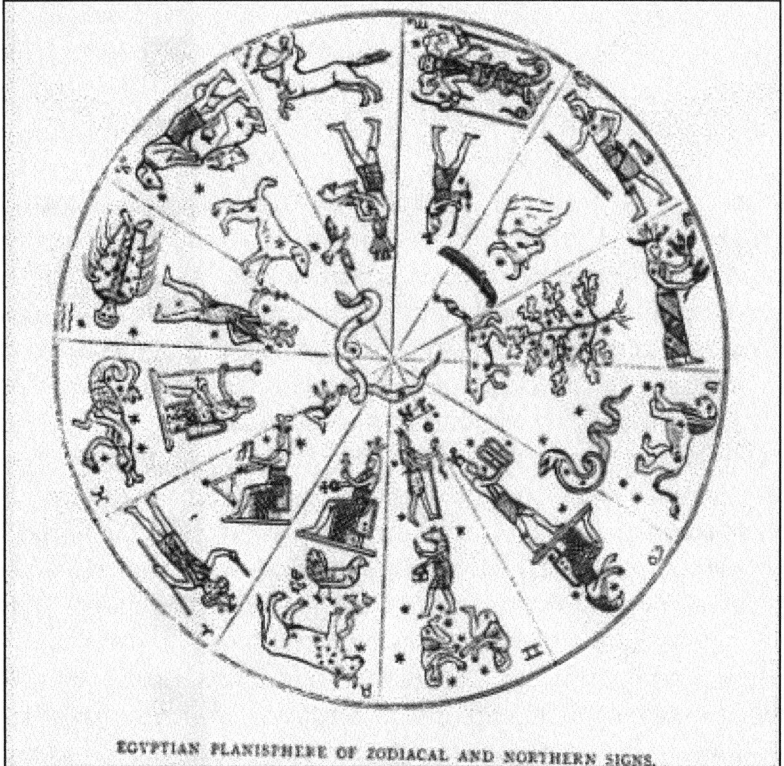

EGYPTIAN PLANISPHERE OF ZODIACAL AND NORTHERN SIGNS.

Figure B Draconis (Dragon, Serpent) had control (primary positioning)
of the celestial mount (stellar heaven) for 3 astrological ages, commenceing
in the era of Gemini and running thru Taurus and Aries. Picture Reference from "The Natural Genesis" by Gerald Massey published in 1903

CHAPTER TWO

The Stellar circumpolar symbolism shows the two Trees (Poles) as the Celestial Pole and the Pole of the Ecliptic. The Serpent is Draconis, and the four rivers are the compass directions

Circle Of Perpetual Apparition - Stellar Garden Of Eden

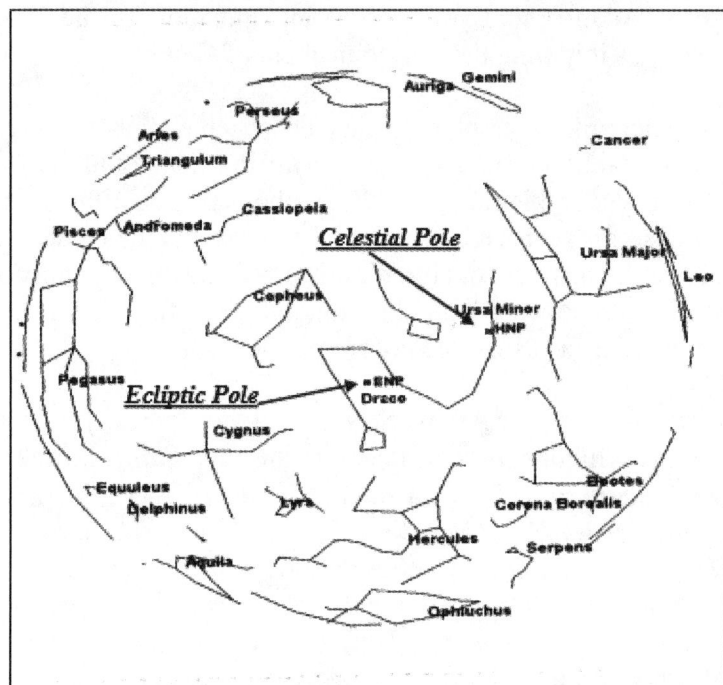

This graphic depicts the celestial Garden of Eden (Circumpolar Constellations) with the Celestial Pole (Tree of Life) located near the star Thuban in the tail of Draconis (the Serpent). The 2nd tree of the garden symbolizes the Ecliptic Pole. Draconis was central to the circumpolar stars (stellar garden) through the eras of Gemini, Taurus, and Aries

An extensive explanation of the Garden of Eden symbolism is given in my book, *Lifting The Gnostic Veil.*

CHAPTER TWO

I have supplied Charts and Graphs on the next few pages - TAKE NOTE of the chart, on page 68, with the Heading: *Astrological Eras and Polar Stations*[1], which matches-up the constellations of the Astrological eras with their Circumpolar counterparts – notice that *Draconis* and *Gemini* moved in tandem into their respective *signal* positions about 6606 BC. Draconis (the Serpent of Eden) took position at the celestial Polar Hub, and Gemini (Gemini Twins symbolize Adam and Eve) entered into position at the Vernal Equinox, thus initiating the astrological era of Gemini.

Also take note of the graphic on page 69 which depicts the Garden of Eden as paralleled under an aspect of the *Solar* and *Seasonal* symbolism. Under this parallel of the symbolism, the Earthly plateau or island itself is seen as the Garden; the Serpent is the Underworld of the lower hemisphere of climatic adversity; the upper hemisphere during the summer represents the tranquil state; the four rivers of Eden symbolize, as usual, the Four Cardinal Points.

ADAM AND EVE REPRESENT THE SUN AND MOON respectively *in this phase* of the symbolism - see quote from the book ***Star Names Their Lore and Meaning by Richard Allen*** ... *"or, to go back to the beginning of things, **Adam** and **Eve**, who probably were intended by the **nude male** and **female** figures walking hand in hand in the original illustration of the Alfonsine Tables, a similar showing appears, however, on the Denderah Planisphere of 1300 years previous."* ..."*and Brown reproduces a Euphratean representation of a couple of small, naked, male child-figures, one standing upon its head and the other standing upon the former, feet to feet; the original **twins** being the **sun** and **moon**, when the one is up the other is generally down"*...

---

[1] Over a Precession Cycle of 25,920 years the vernal equinox is transited by all 12 zodiac constellations, each for a period of 2160 years which constitutes an astrological era; also during the Precession Cycle the Celestial Pole transits through 6 circumpolar constellations

CHAPTER TWO

Astrological Eras And Polar Stations

Gregorian Year	Astrological Era	Polar Station
2034 A.D.	Aquarius	Ursa Minor
126 BC	Pisces	Void
2286 BC	Aries	Draconis
4446 BC	Taurus	Draconis
6606 BC	Gemini	Draconis
8766 BC	Cancer	Hercules
10,926 BC	Leo	Hercules
13,086 BC	Virgo	Lyra
15,246 BC	Libra	Cygnus
17,406 BC	Scorpio	Cepheus
19,566 BC	Sagittarius	Cepheus
21,726 BC	Capricorn	Cepheus
23,886 BC	Aquarius	Ursa Minor

This chart indicates the commencement of each of the 12 Astrological Ages by their zodiac signs,and shows also the constellations that were correspondingly centered at the Celestial Pole during a given Astrological Age. Each Age spans 2160 years; the next Age of Aquarius mathematically commences in the year 2034 CE.

Graphic, Astrological Eras and Polar Stations

CHAPTER TWO

Garden Of Eden In Solar Symbolism

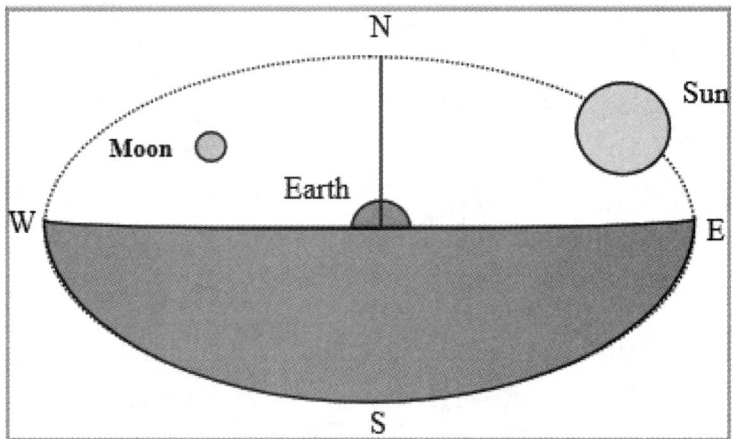

This is a pictographic representation of the *Garden of Eden allegory* focused on the *solar symbolism*. This particular symbology shows seasonal symbolism: the garden is the *upper hemisphere* when the sun is in high declination above the celestial equator, the two trees of the garden are the equinoctial points, vernal and autumnal; the serpent is the darkness of the lower hemisphere, the four rivers are the four compass directions. The sun is like a flaming disc that circuits, sort of like a guardian, around the garden, *yearly* or perhaps *daily*, depending on the focus of the symbolism. The sun and the moon symbolize Adam and Eve.

Graphic, Garden of Eden in Solar Symbolism

CHAPTER TWO

THE PRECEDING QUOTE (from Richard Allen's book) reflects both *Stellar* and *Solar* symbolism, but *we shall remain primarily focused* on the *Stellar* symbolism reflective of the *Circumpolar Constellations,* as this, I believe, is most vivid; however both of these versions run in parallel. FOR EXAMPLE, let us again take note of the pictograph labeled *Garden of Eden Solar Symbolism* on the preceding page - this graphic depicts the seasonally verdant Earth itself as the Eden Paradise, especially the upper hemisphere during the phase of the sun's annual cycle when its declination is above the celestial equator. All of the vital symbols are present in the *solar* mythology as well as the *stellar*, but of course with different designations. The two Trees (Poles, Pillars) are the *Vernal* and *Autumnal* equinoxes, the Serpent is the *Darkness* of the *daily cycle* or Underworld of the *yearly cycle*; the four rivers of Eden represent the four compass directions. Adam and Eve are the sun and moon as indicated by the quote from the Richard Allen book.

FYI - THE STELLAR SYMBOLISM PRECEDED the Solar according to various scholars; be that as it may, the symbolisms are not limited to the stellar and solar categories - also, some symbolisms and allegories may evolve and modify overtime due to cosmic changes that cannot be reflected accurately without adjustments to the mythological tales. FOR EXAMPLE when the Astrological Age transits from one zodiacal sign to another, for instances such as from Gemini to Taurus and from Taurus to Aries, and on and on; then consequently in order to maintain synchronism between the symbolisms and their underlying counterparts, it becomes necessary that any symbolisms or allegories referring to the vernal equinox must be modified in sync with the astronomical charting - consequently, a symbolic reference to the vernal equinox would necessarily change types, from twins (Gemini), to Bulls (Taurus), to Rams (Aries) etc. The core of the mythical tales would remain intact but the mythological designations employed to tell the various stories would modify overtime in accordance with the changing dynamics of the cosmos - cultural inputs are also a factor. Also, perspicuity must be utilized if and when the allegory is written from a *unique geocentric perspective,* that references horizon, azimuth, and altitude, rather than a *global perspective,* which references the celestial equator, right ascension, and declination, and there other contingencies also.

CHAPTER TWO

Universe as Macrocosm and Man as Microcosm

AS A REMINDER, we are bringing forth light on the symbolism of the Garden of Eden mythology, but not just *any* light or a fanciful conception. We are unfolding the *original* esoteric light which was born out of the original astrotheological arcana. Astro-theology (star religion) is the original *intellectual* link between Heaven, Earth, and *Man*, a link that helped nurture and elevate Man from the status of a smart earth creature into the lofty realms of divine numinous kinship with the infinite source. *Man* studied himself and, likewise through his study and observations of the universe, *Man* unfolded vital secrets of the cycles of the cosmos; secrets that unveiled *striking typological relationships and parallels* between the human species and the heavens above. *Man* found relationships in the cycles of the cosmic lights that seem prototypical to the biological cycles and proportions of Man; such as the **gestation cycle** of the sun at 280 days, from March 21 to Dec. 25, being an exact match for the gestation of Man at 280 days; and the light cycle of the Moon at 28 days being an exact match for the woman's **menstrual cycle** at 28 days. *Man* gazed upward to the heavens, intensely cogitating the purport of the associative numbers that linked the human species with the heavenly arc; and thereafter, in pantheistic awe, concluded and declared, that, indeed, *by the numbers, Man* had been created in the image and likeness of the cosmic god.

Scholarly speculations in regards to the Garden of Eden Tale

BUT MORE TO THE POINT of our subject within this chapter, i.e. *the Garden of Eden myth* - we, of this generation, are not the first to see the idiocy of the Eden saga as literally presented in the bible. Historically, we find many great thinkers, earnestly trying their utmost to extrapolate, to some degree, a rational and coherent message from between the lines of the Eden composition, and similar cultural tales that are held dear by many faithful devotees. SOME have reckoned **Adam** as *intellect* and **Eve** as *passion* and the forbidden fruit as a tug in between these traits, with the **Serpent** as the great tempter egging us on to give in to our sensual and sentient appetites. THE METAPHYSICS have proffered the interpretation that **Eden** represents the Divine Consciousness from which we have fallen, that we should strive to purify and cleanse out psyche so that we can again be in conscious unity with

CHAPTER TWO

the divine within his Garden of divine consciousness. **Philo Judaeus**, the renowned Jewish theologian of Alexandria Egypt, who lived at a time more or less contemporaneous to the mythical Jesus of Nazareth suggested the interpretation that the Garden of Eden symbolized the human soul, that the Tree of Life symbolized Religion, which is the pathway to eternal life for the faithful believer; that the Tree of the Knowledge of Good and Evil was the pathway by which the soul discerns the choices of righteousness as opposed to sin; that the four rivers of Eden symbolized prudence, temperance, courage, and justice. **Maimonides** saw, in the mythological Eden Saga, the psychic emergence of Man from the animal state wherein moral discernment is not perceived, into the elevated human, with rational intellect, whereby Man becomes endowed with abstract reasoning, moral discernment, human ethics and the like.

THERE ARE MANY, MANY INTERPRETATIONS of the Eden saga that have developed (and are still developing) after these many thousands of years since the writings were first exposed. The interpretations vary, but nevertheless, all of the postulations are threaded by one common fiber, and that fiber is the quest, the endless quest to somehow extract a reasonable, rational, and coherent religious message from out of the folds of this puzzling and enigmatic Judaic tale, which innumerable monotheists insist is divinely inspired. The Eden saga, as literally written, is a palpable fairy tale that even a child would fervently reject as conveying a message of cardinal truth, if not told that the story came out of the bible.

But within the folds of astro-theology we are not dealing with mere interpretations, even though some postulations may have intellectual and/or spiritual merit, but rather we are focused on the *primeval origins* of the Eden myth and other similar allegories; and we hereby do ardently declare that the provable origin is discoverable within the matrix of ancient astro-theological symbolism. THE TRUE GENESIS of our religious literature, bequeathed to us through the cultural conduits of ancient mythological allegories, lies in cosmic symbolism; that is to say, the recording of astronomical phenomena in a mythological format.

CHAPTER TWO

The house of religion has been constructed upon the foundations of cultural mythologies, and our ancient mythologies were all engendered, to a significant degree, by man's anthropomorphizing the forces and faces of nature, cosmic and environmental.

Eden Stellar Symbolism verses Eden Solar Symbolism

As we further analyze the arcane aspects of biblical symbolism, projected as a mythological expression of astronomical phenomena, we are primarily focused on the *stellar* circumpolar symbolism relative to the Eden tale. We are also reviewing correlative aspects of the *solar-equinoctial*[1] symbolism which follows, in conformity to the star-symbology, the same parallels or typology as the stellar mythos. We have already unfolded the underlying identities of the main allegorical players of the Eden saga as found under the stellar circumpolar symbolism. THE GARDEN of Eden itself is the *Circle of Perpetual Apparition*, that is to say, the celestial plateau of circumpolar constellations that are always visible, and never set below our horizon. The Tree of Life and the Tree of the Knowledge of Good and Evil symbolize the *Celestial Pole* and the *Pole of the Ecliptic* respectively. The Serpent of the Garden symbolizes the constellation *Draconis*. The Four Rivers emanating from the Garden of Eden symbolize the *Four Cardinal Directions*; North, East, South, and West. Adam and Eve reflect the nude or semi-nude figures of the zodiacal constellation Gemini, the Twins *Castor* and *Pollux*. The term Eden indicates wilderness, the uncharted celestial seas of cosmic space; the celestial Garden of Eden was seen as an elevated island, a plateau, a mountain in the north which never succumbed to the figurative cosmic sea that surrounded it. All other stars were eventually swallowed by the cosmic sea, not to be seen until their reemergence in another cycle; but not the circumpolar stars, they lived (were visible) always and forever.

---

[1] Charting of the circumpolar stars involves tracking the transitions of the Celestial Pole through 6 circumpolar constellations over a Precession period of 25,920 years. Charting the Equinox involves tracking the transitions of the 12 zodiacal constellations as they each transit the vernal equinox for 2160 years, making a total of 25,920 years for a complete revolution of all 12 zodiac signs.

CHAPTER TWO

As REGARDS the Eden allegory reflective of *solar symbolism,* the symbolism is primarily reflective of seasonal transition between the two extremes of summer and winter. Summer or *delight*, if you will, occurs in that span when the sun is at *positive* declination; while on the other hand, winter or *torment* encroaches after the sun falls or is *cast out* of the upper hemisphere into *negative* declination[1]. So Eden, in this solar phase of the symbolism, represents the Earth as a paradise in summer, *but after the fall* of Adam and Eve i.e. the fall of the sun and moon into the lower hemisphere, Earth then becomes a habitat of struggle and torment. In this solar-equinoctial phase of the symbolism the Serpent symbolizes the lower hemisphere of adversity; the lower hemisphere signifies opposition and contention to the upper world. The four rivers are, of course, the four compass directions of North, South, East, and West. The two trees of Eden, that is, the *Tree of Life*, and the *Tree of the Knowledge of Good and Evil* signify the two equinoxes. Exegetically, I am somewhat conflicted on the placement of the tree symbols because the allegorical attributes of the trees are, to a great extent, interchangeable for both the vernal and the autumnal equinoxes. The Hebrews celebrate their New Year in the spring circa the Passover (passing of the sun over the vernal equinox) as the sun enters *new life* as it emerges from the bondage of of the underworld (lower hemisphere); the Hebrews also commemorate the New Year in the Fall at *Rosh Hashanah*; this holy day commemorates the Creation of the world, the birth of life. The Tree of the Knowledge of Good and Evil highlights contention with Satan represented as the serpent - both the vernal and the autumnal equinoxes are points of contention between the upper and lower domains. The Tree of the Knowledge of Good and Evil is a symbolic reference to some form of Judgement and/or Balance I am sure - this is seen by the scales of opposing polarities (good verses evil) hanging from the Tree; these judgmental attributes are reflected in both equinoctial intersections.

---

[1] *Declination refers the the distance of the sun ,in degrees, above or below the Celestial Equator*

CHAPTER TWO

Most significantly the Trees of Eden mark the line of division (contention) between the sacred and the profane in a religious context, just as the equinoctial points mark the line (Celestial Equator) of the opposing upper and lower cosmic domains.   The region above the equinoxes is symbolic of that which is spiritual and godly, so to speak, within the symbolism, whereas the region below the equinoxes denotes materialism and opposition**.**

Witness quote: *Book Two, The Astrological Foundation of The Christ Myth:*

"The Evolution from astronomy to Religion *was done by adapting religious correlations* **to** *the opposing spheres(the region below the equinoxes verses the region above the equinoxes) of natural contention.* **The forces** *of the northern hemisphere , in their religious parallels, represented the positive spiritual natures. The Forces of the Southern Hemisphere represented the negative instinctive natures.* **The Never Ending War of the Sun (Light) to overcome or destroy darkness** *,* <u>*in it's Religious Parallels*</u>*, became the Never Ending Struggle of Man's Spiritual Nature to Dominate his Carnal (beastly) Nature.* **Under it's Religious applications**, *Mythology made the following morally linked transformations - The Darkness of the underworld , in it's religious context, became The Region of Death, Evil, and Matter (Materialism). The Light of the Upperworld became the Region of Life(everlasting), Goodness, and the Divine Spirits.*

The Lord of the Underworld became an opposing Devil, *a Seducer, an accuser. He was Evil, just for the sake of being evil. The Devil wanted God's creation(humanity) to serve Him(the devil). The devil(from the mythological underworld, now rendered Hades (hell) in it's religious context) became the Tempting spirit that encouraged mankind to give in to their Carnal Nature. The Devil became the opponent to morality. The devil was an advocate of licentiousness, materialism, and hedonism, the consequences of which, are Death.*

The Vernal Equinox (in its religious application) now became an entrance way, a Gate to Paradise(Heaven). The subjects passage from the lower world(world of matter) to the upper world(spiritual world) was not guaranteed. The Subject now had to qualify, he had to be Judged. Did he give in to the Evils of the underworld, or did he remain faithful to

CHAPTER TWO

the Lord of Light (Good)? His Fate weighed in the Balance. Satan was the Accuser of the Subject, because he wanted to keep his victim in Hell, or send his Victim to the lowest regions of hell(Capricorn) into his Pit. The heavenly region above the equinoxes was viewed as a land of delights, A verdant Garden (of Eden). **In some cases** *the region was viewed as filled with Heavenly Angels nourished with Sweet Milk and Honey"*

Serpent of Eden as depicted in Solar Symbolism

AND THERE WERE TWO VERSIONS to the *serpent* symbolism, not just one. The polar *stellar* serpent is correct as Draconis, but there also existed, symbolically, the *serpent of darkness* of the *solar* mythology. The serpent of darkness is the same throughout all changes of the zodiacal eras – this serpent symbolizes the darkness of the Egyptian underworld that consumed the light of the sun *daily* as it fell below the horizon into its lair – this symbolizes the split of light and darkness within the *24-hour cycle*. IN TERMS OF THE ANNUAL cycle, the serpent of darkness, or underworld, is duplicated as the serpent of the lower region beneath the equinoxes, that is to say, the span, or path of the sun, from the autumnal equinox through the winter solstice on to the vernal equinox. This region (southern hemisphere is where the suns power is weakened as it falls to its lowest declinations during the Fall and Winter seasons.

Take note of the following passage from Genesis whereas the mythical god of the bible imposes punishment on the serpent and Adam and Eve for their transgressions
Genesis 3: 11-15

[11]And he said, Who told thee that thou *wast* naked? Hast thou eaten of the tree, whereof I commanded thee that thou shouldest not eat? [12]And the man said, The woman whom thou gavest *to be* with me, she gave me of the tree , and I did eat. [13]And the LORD God said unto the woman, What *is* this *that* thou hast done? And the woman said, The **serpent** beguiled me, and I did eat.

[14]And the LORD God said unto the *serpent*, Because thou hast done this, thou *art* cursed above all cattle, and above every beast of the field; upon thy

CHAPTER TWO

belly shalt thou go, and dust shalt thou eat all the days of thy life: 15And I will put enmity between thee and the woman, and between thy seed and her seed; it shall bruise thy head, and thou shalt bruise his heel.

The biblical editors made a reference to enmity between the serpent and Eve and also the progeny of both. Progeny or seed in this sense of the symbolism means recurring cycles. *This serpent* that is fated to be the eternal enemy of Eve and the children of Adam and Eve is the *Serpent of darkness*, of the underworld. Eve seems to symbolize the sun in the context of this parable or possibly both Adam and Eve collectively symbolize the the force of light, but regardless, the primary point of the symbolism are the references to the *bruising of the head* of the serpent and of the *heel* of the seed (progeny) of Adam and Eve. This allegory goes far back into ancient Egyptian symbolism to a time preceding when the symbols were humanized.

Take note of the following Egyptian pictograph on page 78, wherein the biblical verse previously cited and now reiterated is clearly symbolized - *15And I will put enmity between thee and the woman, and between thy seed and her seed; it shall bruise thy head, and thou shalt bruise his heel.* -

You will notice that in the Egyptian pictograph hereby presented that significant components of the Eden saga and the biblical verse just cited are symbolically pictured and readily identifiable. The Serpent and its Tree are shown, also conflict between the Head (of the Serpent of Darkness) and Heel (of the cat i.e. the seed of Adam and Eve representing,in this case, the forces of light). Clear conflict between the opposing forces of light and darkness is demonstrated by the appearance of the knife in the grasps of the feline. I think that it is palpably clear that the Hebrews have brought forth an *old symbolism of conflict between light and darkness* repackaged, slightly revised, and labeled under their own cultural brand.

CHAPTER TWO

Graphic of Tree, Serpent, and Cat

Artist reproduction of ancient Egyptian graphic - the cat symbolizes the sun cutting away at the serpent of darkness. Reference "From Fetish to God In Ancient Egypt" by E A Wallis Budge, published 1934

In the artist recreation of an Egyptian graphic, we see the cat in conflict with the serpent. The *Heel* of the cat (Eve) is pressed upon the *head* of the *serpent* and hence the serpent's nearest bite is at the Heel of the cat. The cat symbolizes the sun and the serpent symbolizes darkness. This picture symbolizes the eternal war between light and darkness under the allegory of conflict between a sacred animal that sees in the dark and is a symbol of the sun - and the slinking serpent. The cat holds a knife with which it shall hack away at the serpent – first it will decapitate the serpent and afterwards, in degrees, hack off portions of the serpent's body

CHAPTER TWO

progressively. This hacking away of the serpent of darkness, in parts, represents the incremental hacking away of darkness by the sun as it progresses though the night. Thus this is the original (or one of the original) Egyptian version of the conflict between light and darkness typed as a cat and a snake - and the Hebrew rendition involving Eve and the snake is clearly derived from it.

IN REVIEW, within this chapter we have discussed the origin of the Judaic religion on which, of course, the bible is based. The ancient matrix of Judaism was in the *Near East,* and it is certain that Judaism must have been significantly influenced by the dominant cultures of the Near East Region, which anciently included *Egypt, Sumer, Babylonia, Persia, Anatolia, Canaan,*and of course *Greece* during the phase of Hellenism that influenced that region. Any cultural effects on Judaism, of course, must have had ripple effects on Christianity and Islam, being that these two religions are the undeniable offsprings of Judaism, and all share the concept that the ancient patriarch Abraham was the father of their several creeds.

We have focused on the Creation story of Genesis, and we have made comparisons between the Judaic version of Creation and the Egyptian version so as to expose the glowing similarities between the two. We have postulated, with certain proofs, that the Jewish rendition shows significant parallels to the Egyptian rendering. We have further asserted that the biblical Creation story as well as the Egyptian are allegorical representations of astronomical phenomena. We have expressed the fact that there are multiple levels of astro-theological symbolism which include *Stellar Symbolism, Solar Symbolism*, and some other very interesting categories - we have exemplified some of these categories within this chapter.

The biblical Creation story details the creation of the world and also details the creation of the human race. We have challenged this narrative as allegorical and not at all historical. We have noted that the bible proffers to separate accounts of the creation of humankind,

CHAPTER TWO

and that one family was allegedly created in the image of god, while the other family was allegedly created from the soil of the earth. We have offered that these two separate creations carry implications of *two different natures* existent within humans, one *numinous* and the other *geotic*.

We have also referenced the assertion of the bible that Man has been created in the image and likeness of god - we have suggested that this refers to the *Macrocosm* and the *Microcosm*, that the Macrocosm is the *Cosmic Domain* itself and that the Microcosm is Man (the human race) itself. Anciently the cosmic domain was perceived as the Dome of the heavens,consisting, most notably, of five wandering stars (Planets) , two luminaries, and nine hierarchies or levels of ascendancy, with the ninth level representing Heaven or infinity itself. These levels included the Moon, Mercury, Venus, Sun, Mars,Jupiter, Saturn, The Stars, then Infinity. The planets[1] Uranus, Neptune, and Pluto were not included in the ancient symbolism. We have further postulated that Man being created in the image and likeness of god does not refer to appearance per se but rather to proportions and numbers relevant to human biology and other factors. We suggest that the rhythm of Man is in tune with the rhythm of the universe, that is to say, from a perspective that situates the Earthly island or plateau as the center of the universe, as was visualized by the ancestors.

---

[1] In the ancient symbolism, Uranus refers to the Sky, Neptune to the Seas or encircling Ocean, and Pluto to the Underworld - not to the planets that we now call by those names that just recently came into the scopes of our modern telescopes. Ancient symbolism, to the best of my knowledge, was based on those cosmic lights visible to the naked eyes.

CHAPTER THREE

Chapter Three

Exploring Stellar, Solar, Seasonal, and 24-hour Cycles and their Parallels as Expressed in Biblical Symbolisms

Major Aspects Of Astronomical Correlations And Symbolisms

Mythology illustrates its symbolisms at various levels of understanding, relevant to the physical reality on which the myth is focused. The allegory cannot be held to just one interpretation because the applications of the myths are not singular but rather are multiple, in line with the various levels of symbolism, such as Lunar, Stellar, Solar, Environmental - plus varied subcategories of possibly more intense focus, more pinpointed if you will – and there are social applications also. Interpretations are sometimes made more intricate because of language and cultural inputs. The accurate interpretations must and do parallel each other but may refer to different time-frames and/or different astronomical or environmental aspects. The picture of the cosmos is constantly changing, at the rate of one degree every seventy-two years – so this physical change in the coordinates of the starry signpost must, in tandem, produce change in *their* mythical appellations. The stories remain the same or similar but the players of the parts evolve and transfer, according to the positions of the various starry signpost. For instance 4000 years ago (in the era of Aries) the vernal equinox was symbolized as a Lamb but 6000 years ago (in the era of Taurus) the vernal equinox was symbolized as a Bull. The appellations or designates of or for the symbolisms of this cardinal point (vernal equinox) shift with Time, making one complete astrological shift in 2160 years. Likewise with all other astronomical coordinates – the other coordinates must, of course, shift also in sync with the vernal equinox. The mythical appellations, titles or names or nuances of all are transferring - or evolving toward mythological adjustments, because of the precession cycle that shifts at the rate of

CHAPTER THREE

one degree every 72 years. Therefore in some cases the symbolism can become very intricate if it hones in on coordinate variations of only a few degrees of arc. Some of you have probably already noticed that in reading the bible you find the same theme repeated over and over again, with different players and small variations, but the central plot is basically unchanged. This is because the bible is, in fact, retelling the same astronomical stories (cycles) (mythologically veiled) over and over again. The nature of cycles is repetition – the celestial entities repeat their courses without deviation throughout eternity, as far as we can tell - but the starry signposts that track the movements of the cycles shift with Time, as a result of precession and other factors. A good way to visualize the effects of precession is to imagine the world centered as a fixed theatrical Stage, surrounded by a circular wall covered with directional graphics (that mark the compass directions, East, South, West, North and points in between) that is revolving around the stage, so that the directional markers on the wall do not accurately point to the true compass directions, because of the constant movement of the wall. So precession causes us to lose our sense of direction, astronomically - therefore it was incumbent upon the ancients to develop a system that tracked the rate of precession, and thereby provide a means of accurately gauging the compass directions – which is essential to the correct tracking of Time cycles. The underlying esoteric purpose of the bible *(a Registry of Astronomical Data)* and/or religious scriptures in general, of whatever faith, formulated as symbolical reflections of natural phenomena, is to track the movements of celestial cycles, including the cycle of precession. TAKE NOTE of these biblical tales and their similarities:

Both Abraham (of the Old Testament and father of Isaac) and Zacharius (of the New Testament and father of John The Baptist) were recorded in the bible as old men with old barren wives that were visited by deities and subsequently were miraculously endowed with the ability to conceive. Read the following passages and I'm sure you will agree that the same mythological theme has been repeated in the two tales under a different cast of players but the plots are of the same basis.

CHAPTER THREE

Genesis 17:15 through Genesis 17:19

15And God said unto Abraham, As for Sarai thy wife, thou shalt not call her name Sarai, but Sarah *shall* her name *be*. 16And I will bless her, and give thee a son also of her: yea, I will bless her, and she shall be *a mother* of nations; kings of people shall be of her. 17Then Abraham fell upon his face, and laughed, and said in his heart, Shall *a child* be born unto him that is an hundred years old? and shall Sarah, that is ninety years old, bear? 18And Abraham said unto God, O that Ishmael might live before thee! 19And God said, Sarah thy wife shall bear thee a son indeed; and thou shalt call his name Isaac: and I will establish my covenant with him for an everlasting covenant, *and* with his seed after him.

Genesis 21:1 through Genesis 21:2

1And the LORD visited Sarah as he had said, and the LORD did unto Sarah as he had spoken. 2For Sarah conceived, and bare Abraham a son in his old age, at the set time of which God had spoken to him.

Luke 1:18 through Luke 1:24

18And Zacharias said unto the angel, Whereby shall I know this? for I am an old man, and my wife well stricken in years. 19And the angel answering said unto him, I am Gabriel, that stand in the presence of God; and am sent to speak unto thee, and to show thee these glad tidings. 20And, behold, thou shalt be dumb, and not able to speak, until the day that these things shall be performed, because thou believest not my words, which shall be fulfilled in their season. 21And the people waited for Zacharias, and marvelled that he tarried so long in the temple. 22And when he came out, he could not speak unto them: and they perceived that he had seen a vision in the temple: for he beckoned unto them, and remained speechless. 23And it came to pass, that, as soon as the days of his ministration were accomplished, he departed to his own house. 24And after those days his wife Elisabeth conceived, and hid herself five months, saying,

And we have an episode duplicated in regards to Abraham and Isaac – it happened that Abraham had occasion to lie and claim that Sarai

CHAPTER THREE

was his *sister* rather than his *wife* and lo and behold the identical episode is repeated under the type of Isaac and Rebekah.

Genesis 12:10 through Genesis 12:13

[10]And there was a famine in the land: and Abram went down into Egypt to sojourn there; for the famine *was* grievous in the land. [11]And it came to pass, when he was come near to enter into Egypt, that he said unto Sarai his wife, Behold now, I know that thou *art* a fair woman to look upon: [12]Therefore it shall come to pass, when the Egyptians shall see thee, that they shall say, This *is* his wife: and they will kill me, but they will save thee alive. [13]Say, I pray thee, thou *art* my sister: that it may be well with me for thy sake; and my soul shall live because of thee.

Genesis 26:6 through Genesis 26:7

[6]And Isaac dwelt in Gerar: [7]And the men of the place asked *him* of his wife; and he said, She *is* my sister: for he feared to say, *She is* my wife; lest, *said he*, the men of the place should kill me for Rebekah; because she *was* fair to look upon.

THIS ALSO MUST BE REMEMBERED – the conflict or contention between biblical brothers is repeated consistently within the scriptures, such as the conflict between Cain and Abel, Isaac and Ishmael *and* Esau and Jacob.

Also, the events surrounding the births of **Moses** and **Jesus** clearly indicate that the same theme has been repeated under two different casts of players. Both prophets were born under circumstances whereas their lives at birth were under threat. And in both cases there was the wholesale slaughter of all male offspring under a certain age or at birth. The similarities are vivid and it's very easy to see that the stories are duplications of the same plot. The *common theme* to each story is the *killing* of the newborns and the *flight* or *hiding* of the child prophet.

CHAPTER THREE

Matthew 2:13 through Matthew 2:16

13And when they were departed, behold, the angel of the Lord appeareth to Joseph in a dream, saying, Arise, and <u>take the young child and his mother, and flee</u> into Egypt, and be thou there until I bring thee word: for <u>Herod will seek the young child to destroy him.</u> 14When he arose, <u>he took the young child and his mother by night</u>, and departed into Egypt: 15And was there until the death of Herod: that it might be fulfilled which was spoken of the Lord by the prophet, saying, Out of Egypt have I called my son.

16Then Herod, when he saw that he was mocked of the wise men, was exceeding wroth, and sent forth, and <u>slew all the children that were in Bethlehem,</u> and in all the coasts thereof, from two years old and under, according to the time which he had diligently inquired of the wise men.

Exodus 1:15 through Exodus 1:22

15And the king of Egypt spake to the Hebrew midwives, of which the name of the one *was* Shiphrah, and the name of the other Puah: 16And he said, When ye do the office of a midwife to the Hebrew women, and see *them* upon the stools; <u>if it *be* a son, then ye shall kill him:</u> but if it *be* a daughter, then she shall live. 17But the midwives feared God, and did not as the king of Egypt commanded them, but saved the men children alive. 18And the king of Egypt called for the midwives, and said unto them, Why have ye done this thing, and have saved the men children alive? 19And the midwives said unto Pharaoh, Because the Hebrew women *are* not as the Egyptian women; for they *are* lively, and are delivered ere the midwives come in unto them. 20Therefore God dealt well with the midwives: and the people multiplied, and waxed very mighty. 21And it came to pass, because the midwives feared God, that he made them houses. 22And Pharaoh charged all his people, saying, <u>Every son that is born ye shall cast into the river,</u> and every daughter ye shall save alive.

Exodus 2:1 through Exodus 2:10

1And there went a man of the house of Levi, and took *to wife* a daughter of Levi. 2And the woman conceived, and bare a son: and when she saw him that <u>he was a goodly child, she hid him</u> three months. 3And when she

CHAPTER THREE

could not longer hide him, she took for him an ark of bulrushes, and daubed it with slime and with pitch, and put the child therein; and she laid *it* in the flags by the river's brink. 4And his sister stood afar off, to wit what would be done to him.

5And the daughter of Pharaoh came down to wash *herself* at the river; and her maidens walked along by the river's side; and when she saw the ark among the flags, she sent her maid to fetch it. 6And when she had opened *it*, she saw the child: and, behold, the babe wept. And she had compassion on him, and said, This *is one* of the Hebrews' children. 7Then said his sister to Pharaoh's daughter, Shall I go and call to thee a nurse of the Hebrew women, that she may nurse the child for thee? 8And Pharaoh's daughter said to her, Go. And the maid went and called the child's mother. 9And Pharaoh's daughter said unto her, Take this child away, and nurse it for me, and I will give *thee* thy wages. And the woman took the child, and nursed it. 10And the child grew, and she brought him unto Pharaoh's daughter, and he became her son. And she called his name Moses: and she said, Because I drew him out of the water.

These are a few examples of biblical duplications in terms of basic story lines – this policy is consistent within the bible. The bible is a Registry of Astronomical Phenomena written in a Mythological Format – it (the bible) records the cycles of Time. The cycles of Time repeat themselves, they do not change – but the coordinates that mark and identify the cycles, the starry signposts that track the cycles, if you will, do in fact modify and transfer with time, due to the process of Precession. Hence the allegorical tales are repeated, incorporating the same basic themes but under varying titles (symbols) and circumstances (coordinates). This is an important point.

Witness quote from <u>Book One, The Astrological Foundation Of The Christ Myth</u>:

"I should mention at this juncture that Natural Truth (that is truth governed and in accord with divine and natural law, i.e.. God's creative law) is as a Spiral ascending from a Divinely perfected core.

CHAPTER THREE

Each level of the spiral, expanding to infinity, represents a different Level of Truth. The levels are <u>Moral-Sociological, Solar-Lunar, Stellar, Mystical-Religious</u>. That which is Moral-Sociological charts the social, governmental, ethical guidelines of humanity. That which is Solar-Lunar charts the Mythos reflective of the Solar System. That which is Stellar Charts the Mythos reflective of the expanding Cosmos That which is Mystical-Religious placates and serves the Emotions, Fears, and Hopes of humanity. So, although the various levels of the Ladder or Spiral may differ in content, the Harmony of the Truth is unaltered and is exact. Any deviation from exactness is a deviation from Truth."

I wrote that paragraph in *Book One* in order to emphasize the fact that allegorical Truth (symbolism) runs in parallel even when the surface content of the myths seem different. Of course cultural and language differences can bring variations to the tales and I have already noted above how starry names and titles (that serve as signpost to mark the compass directions and points in between) change or transfer with the march of time – as I noted, the cycles are constant but the background of stars (the wall of cosmic space that surrounds us) by which we measure the rate and movement of the cycles is not fixed, but is also moving westward at the rate of one degree every seventy-two years which accumulates to thirty degrees in 2160 years (an Astrological Age). This background of stars completes its elliptical revolution in the span of 25,920 years, and then repeats. But the ingeniousness of the ancients in formulating these mythical tales (which may hold possible variations in allegorical content but *without* significant variations in the underlying astronomical messages) goes further to denote the keen wisdom of those ancient sages. They have fine-tuned the process of allegorical illustrations with such precision that even if the subject of the tale is only applicable to one phase of the symbolism, in terms of initial focus, for instance lunar, it will nevertheless fit to form flawlessly when applied to the Stellar and/or Solar realities. In the pages immediately following we shall explore important parallels to the various phases of the symbolisms, Stellar, Solar and Lunar. We shall

CHAPTER THREE

provide decipherments to biblical tales at multiple levels of mythological interpretations so as to buttress and reinforce the observations that I have just previously made.

We shall now expand on the quote from above (from Book One), not in terms of how our social and political attitudes have been affected by mythology – that discussion is not in our focus right now. However we need to explore in more precise detail the various categories of natural phenomena and how the ancients have symbolically illustrated these astronomical and environmental phenomena, mythologically and biblically. Our evaluations and interpretations of biblical mythology within this book are primarily focused on three cosmic categories and one environmental category. Cosmically, we are focused on *Circumpolar, Equinoctial and Diurnal/Nocturnal symbolism* and environmentally our target is the *Agricultural symbolism*, which we shall bring into focus a little later. Many of the biblical mysteries can be made clear when explained within the scopes of the aforementioned cosmic categories of symbolisms. Our task at this juncture is to examine the various cosmic symbolisms, in terms of the underlying astronomical facts and the mythical renditions of those cosmic realities.

Circumpolar, Equinoctial and Diurnal/Nocturnal Symbolism

This section is important - Circumpolar symbolism is a category of the stellar symbolism i.e. time tracking based on the apparent movement of the stars. **In the case of Circumpolar symbolism** we are concerned mainly with the six primary polar constellations, which are *Lyra, Hercules, Draconis, Ursa Minor, Cepheus and Cygnus*.

The constellation of *Ursa Major* must be included as a 7th companion to the Circumpolar constellations – it is, in fact, the most prominent of all the polar star groupings, because of its well known component known as the *Big Dipper*. But Ursa Major does not actually touch the axis of the celestial North Pole, in the process of precession, as do the other six official circumpolar constellations. However Ursa

CHAPTER THREE

Major (The Great Bear) is an indispensable participant, on which much mythological symbolism is based.

The tracking of the circumpolar stars (constellations) means the tracking of their movement *toward* and *away* from the point of celestial polar axis, situated at 90 degrees positive declination. I am referring to gradual shifting of the six polar constellations that completes their cycle in twenty-five thousand nine hundred and twenty years, and is directly related to the precession of the equinoxes. This point of the celestial polar axis is considered as the Station of the pole – in the symbolism this point is referred to as the *Throne, The Mount, The Mount Of The North, The Kingdom, The Government (Governor), The Tree Of Life* and by other descriptive appellations. The region of the celestial pole stars is the cosmic space within 30 degrees of the celestial axis – this is the region of the non-setting stars – stars that are always visible throughout the year. As I explained in Book Three, this celestial polar hub is the original celestial object (region) on which the symbolism of the mythical heaven is based. The latitude of Cairo Egypt near the pyramids of Giza is about 30 degrees north, likewise with the latitude of Jerusalem at about 31.5 degrees north. These two ancient centers of astronomical observation have latitudes that are in direct relation to the circumpolar space that I suggest is the cosmic region of the ever-living stars of the mythical heavenly paradise. If you are not familiar with the innate relationship between planetary latitude and the celestial circumpolar region – please refer to a handbook on astronomy. I have explained the relationship between planetary latitude and the celestial circumpolar region in Book Three.

We have explained previously, in the forgoing chapters that the ancients referred to Outer Space as Waters i.e. Celestial Waters. They imagined that the celestial entities were afloat upon the celestial waters of space. Heaven, that is the Mount of the North (the region within 30 degrees or so of the celestial polar axis), was visualized as an island, an oasis, a heavenly land that rested on top of the celestial waters. Those waters or seas that lay outside of the region of the Mount were considered as outside of the heavenly domain – *this is strictly in regards to the circumpolar symbolism.* The Mound, or

CHAPTER THREE

Mount or Island of the circumpolar heaven or paradise was mythically seen as surrounded by waters or seas that were antagonistic to the heavenly abode. The waters or seas outside of the heavenly boundaries lay within the boundaries of Satan or within the celestial Wilderness (below 60 degrees north declination) where one may be subject to the attacks of Satan – in Satan's lair, as it where– *this is strictly in regards to the circumpolar symbolism*. So when constellations, that usually circuited within the immediate vicinity of the celestial pole or within the region of the Celestial Mount, were seen gravitating away from the polar axis and toward the celestial waters or seas below the boundaries of the circumpolar stars, as a result of shifting caused by precession, this was described in the picturesque language of the ancients, as being cast out of heaven – or cast out of paradise or removed from the Throne or Deviation or something mythologically similar. We are forming a foundation for biblical interpretations *relevant to the circumpolar stellar symbolism* that shall soon follow.

Equinoctial Symbolism is a category of the Solar mythology – that is the tracking of Time based on the changing coordinates of the sun as it makes its apparent annual journey around the earth – with special interest to the *background of stars* that denote the position of the sun as it crosses the vernal equinox. Within the solar symbolism the Mount is the point of the vernal equinox. *The vernal equinox of the* _solar_ symbolism *parallels the celestial axis of the* _circumpolar_ symbolism. Within the solar symbolism, it is the vernal equinox that *most often* is the *Mount, the Throne, The Marriage, The Wedding, The Tree in the midst of the Garden of Eden, The Beginning of Days, The Resurrection, The Deliverance, The Crossing, The Victory, The Overthrowing, The Twin, The Gateway* and various other descriptive appellations.

WITHIN THE SOLAR SYMBOLISM we have two seas or sections of celestial waters – they are the *upper* waters of the cosmic *northern* hemisphere and the *lower* waters of the cosmic *southern* hemisphere. The line of *division* between the two is the *celestial equator* – the celestial equator intersects the ecliptic at the vernal equinox on the east and the autumnal equinox on the west. The lower waters, seas

CHAPTER THREE

most often symbolize *Matter, Satan, Opposition, Rebirth, Egypt, The Dragon, The Serpent, The wilderness, The Desert, The Red Sea, The Harlot* and various other descriptive appellations.

The upper waters most often symbolize *Spirit (as opposed to matter), Gardens, Blessings, Freedom, Liberation, Escape, Growth, Warmth* and other characteristics that tend to counteract the efforts of Satan, the lower waters.

Diurnal/Nocturnal symbolism is a category of the Solar mythology – as it relates to the *daily* day and night cycle of the sun in its apparent 24-hour journey around the earth. Within the Diurnal/Nocturnal symbolism the Mount is the eastern horizon, at dawn. When the sun mounts the crest of the eastern horizon at the break of day, this is synonymous to the king of the morning mounting his throne and *parallels* the sun reaching the vernal equinox, in the Equinoctial Symbolism. The symbolism of the Diurnal/Nocturnal mythology is basically identical to that of the Equinoctial mythology but the *Diurnal/Nocturnal allegory relates to the 24-hour cycle* while the Equinoctial mythology relates to the annual cycle of the sun.

We are about ready to commence our decipherment of selected biblical passages, but there is some more information that I would like my readers to peruse pursuant to that objective concerning Dualism and related aspects. But first - the next few pages include graphics that picture the twelve astrological stations of the celestial pole transited by the circumpolar stars during the Great Year of 25,920 years. These graphics show the positions of the circumpolar constellations relative to the northern celestial axis, at the commencement of each of the 12 astrological eras. This enables us to view the gradual shifting of the polar constellations over this long period of 25,920 years. Much of the biblical allegory *that is focused on stellar symbolism*, is actually describing the movement from age to age that is pictured in these graphs, hence the graphs will be of immense aid as a reference when we commence our circumpolar interpretations

CHAPTER THREE

Graphic Of Circumpolar stars during Virgo Era

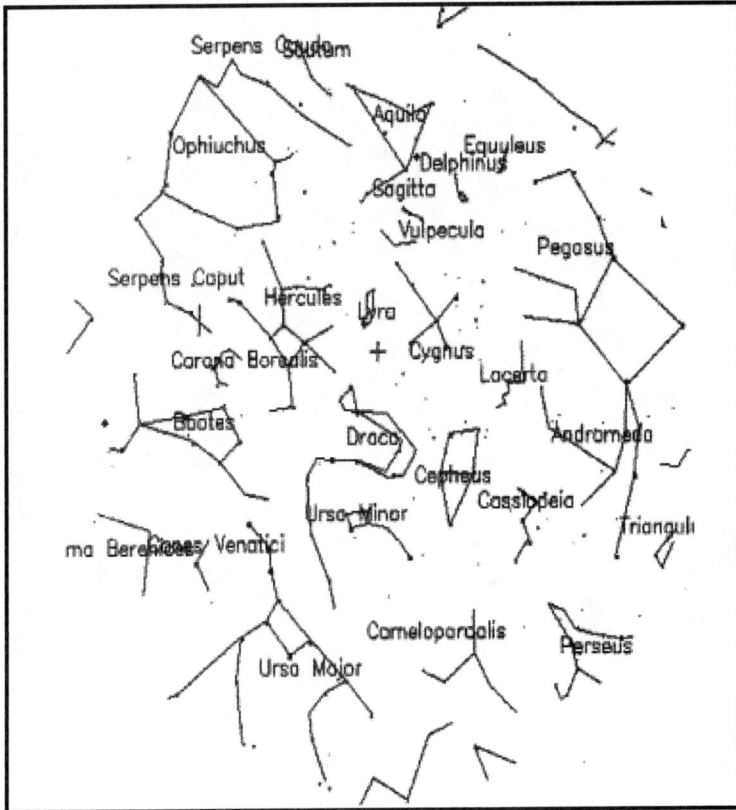

Figure G: Circumpolar view of Virgo era 13,086 BC. The + marks the celestial polar axis

CHAPTER THREE

Graphic Of Circumpolar stars during Leo Era

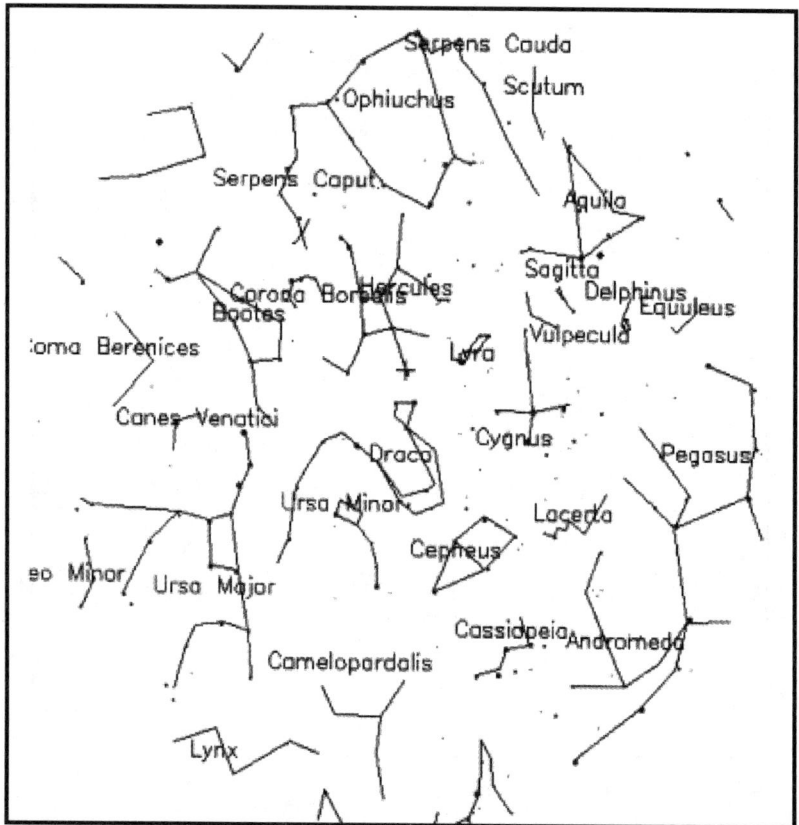

Figure H: Circumpolar view of Leo era 10,926 BC. The + marks the celestial polar axis

CHAPTER THREE

Graphic Of Circumpolar stars during Cancer Era

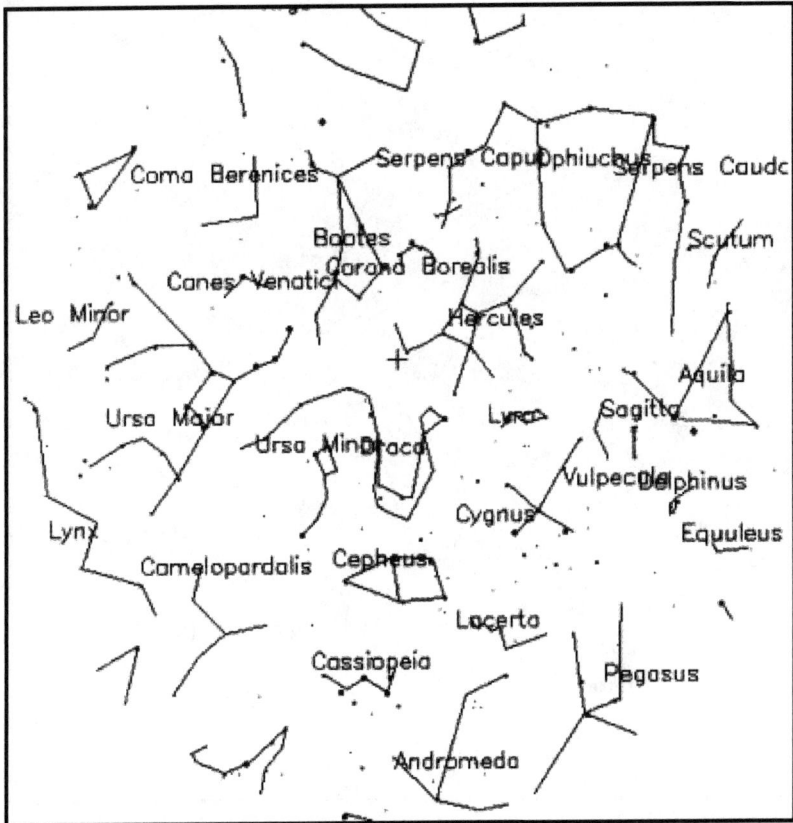

**Figure I: Circumpolar view of Cancer era 8,766 BC.
The + marks the celestial polar axis**

Graphic of Circumpolar Stars during Cancer Era

CHAPTER THREE

Graphic Of Circumpolar stars during Gemini Era

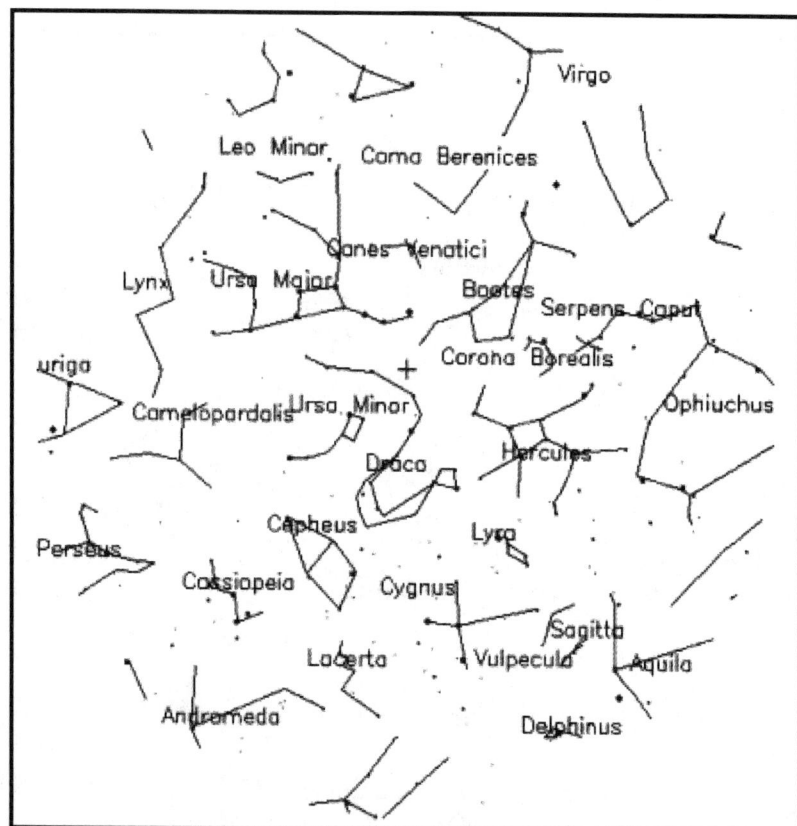

Figure J: Circumpolar view of Gemini era 6606 BC. The + marks the celestial polar axis. This era marks the beginning of the 6480 year (i.e. 3 astrological eras) reign of Draconis at the celestial pole.

CHAPTER THREE

Graphic Of Circumpolar stars during Taurus Era

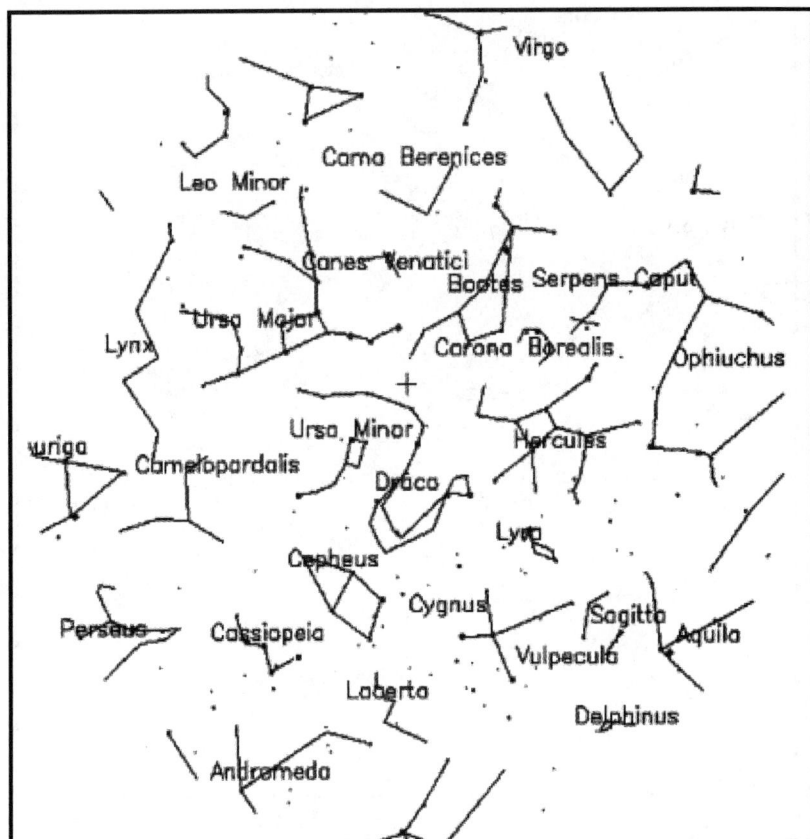

**Figure K: Circumpolar view of Taurus era 4446 BC.
The + marks the celestial polar axis**

CHAPTER THREE

Graphic Of Circumpolar stars during Aries Era

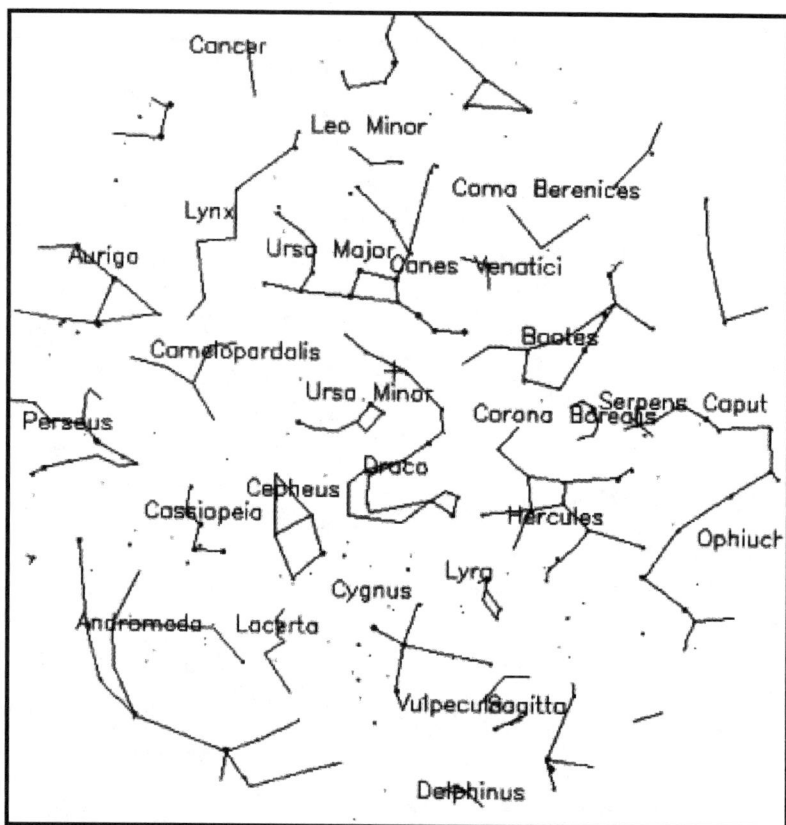

Figure L: Circumpolar view of Aries era 2286 BC.
The + marks the celestial polar axis

CHAPTER THREE

Graphic Of Circumpolar stars during Pisces Era

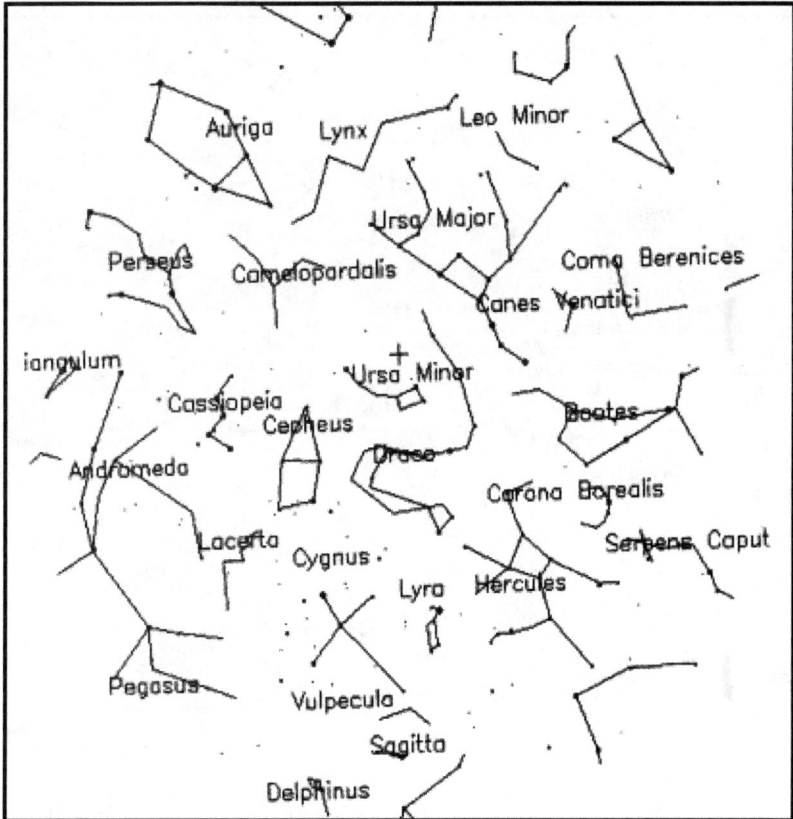

**Figure M: Circumpolar view of Pisces era 126 BC. The +
marks the celestial polar axis. The Pisces era is marked by
the removal of Draconis from the polar mount (stellar
heaven)by Ursa Minor, the child of Ursa Major.**

CHAPTER THREE

Graphic Of Circumpolar stars during Aquarius Era

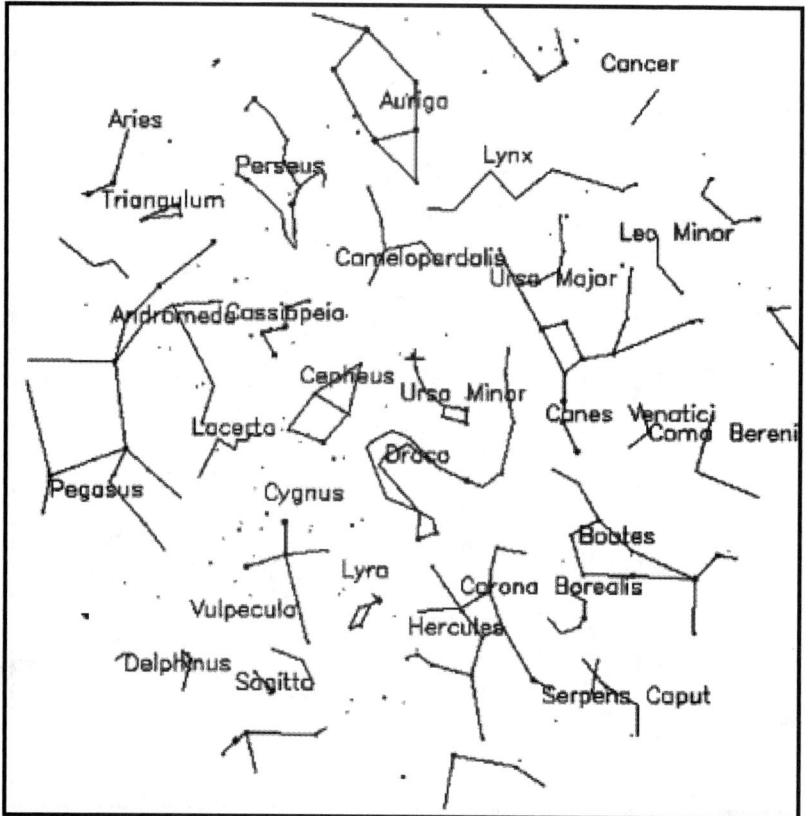

Figure N: Circumpolar view of Aquarius era 2034 AD (23,886 BC). The + marks the celestial polar axis

Graphics of Circumpolar Stars during Aquarius Era

CHAPTER THREE

Graphic Of Circumpolar stars during Capricorn Era

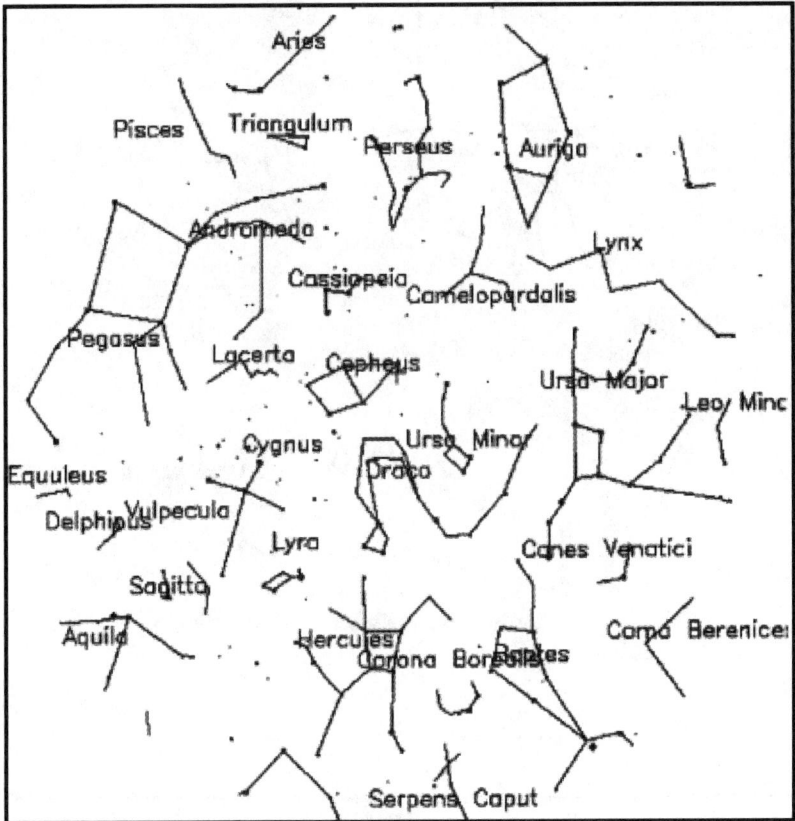

**Figure O: Circumpolar view of Capricorn era 21,726 BC.
The + marks the celestial polar axis**

Graphic of Circumpolar Stars during Capricorn Era

CHAPTER THREE

Graphic Of Circumpolar stars of Sagittarius Era

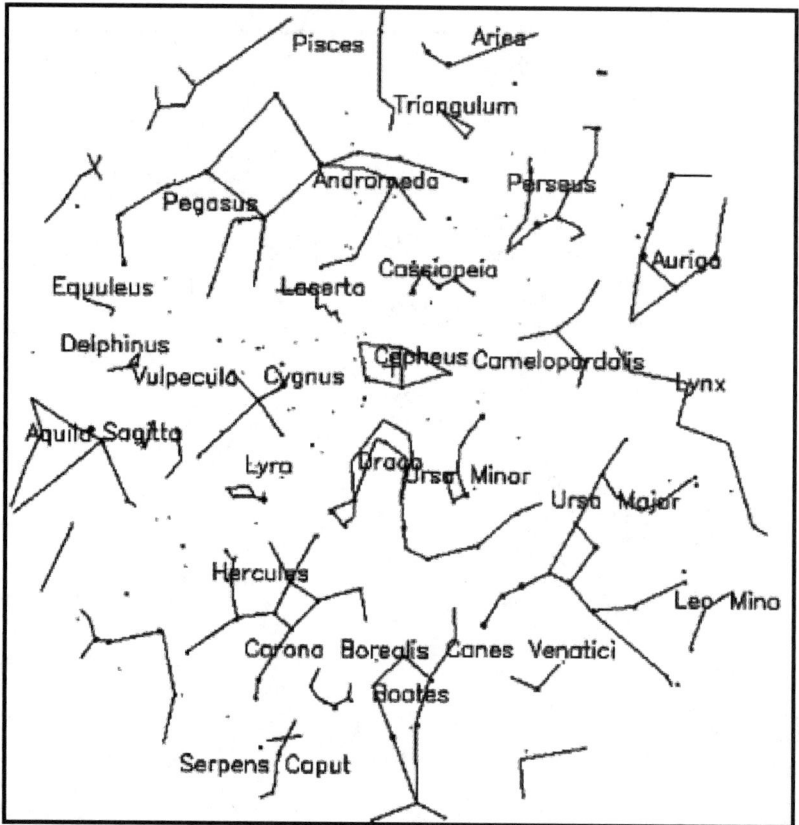

**Figure P: Circumpolar view of Sagittarius era 19,566 BC.
The + marks the celestial polar axis**

CHAPTER THREE

Graphic Of Circumpolar stars during Scorpio Era

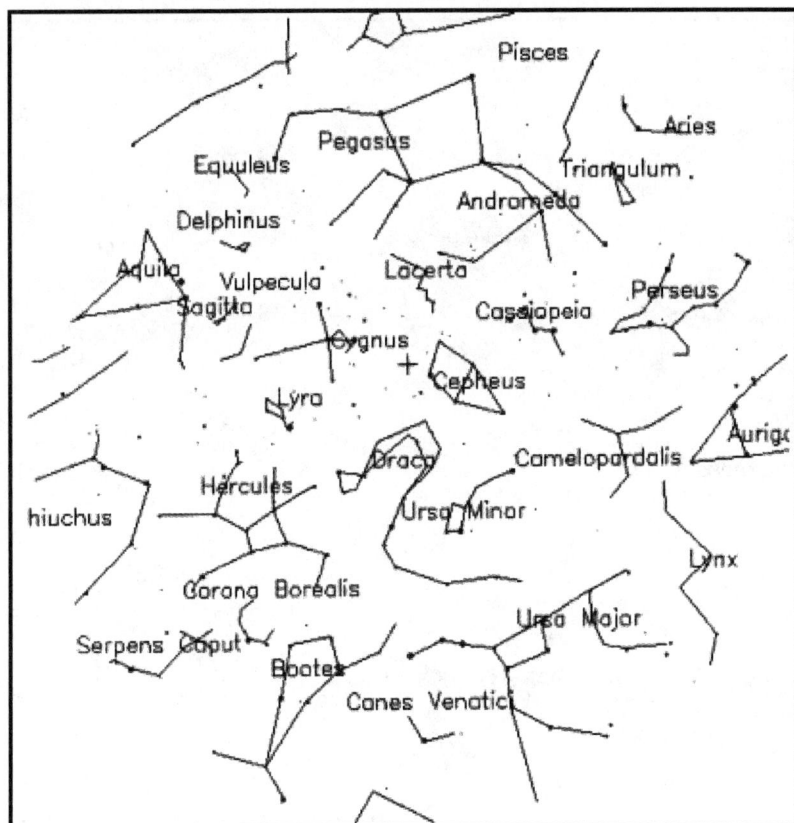

**Figure Q: Circumpolar view of Scorpio era 17,406 BC.
The + marks the celestial polar axis**

CHAPTER THREE

Graphic Of Circumpolar stars during Libra Era

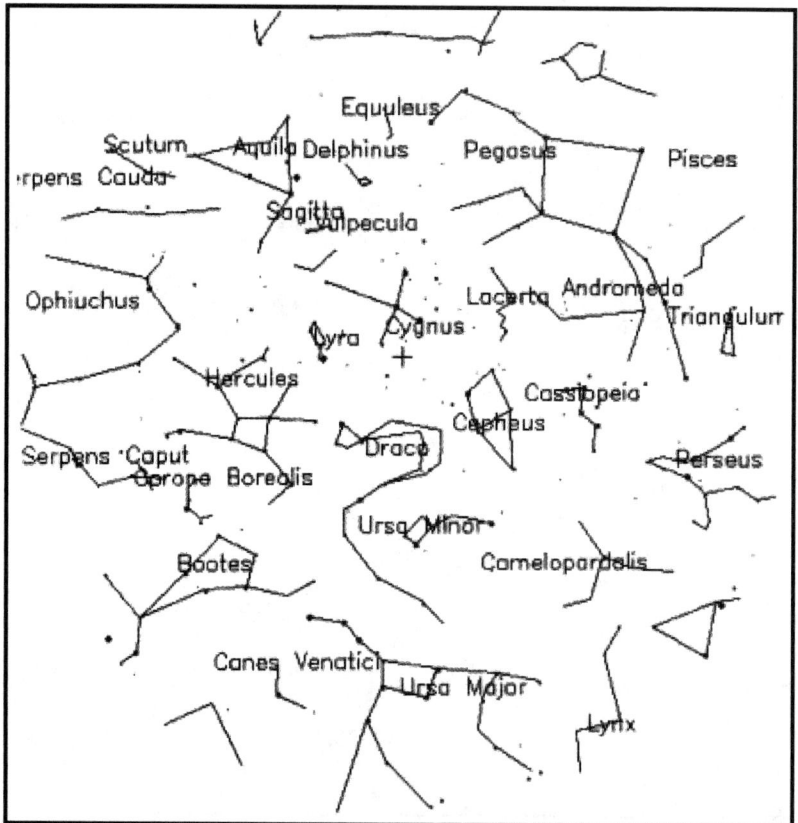

**Figure R: Circumpolar view of Libra era 15,246 BC.
The + marks the celestial polar axis**

CHAPTER THREE

Dualism – The Devil Is The Backside Of God

THE BIBLE IS ALL ABOUT CONFLICT, *conflict between the positive and negative forces of nature* that is symbolized, mythologically, as contention between God and the Satan. Religiously, this conflict is pictured as war between good and evil, but of course, physical Nature is not capable of moral discernment; it does not discern between Good and Evil. All earthly nature is in a feeding frenzy seeking to sustain life by consuming other life - when we become sick it is because some *life form* is feeding on us. This *kill or be killed axiom* that pervades physical earthly nature is bequeathed to us by our Creator is the logical conclusion – this system is neither good nor evil but integral and seemingly necessary for the perpetuation of life. The concept of god as a beneficent deity and the devil as an evil demon does not wash in the decipherment of biblical mythology, in fact in many cases the interpretations show that god is dual-natured, that actually the true identity of the devil is as the *backside of god*.

Within mythology the dual nature of god is sometimes shown as two separate apposing forces, namely Satan and god, in their many various titles - but at other times the dual nature of god is shown in an androgynous form, i.e. a singular form with both natures engrained in one entity and in conflict with each other - within separate time-frames, a split personality, if you will.

Of course, as regards astro-theology, the image of god, in one of its mythical forms, symbolizes the sun – hence a god with a dual nature is representative of the physical sun as having a dual nature or effect (for instance, positive polarity when the sun occupies the northern hemisphere verses negative polarity as it traverses the southern hemisphere). **Mythologically, the sun may take on the descriptive characteristics of the celestial region that it transits,** so that while transiting the underworld the sun may be symbolized in a non-positive light, in some cases. One instance of the duality of a god symbol is found in the case of the god Oaanes, who was half fish and

CHAPTER THREE

half man – this shows two aspects in one god. The ancient Egyptians illustrated a dual natured deity under the singular form of Horus and Set, with Horus as the deity of *Light* and Set as the deity of the *Underworld* in regards to the annual cycle or *Night Time* in regards to the twenty-four hour cycle, and both sharing one body. See picture on the following page.

CHAPTER THREE

Graphic Horus-Set

THE DUAL GOD HORUS-SET.

Figure S:Egyptian Deity Horus-Set depicted as a dual god.
Reference "The Gods Of The Egyptians Volume 2"
by E Wallis Budge, published in 1904

Graphic Of Horus-Set

CHAPTER THREE

The biblical symbolism shows two gods, the *god of matter* and the *god of spirit* – the god of matter rules the cosmic southern hemisphere in the solar mythology and the god of spirit rules the upper regions, the cosmic northern hemisphere, and their conflict is eternal. This godly dualism is indicated in the first chapters of Genesis under the creation saga – the bible shows man or mankind created twice over. Some view this as a mistake on the part of the biblical editors, but actually the dual creation matches the symbolism of two gods with two antagonistic sons. See the following verses:

Genesis 1:26 through Genesis 1:28
26And God said, Let us make man in our image, after our likeness: and let them have dominion over the fish of the sea, and over the fowl of the air, and over the cattle, and over all the earth, and over every creeping thing that creepeth upon the earth. 27So God created man in his *own* image, in the image of God created he him; male and female created he them. 28And God blessed them, and God said unto them, Be fruitful, and multiply, and replenish the earth, and subdue it: and have dominion over the fish of the sea, and over the fowl of the air, and over every living thing that moveth upon the earth.

Genesis 2:4 through Genesis 2:6-7
4These *are* the generations of the heavens and of the earth when they were created, in the day that the LORD God made the earth and the heavens, 5And every plant of the field before it was in the earth, and every herb of the field before it grew: for the LORD God had not caused it to rain upon the earth, and *there was* not a man to till the ground. 6But there went up a mist from the earth, and watered the whole face of the ground. 7And the LORD God formed man *of* the dust of the ground, and breathed into his nostrils the breath of life; and man became a living soul.
Genesis 2:18
18And the LORD God said, *It is* not good that the man should be alone; I will make him an help meet for him.

CHAPTER THREE

Genesis 2:21 through Genesis 2:25

21And the LORD God caused a deep sleep to fall upon Adam, and he slept: and he took one of his ribs, and closed up the flesh instead thereof; 22And the rib, which the LORD God had taken from man, made he a woman, and brought her unto the man. 23And Adam said, This *is* now bone of my bones, and flesh of my flesh: she shall be called Woman, because she was taken out of Man. 24Therefore shall a man leave his father and his mother, and shall cleave unto his wife: and they shall be one flesh. 25And they were both naked, the man and his wife, and were not ashamed.

According to the biblical passages just rendered, from the first chapter of Genesis, humankind was created in the first stages of creation, on the 6th day of the process; however in the second chapter of Genesis god seems to have forgotten that *they* (the gods) had already created mankind and states that there was no one to tend the ground, hence he (god) created a single earthman, subsequently named Adam because he was formed from out of the earth (Adamah). The key to recognizing this second man that was created by god and called *Adam* is in the name *Adam* itself. This term *Adam* means red and actually red earth when we consider that it is stated that *Adam* was created form the soil, *Adamah*. This Hebrew word *Adamah* means earth, ground, soil according to the biblical dictionaries and *Adam means red*, hence Adam was made from red mud. The term red is key, the editors use it to refer to the *Satan*, the *underworld* and to that which apposes the spiritual creation. Note the following passages:

Genesis 25:25

25And the first came out red, all over like an hairy garment; and they called his name Esau.

Exodus 13:18

18But God led the people about, *through* the way of the wilderness of the Red sea: and the children of Israel went up harnessed out of the land of Egypt.

CHAPTER THREE

Revelation 6:4

4And there went out another horse *that was* <u>red</u>: and *power* was given to him that sat thereon to *take peace from the earth*, and that they should kill one another: and there was given unto him a great sword.

Revelation 12:3 through Revelation 12:4

3And there appeared another wonder in heaven; and behold a great <u>red</u> dragon, having seven heads and ten horns, and seven crowns upon his heads. 4And his tail drew the third part of the stars of heaven, and did cast them to the earth: and the dragon stood before the woman which was ready to be delivered, for to devour her child as soon as it was born.

The term *red*, in every case, is used to denote *apposition* and *malevolence* – that is the true biblical symbolism for the term *red*. Note that *Esau* who was *red* was an opponent to the spiritually chosen Jacob. In Exodus the *Red Sea* is connected to the term *Wilderness* which is another form of the underworld symbolism. In Revelations the term *red* describes a Horse whose rider took peace from the world. Also in Revelations that great evil Dragon is described as *red*, and Adam was made of *red mud*! In the esoteric symbolism Adam represents Matter in opposition to Spirit and Adam's creator was the god of Matter and not the god of spirit. This *god of Matter* was called the Demiurge by Plato – i.e. a force that mesmerizes humanity, and deceives humanity with the illusion of spirituality that is actually debased materialism. The first Creation of humans, those that were created in the *image* of god represent or seem to represent a true spiritual creation that was created in *god's likeness*. Under the *solar* symbolism the upper region is synonymous to spirituality in some phases.

The first creation of humans, male and female, evidently have been supplanted by the second creation of Adamites. It is interesting to note that, according to the bible, we humans, or the House of Israel primarily, are descended from Adam who was created out of mud (Red Earth). The bible gives a detailed account of the Adamite lineage, through the Children of Israel, but *nothing* is mentioned of the lineage of those that were created in the image and likeness of

CHAPTER THREE

god, as given in the *first* chapter of Genesis. So the question looms - did the biblical editors accurately represent their intent by stating that two separate branches of humanity were created - one in the likeness of god and the other from red mud. Most people seem to think that these two separate creations of humankind are simply two contradictory versions of a single event., and they choose to overlook or disregard the discrepancies between the two. It is not unusual for people to look pass or away from that which they do not readily understand; and, in truth, these biblical passages are subject to *gross* misinterpretations by some nefarious types. Symbolically, there is a deeper purport to these two distinct creations - they point to two categories of human thinking, existent to some extent in every branch of humanity, that is to say, the Numinous, and in opposition, the Geotic. The *Numinous* are innately inclined toward divine illumination; they are intellectually receptive to connecting with the divine. The Geotics are ruled or guided by their earthly instincts and sentient appetites; they are mesmerized by the illusions of the material world and they refuse to sincerely accept, as valid or worthwhile, any concept that cannot be empirically verified. We know that humans are the only animals that have a concept of divinity, but unfortunately, that supernal trait seems to be suppressed or underdeveloped within the psyche of some of us.

It behooves us to delve into the esoteric aspects and cultural genesis of religion in order to truly understand the biblical interpretations that we shall soon render, that have been significantly impacted by the adherents to certain arcane persuasions. Of course we all know that it's *impossible* to point to a definite point in time when mankind was *actually* created, whether from earth or spirit – these biblical passages have reference to cultural and theological concepts. The seminal, astrotheological origins will become more apparent and understandable as we go along.

One significant hint as to the sensible interpretation of creation is given in the bible, in Genesis 2 verses 19 and 20, whereas god gives Adam the authority to name the elements of creation i.e. animals, trees etc. "Genesis 2:19-20 And out of the ground the LORD God formed every beast of the field, and every fowl of the air; and brought them unto

CHAPTER THREE

Adam to see what he would call them: and whatsoever Adam called every living creature, that was the name thereof."... THE ACTUAL FIRST CAUSE or creation that humankind witnessed is the one that man participated in and actually governed, that is *creation born out of discernment.* When mankind came on the scene, so to speak, the world existed as an amorphous mass, and that was chaos. The lack of designations and boundaries and sections and titles engenders social and developmental chaos. When man first gazed upon the starry heavens, witnessing that great mass of billions of undesignated untitled unnamed lights, he was viewing from within the darkness of intellectual chaos. But when he began to group those lights into constellations and permanently name the constellations and the stars – that action was the first creation. Something that did not exist before had been created out of chaos – that is the discernment and permanent naming of the star groups and stars actually created those elements conceptually. The same goes for all parts of nature – take the forest for example made up of thousands of types of trees – when the types are undesignated chaos ensues. But when man delves into the forest and examines and discerns the different types of trees – each time he names a tree, it has in intellectual fact been created. Mankind is the father of creation when we understand its true fundamental and practical meaning. That which accurately defines the world's creation is a very important subject that is grossly misunderstood by most - we shall examine this issue more deeply later in the book.

The duality of god as symbolized in the bible gives two contradictory images to the deity, which are reflective of the two contrasting effects of the sun upon the earth, dictated by its declinations in the upper hemisphere during Spring-Summer or lower hemisphere during Fall-Winter.

The duality of god in biblical mythology, is further indicated by the Jewish festivals of *Passover* and *Rosh Hashanah* (New Years). Passover marks the suns entrance into the upper region and Rosh Hashanah marks the suns entrance into the underworld – the vernal equinox (marked by Passover) and the autumnal equinox (marked by Rosh Hashanah) are the Gateways to the apposing regions of the

CHAPTER THREE

alternate gods. The two festivals are declaring homage to separate gods or influences we might say; Spring-Summer brings relief and comfort, while Fall-Winter is oppressive and punishing.

Also, the gods of the *Old Testament* and the *New Testament* do not mesh and this can be interpreted as a conflict between materialism (god of Matter) and spiritualism (god in the Spirit). The god of the Old Testament is a *Patron* god that seeks to exalt his chosen people above all others as rulers and guides – Yahweh is a nationalistic totem, if you will. The god of the Old Testament is narrowly focused on one people or nation – it's as if the world outside of Israel does not exist, except as fodder or adversaries to his chosen. The god of the New Testament is a Universal (Catholic) god (the word Catholic means universal) that reaches out to humanity in total in a proselytizing way in order to save and prepare humanity for so-called spiritual salvation. The possible indication is that not only did the new religious order grow out of the old order but was originally founded in direct opposition to the old religious order, or was made to appear that way.

As I noted at the beginning of this section – the bible is all about conflict, the eternal war between the positive and negative forces within the realms of cosmic and environmental nature, illustrated in a mythological format. And we have described and are describing some of the categories under which the mythology is penned, namely *Circumpolar, Equinoctial, Diurnal/Nocturnal and Agricultural* symbolism.

War In Heaven Between The Dragon And The Woman's Seed

I noted earlier in this chapter that the bible stories are actually repetitions of the same basic plot or theme with different characters playing the parts. Now I would like to further exemplify that point with reference to the 12th chapter of Revelations.

Revelation 12:1 through Revelation 12:6
[1]And there appeared a great wonder in heaven; a woman clothed with the

CHAPTER THREE

sun, and the moon under her feet, and upon her head a crown of twelve stars: 2And she being with child cried, travailing in birth, and pained to be delivered. 3And there appeared another wonder in heaven; and behold a great red dragon, having seven heads and ten horns, and seven crowns upon his heads. 4And his tail drew the third part of the stars of heaven, and did cast them to the earth: and the dragon stood before the woman which was ready to be delivered, for to devour her child as soon as it was born. 5And she brought forth a man child, who was to rule all nations with a rod of iron: and her child was caught up unto God, and *to* his throne. 6And the woman fled into the wilderness, where she hath a place prepared of God, that they should feed her there a thousand two hundred *and* threescore days.

I must say that these verses sound very mesmerizing and apocalyptic and ring of great foreboding and awe. But, in truth, this is just an extravagant, overblown version of the oft repeated theme of mythical, biblical and Quranic scriptures - that is describing the circumstances attendant to the birth (rebirth) of the sun, as it crosses the vernal equinox in the spring of the year. These verses are a retelling of the myth of the birth of Jesus as well as the escape (birth) of Israel from Egypt. All are allegorical representations of the same underlying astronomical reality – i.e. the cosmic state of affairs attendant to the annual emergence of the sun from the depths of the underworld at the crossing of the vernal equinox (the Passover if you will).

The cardinal factors contained in these passages, from Revelations, is that a woman is pregnant at the point of delivery – that malevolent forces are in apposition to the successful birthing of her male child (that is considered divine, destined to rule and chosen) – that after the birth of the child it was incumbent upon the woman that she flee or hide the child for his and her protection from the pursuing Dragon. This is the plot of the story and it is simply *retold* under a new guise, as is the case repeatedly within the bible. Let us now make some comparisons that will substantiate my observations most clearly, by reading the other biblical verses that revolved around this same plot – and then I will interpret the symbolism.

CHAPTER THREE

Concerning the birth of Jesus:

Matthew 1:18 through Matthew 1:25

[18]Now the birth of Jesus Christ was on this wise: When as his mother Mary was espoused to Joseph, before they came together, she was found with child of the Holy Ghost. [19]Then Joseph her husband, being a just *man*, and not willing to make her a public example, was minded to put her away privily. [20]But while he thought on these things, behold, the angel of the Lord appeared unto him in a dream, saying, Joseph, thou son of David, fear not to take unto thee Mary thy wife: for that which is conceived in her is of the Holy Ghost. [21]And she shall bring forth a son, and thou shalt call his name JESUS: for he shall save his people from their sins. [22]Now all this was done, that it might be fulfilled which was spoken of the Lord by the prophet, saying, [23]Behold, a virgin shall be with child, and shall bring forth a son, and they shall call his name Emmanuel, which being interpreted is, God with us. [24]Then Joseph being raised from sleep did as the angel of the Lord had bidden him, and took unto him his wife: [25]And knew her not till she had brought forth her firstborn son: and he called his name JESUS.

Matthew 2:1 through Matthew 2:4

[1]Now when Jesus was born in Bethlehem of Judaea in the days of Herod the king, behold, there came wise men from the east to Jerusalem, [2]Saying, Where is he that is born King of the Jews? for we have seen his star in the east, and are come to worship him. [3]When Herod the king had heard *these things*, he was troubled, and all Jerusalem with him. [4]And when he had gathered all the chief priests and scribes of the people together, he demanded of them where Christ should be born.

Matthew 2:13 through Matthew 2:16

[13]And when they were departed, behold, the angel of the Lord appeareth to Joseph in a dream, saying, Arise, and take the young child and his mother, and flee into Egypt, and be thou there until I bring thee word: for Herod will seek the young child to destroy him. [14]When he arose, he took the young child and his mother by night, and departed into Egypt: [15]And

CHAPTER THREE

was there until the death of Herod: that it might be fulfilled which was spoken of the Lord by the prophet, saying, Out of Egypt have I called my son.

16Then Herod, when he saw that he was mocked of the wise men, was exceeding wroth, and sent forth, and slew all the children that were in Bethlehem, and in all the coasts thereof, from two years old and under, according to the time which he had diligently inquired of the wise men.

Concerning the persecution of Israel and the killing of her male children:

Exodus 1:9 through Exodus 1:10
9And he said unto his people, Behold, the people of the children of Israel *are* more and mightier than we: 10Come on, let us deal wisely with them; lest they multiply...

Exodus 1:15 through Exodus 1:16
15And the king of Egypt spake to the Hebrew midwives, of which the name of the one *was* Shiphrah, and the name of the other Puah: 16And he said, When ye do the office of a midwife to the Hebrew women, and see *them* upon the stools; if it *be* a son, then ye shall kill him....

Exodus 1:22
22And Pharaoh charged all his people, saying, Every son that is born ye shall cast into the river...

Concerning the birth (escape) of Israel, Passover:

Exodus 12:2 through Exodus 12:3
2This month *shall be* unto you the beginning of months: it *shall be* the first month of the year to you. 3Speak ye unto all the congregation of Israel, saying, In the tenth *day* of this month they shall take to them every man a lamb, according to the house of *their* fathers, a lamb for an house:

Exodus 12:17 through Exodus 12:18
17And ye shall observe *the feast of* unleavened bread; for in this selfsame day have I brought your armies out of the land of Egypt: therefore shall

CHAPTER THREE

ye observe this day in your generations by an ordinance for ever. [18]In the first *month*, on the fourteenth day of the month at even, ye shall eat unleavened bread, until the one and twentieth day of the month at even.
Exodus 12:30 through Exodus 12:31

[30]And Pharaoh rose up in the night, he, and all his servants, and all the Egyptians; and there was a great cry in Egypt; for *there was* not a house where *there was* not one dead. [31]And he called for Moses and Aaron by night, and said, Rise up, *and* get you forth from among my people, both ye and the children of Israel; and go, serve the LORD, as ye have said.

Concerning the flight of Israel into the wilderness, the pursuit by Pharaoh, his death:

Exodus 13:17 through Exodus 13:18

[17]And it came to pass, when Pharaoh had let the people go, that God led them not *through* the way of the land of the Philistines, although that *was* near; for God said, Lest peradventure the people repent when they see war, and they return to Egypt: [18]But God led the people about, *through* the way of the wilderness of the Red sea: and the children of Israel went up harnessed out of the land of Egypt.

Exodus 14:8 through Exodus 14:9

[8]And the LORD hardened the heart of Pharaoh king of Egypt, and he pursued after the children of Israel: and the children of Israel went out with an high hand. [9]But the Egyptians pursued after them, all the horses *and* chariots of Pharaoh, and his horsemen, and his army, and overtook them encamping by the sea, beside Pihahiroth, before Baalzephon.
Exodus 14:19

[19]And the angel of God, which went before the camp of Israel, removed and went behind them; and the pillar of the cloud went from before their face, and stood behind them:
Exodus 14:21 through Exodus 14:23

[21]And Moses stretched out his hand over the sea; and the LORD caused the sea to go *back* by a strong east wind all that night, and made the sea

CHAPTER THREE

dry *land*, and the waters were divided. 22And the children of Israel went into the midst of the sea upon the dry *ground*; and the waters *were* a wall unto them on their right hand, and on their left. 23And the Egyptians pursued, and went in after them to the midst of the sea, *even* all Pharaoh's horses, his chariots, and his horsemen.

Exodus 14:26 through Exodus 14:28

26And the LORD said unto Moses, Stretch out thine hand over the sea, that the waters may come again upon the Egyptians, upon their chariots, and upon their horsemen. 27And Moses stretched forth his hand over the sea, and the sea returned to his strength when the morning appeared; and the Egyptians fled against it; and the LORD overthrew the Egyptians in the midst of the sea. 28And the waters returned, and covered the chariots, and the horsemen, *and* all the host of Pharaoh that came into the sea after them; there remained not so much as one of them.

Symbolism Of Dragon's Threat To Divine Birth Interpreted

I trust that you have read through all of the biblical verses above, *diligently* – if so, we are ready for our decipherments. The astronomical reality that is the bases for all of these tales above, is the birth of the sun that occurs about March 21 each year as the sun on the path of its ecliptic intersects the celestial equator at the point of the vernal equinox. This is the most momentous seasonal occurrence of every year, because it marks the beginning of Spring which marks relief from the oppressive demons of winter and promises salvation to the inhabitants of earth with warm and moist summer weather that is conducive to ample crop production.

The verses in Revelations describe a pregnant woman that is going through the pains of labor and is threatened by a Dragon that intends to kill and eat her child at birth. The woman is described as being adorned with the sun and moon and also with 12 stars about her. The description of the Dragon is equally bizarre – he has 7 heads and 10 horns, is red in color and has a gigantic tail that is capable of pulling stars from the sky. The woman gives birth to her child, snatches it

CHAPTER THREE

up and runs for her and the child's life and is pursued by the Dragon – she finds safety in the wilderness under the protection of her deity. **This is the interpretation** - the Dragon is the serpent of darkness and/or the Underworld – the ancients used the term Dragon and serpent, among other terms, to describe the demon that was unseen in darkness. The Dragon was the evil lurking monster that attacked and killed the Light of the sun, in the picturesque language of the ancients. The woman is the cosmic mother that gives birth to the sun - she is the actual infinite sky, the cosmos from which the sun is birthed and the 12 stars represent the 12 zodiacal constellations that surround the sky. See the graphic on the next picture page - drawn from an ancient Egyptian Relief, which depicts the cosmic mother giving birth to the sun. The threat of the Dragon to eat the child means the threat of the Underworld to eat (consume) the light of the newborn sun in its infancy (at the vernal equinox) before it grows to maturity and is able to withstand and defeat the forces of darkness/Underworld. See graphic on the second picture page which shows an ancient Egyptian mural of a crocodile (Dragon) pursuing after a pregnant hippo (cosmic mother) – the newborn baby male hippo is protruding from the mother hippo's rear, about to be delivered – and the crocodile is seeking to consume the newborn.

THE SEVEN HEADS AND TEN HORNS of the Dragon symbolize the 7th month and 10th day of the month – which was the occasion of the transit or the festival that marked the transit of the sun across the vernal equinox. The wilderness is the interval of time, after the sun crosses the equinox, but before it gains its summer strength when it is weak and vulnerable to the attacks of the winter darkness (or cold) and there is more. Now, with these interpretations in mind, let us revisit the biblical passages above and prove the accuracy of our findings.

My contention is that all of the biblical verses above are allegorical tales reflective of the same underlying astronomical reality, but retold under different settings –the same story with different actors. These verses from all three chapters of the bible carry the same plot – that is *Revelations 12:1-5, Matthew 1:18-25, 2:1-4, Exodus 1:10, 15-16,*

CHAPTER THREE

22 - all describe the coming birth of a chosen, divine child or people and an enemy that seeks to prevent the birth. The *man-child* of Revelations is an individual and *Jesus* of Matthew is an individual whereas the *Israelites* of Exodus are a tribe, but all symbolize the physical sun. In Revelations the enemy is a Dragon, in Matthew the enemy is called Herod and in Exodus the enemy is called Pharaoh – actually Pharaoh is the Dragon also, as well as Herod - the bible actually refers to Pharaoh as a Dragon – See the following biblical passage:

Ezekiel 29:3

³Speak, and say, Thus saith the Lord GOD; Behold, I *am* against thee, **Pharaoh** king of *Egypt, the* **great dragon** *that lieth in the midst of his rivers,* which hath said, My river *is* mine own, and I have made *it* for myself.

Here Pharaoh is clearly equated with the Dragon. Pharaoh, the Dragon and Herod are all the same allegorically. The storyline for Israel is escape from bondage rather than birth, but escape is actually synonymous to birth or rebirth – being freed from bondage is a new birth in terms of the symbolism, without doubt. Of course the actual birth that is being described by all three tales is the birth of the sun at the vernal equinox.

I EXPLAINED that the Dragon with **7 heads** and **10 horns** actually symbolized the 7th month and the 10th day of the month – the commemoration of the Jewish Passover *starts* in the 7th month and 10th day – this is biblical. And since the Dragon is the demon of darkness, the editors used the month and day that measures and commemorates the defeat of the fiend (at the time of his final attack on the light of the sun) to describe this demon of darkness/Underworld. The month of Abib, now called Nisan is the 7th month of the Jewish civil year. See the following verse whereas the Israelites are instructed to commemorate their new birth (escape from Egyptian bondage):

CHAPTER THREE

Exodus 12:2 through Exodus 12:3

²This month *shall be* unto you the beginning of months: it *shall be* the first month of the year to you. ³Speak ye unto all the congregation of Israel, saying, In the **tenth** *day* of this month they shall take to them every man a lamb, according to the house of *their* fathers, a lamb for an house:

This is vivid – the commemoration of the event was set as the 1ˢᵗ month and 10ᵗʰ day of the Jewish religious year – *this is actually the 7ᵗʰ month and 10ᵗʰ day of the Jewish civil year,* that was symbolically expressed as a Dragon with 7 heads and 10 horns.

The remainder of the verses that I have cited above describe the flight of the child and mother into the wilderness, and the Dragons pursuit or Herod's pursuit – Revelations says that the Dragon sent a flood to carry away the woman and child to their death, but the earth opened up and swallowed the flood and saved the mother and child. The Israelite version says the Pharaoh and his army were carried away to their death by the flood (waters) of the red sea in his attempt to pursue the newborn (birth of freedom or escape) Israelites – the similarities of these Tales indicate the sameness of their symbolic portent beyond reasonable doubt is my opinion.

Actually the term *Flood* is a term that *may* often refer to the forces of evil, that is the underworld or opposition or the counterforce to the god in the spirit. The ancient Greeks called the Egyptian Set (the mythical devil of darkness and opposition in ancient Egypt) by the name Typhon. Typhon was the demon of darkness and the chief adversary of the god of positive elements. Typhon actually referred to the underworld of the Egyptians that was viewed as a sea of waters, actually stormy waters when we consider the unsettling impact of that region upon the sun deity. We have in this, war between fire and water with fire (sun) as god and Typhon (flood) as the Satan. Trace the meaning of the word Typhon etymologically and this definition will prove true. It takes a good dictionary to get to the true root

CHAPTER THREE
Graphic Of Cosmic Mother

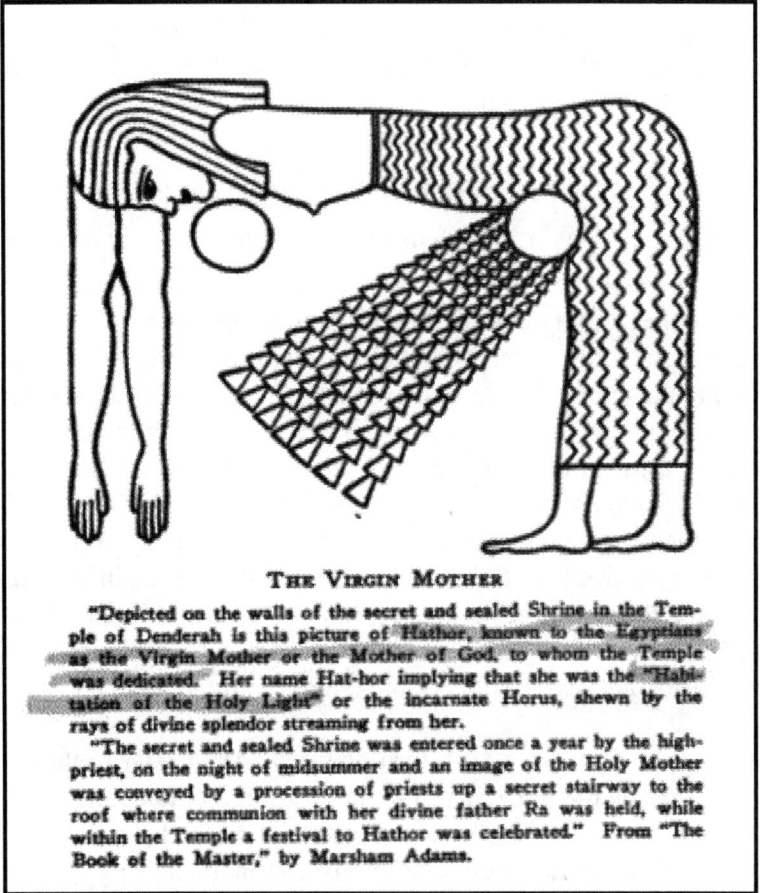

THE VIRGIN MOTHER

"Depicted on the walls of the secret and sealed Shrine in the Temple of Denderah is this picture of Hathor, known to the Egyptians as the Virgin Mother or the Mother of God, to whom the Temple was dedicated. Her name Hat-hor implying that she was the "Habitation of the Holy Light" or the incarnate Horus, shewn by the rays of divine splendor streaming from her.

"The secret and sealed Shrine was entered once a year by the high-priest, on the night of midsummer and an image of the Holy Mother was conveyed by a procession of priests up a secret stairway to the roof where communion with her divine father Ra was held, while within the Temple a festival to Hathor was celebrated." From "The Book of the Master," by Marsham Adams.

Figure T: Egyptian graphic symbolizes the annual rebirth of the sun from the cosmic mother. The sun is reborn on December 25, a type birth also takes place at the vernal equinox in some symbolisms. Reference "The Celestial Ship Of The North" by Valentia Straiton

Graphic Of Cosmic Mother

CHAPTER THREE

Graphic Of Pregnant Hippo pursued by Crocodile that seeks to devour Newborn Child

Figure U: Ancient Egyptian relief depicts the cosmic mother as a pregnant Hippo giving birth to its child. The hippo is pursued by the dragon of darkness/underworld that seeks to devour the child at birth.

CHAPTER THREE

meaning of the word Typhon (Egyptian Set) – so if you have difficulty track the English word *typhoon* which was derived from Typhon and it (typhoon) will lead you to Typhon, the Satan as the flooding waters.

War In Heaven In Terms Of Circumpolar Symbolism
Revelations 12:9-11

9And the great dragon was cast out, that old serpent, called the Devil, and Satan, which deceiveth the whole world: he was cast out into the earth, and his angels were cast out with him. 10And I heard a loud voice saying in heaven, Now is come salvation, and strength, and the kingdom of our God, and the power of his Christ: for the accuser of our brethren is cast down, which accused them before our God day and night. 11And they overcame him by the blood of the Lamb, and by the word of their testimony; and they loved not their lives unto the death.

We have just deciphered the contention between the Dragon of darkness and the newborn sun of light in the *equinoctial phase of the symbolism*. But the ingeniousness of the ancients in formulating these mythical tales goes further to denote the keen wisdom of those ancient sages. They have fine-tuned the process of the allegorical illustration with such precision that even if the subject of the tale is only applicable to one phase of the symbolism, in terms of initial focus, for instance equinoctial, it will nevertheless fit to form flawlessly when applied to other phases of the mythos.

In the circumpolar symbolism the birth is the attainment of the station of the celestial polar axis – this is the point of contention between the Dragon and the Newborn that is destined to rule the world. The circumpolar axis is symbolic of the Throne of God, this point is the hub of our universe from an earthly perspective – our universe revolves around the polar axis. As we noted earlier, the process of precession is such that the circumpolar constellations, in turn, succeed to the position of occupying the throne of the stellar heavens, which is the point of the celestial axis. The transition of powers (constellations), at the throne of the north polar celestial axis,

CHAPTER THREE

was sometimes penned as war between the transiting (contending) constellations in the picturesque language of the ancients. This was the case in reference to the Dragon that was cast out from heaven by the newborn conquering son that removed the Dragon (great deceiver) from the throne of the celestial axis.

According to the biblical verses captioned above, the Dragon was overcome and cast out by the powers of Christ and the blood of the lamb. The reference to the lamb and Christ as the victorious adversaries of the Dragon points to the astrological (zodiacal) eras that marked the intense conflict between the cyclical forces of precession and natural forces of resistance. The war against the Dragon came into focus under the equinoctial era of Aries (the lamb) and was intensified victoriously under the era of Pisces (Christ the Fish).

Now turn back to the series of graphics depicting the circumpolar constellations – go to the graphic labeled Gemini – and note that at the commencement of the era of Gemini, the Dragon ascended the throne of the celestial polar mount, right there at the axis position marked by the cross. The Dragon in terms of the circumpolar mythos is the constellation of Draconis, The Pregnant Mother is the constellation of Ursa Major (the Great Bear) - the male child, destined to rule, is Ursa Minor (the Little Bear). Take note of the positions of the three contenders – the Dragon is flanked on both sides by the mother hippo and her male child who will eventually, in later eras, attack the Dragon and cast the alleged demon into earth (that is downward from the polar heaven).

The war between these contending constellations is displayed with the pictures of time and is quite evident when viewed – so proceed to the next graphic of Taurus and note that the Dragon is couched in his seat with little variation over 2000 years, but a jockeying of positions in definitely in play. Now go to the graphic titled Aries and note that the Dragon sits solidly astride his throne and seems impregnable, but actually this era marks the beginning of his end. The mother and her child are about to attack! Now go to Pisces and

CHAPTER THREE

note that with the mythical coming of Christ and the figurative blood shed by the lamb of Aries, the Dragon has been pushed from the throne. And hail to the era of Aquarius – note that the throne has been completely captured, and the man-child (Ursa Minor) is the undisputed ruler of this era in which we now live, and are enlightened.

Transition of celestial Powers

Much of the bible, and especially much of Revelations of the bible is focused on stellar symbolism, specifically circumpolar symbolism. The primary focus in the stellar allegory is the conflict between the dragon and the newborn child of destiny that is ordained to remove the dragon from his throne, his *heavenly* throne. The throne is the mount of the north, that is the celestial polar hub, the region of the non-setting stars, the primary heaven of stellar mythology.

The dragon is the constellation of Draconis that ascended to the heavenly celestial throne in the era of Gemini. – 6606 BC, in tandem with the Gemini twins, *Adam and Eve,* at the vernal equinox. The dragon (Draconis) was destined to rule (hold primary celestial position) for three astrological ages which approximates 6480 years, thru Gemini, Taurus and Aries. The sages foretold this – they predicted, that astronomically, a savior would unseat the devil (Draconis) and restore the throne to a new generation. This savior, Avatar was destined to be born in the era of Pisces. Of course the uninitiated misunderstood the symbolism of the prophecy and took it as the foretelling of a human savior destined to come to restore humanity spiritually and defeat satanic spiritual influence on mankind.

They saw the mythical Jesus of the Pisces era as the savior and anointed him with the sign of the Fish in the early formative years of the new faith of Christianity. They missed sight of the true savior that was astronomical in reality and actually was and is the configuration of stars that we call Ursa Minor, the Little Bear. Ursa Minor is the anointed child of the great mother bear, Ursa Major.

The unseating of Satan (Draconis) was accomplished under Pisces and the restoration of a new generation is destined for the era of Aquarius. This is

CHAPTER THREE

astronomical wisdom – there are social, spiritual and philosophical implications also, but that is not my focus. Take note of the following three
graphs which depict the circumpolar constellations from the era of Aries
thru Pisces to Aquarius. The defeat of the devil Draconis and the establishment of a new king on the throne in the image of Ursa Minor is clear and
vivid.

CHAPTER THREE

Graphic 1: Aries 2286 BC   **Graphic 3: Aquarius 2034 AD**

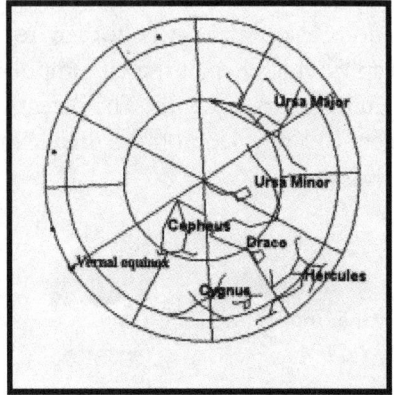

Graphics of Draconis supplanted from Celestial Pole

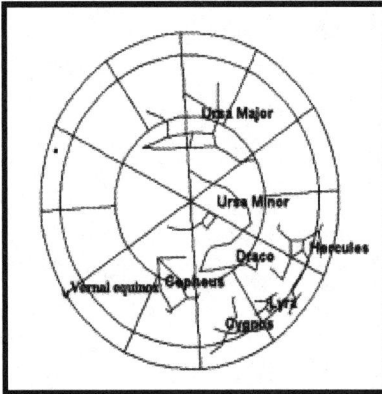

Graphic 2: Pisces 126 BC

Note **Graphic #1** Aries era with Draconis couched directly at the polar axis – Draconis is the stellar dragon, Satan. In the era of Pisces depicted in **Graphic #2**, Satan, the dragon is expelled from the heavenly throne. In **Graphic #3**, Ursa Minor, the child savior of destiny has mounted the throne signaling the commencement of a new Aquarian era that supplants the influence of Satan (Draconis). This is the astronomical prophecy of the coming cosmic savior (Ursa Minor) that some believe also signals the advent of a corresponding human savior.

These Graphics, 1, 2, and 3 depict the supplanting of the constellation Draconis from the central position at the Celestial Polar Hub.The entrance of Ursa Minor into the center of the Celestial Heaven signifies a shift in celestial dominance from Draconis to Ursa Minor

CHAPTER THREE

The Throne In Heaven, The four Beasts And The Twenty-Four Elders

Revelation 4:2 through Revelation 4:4

[2]And immediately I was in the spirit: and, behold, a throne was set in heaven, and *one* sat on the throne. [3]And he that sat was to look upon like a jasper and a sardine stone: and *there was* a rainbow round about the throne, in sight like unto an emerald. [4]And round about the throne *were* four and twenty seats: and upon the seats I saw four and twenty elders sitting, clothed in white raiment; and they had on their heads crowns of gold.

Revelation 4:6 through Revelation 4:7

[6]And before the throne *there was* a sea of glass like unto crystal: and in the midst of the throne, and round about the throne, *were* four beasts full of eyes before and behind. [7]And the first beast *was* like a lion, and the second beast like a calf, and the third beast had a face as a man, and the fourth beast *was* like a flying eagle.

The verses above are clearly an astronomical description of the heavens, centered at the celestial polar axis. The reference to the 24 elders seated about the throne makes this evident. The Twenty-Four Elders symbolize the 24-hours of Right Ascension, that is the 24-hour circles of the daily rotation of the earth. The four beasts are a clear reference to the four cardinal points of the zodiac – the era indicated is the era of Taurus. The **Lion** is of course *Leo*, the **Calf** indicates *Taurus*, the Face of a **Man** indicates the man pouring out the water of *Aquarius*, and the ***Eagle*** was an old name for *Scorpio* used by some cultures of the past – **See Star Names Their Lore and Meaning by Richard Allen Re:** definitions under Scorpio Quote: *"Sir William Drummond asserted that in the zodiac which the patriarch Abraham knew it [Scorpio]was an Eagle; and some commentators have located here the biblical Chambers of the South,..."*

CHAPTER THREE

This description of the circumpolar heavens is further reflected in the book of Ezekiel under the famous description of the Wheel In The Middle Of A Wheel and the four Creatures attendant thereto.

Ezekiel 1:5
5Also out of the midst thereof *came* the likeness of four living creatures. And this *was* their appearance; they had the likeness of a man.
Ezekiel 1:10
10As for the likeness of their faces, they four had the face of a man, and the face of a lion, on the right side: and they four had the face of an ox on the left side; they four also had the face of an eagle.
Ezekiel 1:15 through Ezekiel 1:16
15Now as I beheld the living creatures, behold one wheel upon the earth by the living creatures, with his four faces. 16The appearance of the wheels and their work *was* like unto the colour of a beryl: and they four had one likeness: and their appearance and their work *was* as it were a wheel in the middle of a wheel.

The commentary from Ezekiel matches the passages in Revelations, without question – the editors of Ezekiel used the term Ox instead of Calf in reference to Taurus, which is an insignificant variance – we know that all are of the bovine family. Ezekiel has added more info that helps support our contentions of the throne centered at the celestial axis – his reference to a Wheel in the middle of a Wheel is clearly a description of the circle of the celestial equator which circles the earth at zero declination, the divider of our northern and southern celestial hemispheres. *The circle of the suns ecliptic fits as a Wheel within the Wheel of the Celestial Equator* – the two Wheels move with each other throughout eternity with the progressive shifting of the equinoxes along their eastern and western tangents. Also in *Richard Allen's book, Star Names* under definitions of Ursa Minor Reference the following: *"I have seen no explanation of this, yet frequent references are met with in early records to some mountain located in the North as the seat of the gods and the habitation of life, the South being "the abode of the prince of death and of demons"*

CHAPTER THREE

In the original symbolism going back many millennia, the abode of heaven was viewed as the celestial North and the abode of hell was viewed as the celestial South Polar Region – I covered this issue extensively in *Book Three*.

Babylon The Great Is Fallen

Revelation 17:1 through Revelation 17:2
[1]And there came one of the seven angels which had the seven vials, and talked with me, saying unto me, Come hither; I will show unto thee the judgment of the great whore that sitteth upon many waters: [2]With whom the kings of the earth have committed fornication, and the inhabitants of the earth have been made drunk with the wine of her fornication.

Revelation 17:5
[5]And upon her forehead *was* a name written, MYSTERY, BABYLON THE GREAT, THE MOTHER OF HARLOTS AND ABOMINATIONS OF THE EARTH.

Revelation 18:5
[5]For her sins have reached unto heaven, and God hath remembered her iniquities.

Revelation 18:21
[21]And a mighty angel took up a stone like a great millstone, and cast *it* into the sea, saying, Thus with violence shall that great city Babylon be thrown down, and shall be found no more at all.

Revelation 18:23
[23]And ... for by thy sorceries were all nations deceived.

Revelation 19:2
[2]For true and righteous *are* his judgments: for he hath judged the great whore, which did corrupt the earth with her fornication, and hath avenged the blood of his servants at her hand.

The persistent theme in the selected passages from Revelations of the bible is that Babylon was a harlot, a seducer, corrupter and defiler on a grand scale. She sinned against *high heaven* according to a verse

CHAPTER THREE

cited above, and that is most significant, as we shall see as this decipherment unfolds. The whole earth was touched by the sins of Babylon – the bible forthrightly calls her a whore. But if we read the entire chapters of Revelations, which we do not have the space to duplicate here, we find that before her downfall or condemnation she was the most admired and adored of all the cities of that ancient period. She was rich, glorified and beloved by all merchants (travelers) because she brought wealth, riches and pleasure to all those that came her way, under her guidance.

The bible is a Registry of astronomical phenomena written in a mythological format.

According to the bible she (Babylon) was guilty of sin, corruption and inequity – she was profligate and amoral. And for these abuses she was condemned to utter destruction. I explained in *Book Three* -that when the bible speaks of mortal sin, it is referring to the sin embodied in mathematical error, of *incorrectness*, that is when stars that are looked upon for certain seasonal, yearly and cyclic signals fail in accuracy – they have sinned against high heaven – they have led mankind astray – they have corrupted the populations of the earth by misguiding them. This is the picturesque language of the ancients. When stars fail to give correct guidance, they were accused of deceit, treachery, sorcery and the like and such was the fate of the mythical cosmic ancient Babylon. The cosmic stars were the signpost of the ancients – the merchants traversed the seas by means of the stars for their directions, and the stars signaled the comings and goings of the seasons. The most important stars, above all, in these categories of daily, seasonal, annual and cyclic guidance was that group of stars known as the Great Bear (Ursa Major) – of which the Big Dipper is a part.

The biblical Babylon was Ursa Major, the *Great Bear*, the *Great Mother* – she was the *ever pregnant* (typical of a whore) *mother* hippopotamus with drooping pap's, *Taurt* of the Egyptians and she was the beautiful nymph *Callisto* of the Greeks. Callisto according to Greek mythology was a beautiful nymph that was involved in an intrigue between the mythical deities, Zeus and Hera, which resulted

CHAPTER THREE

in Callisto being expelled into the heavens to spend eternity as the constellation of the Great Bear, forever encircling the celestial polar heavens.

The constellation of the Great Bear was viewed by the ancients as the Mistress of the Night, she was the beacon light that shined in darkness, the guiding light, she Babylon (means gateway) was the gateway to the circumpolar stars – the heaven of stars that never fell below the horizon. She forecast the seasons in their turn by the direction of her tail – she clocked the hours of the night likewise and she was the greatest directional lighthouse of the north – her son, the male hippo, *Ursa Minor,* assisted her and in due course she put him on the Throne, as we have already noted on previous pages of this book.

The bible says that the whole earth was involved with her, and this is patently true – history shows that all of the ancient cultures from every part of the globe, China, Europe, India, Africa, the Americas - all used the Great Bear as their guiding light – she was the lighthouse of the north and the Mistress of the world. Hence the ancients, in their picturesque language referred to the Great Bear as a whore, a harlot because she laid with (served) all (of humanity) – she played the field, so to speak. All who paid the price (in knowledge) were allowed to use her and share her bed (calculate and use her coordinates for guidance and timekeeping).

Witness quotes from Richard Allen's book *Star Names* under the listing for Ursa Major: *"always has been the best known of the stellar groups, appearing in every extended reference to the heavens in the legends, parchments, tablets, and stones of remotest times"* also in speaking of the Indians of the Americas this line is found in his book *"The red men...did not divide the heavens, nor even a belt in the heavens, into constellations. It is a curious coincidence, that among the Narragansetts and the Illinois, the North Star was called the Bear."*

This mythical city, the ancient city of Babylon (The Great Bear) was the delight of the world, the gayest and richest city of all Ages but she was condemned to utter destruction because she provoked god

CHAPTER THREE

by reason of her sins. As I emphasized in *Book Three*, these so-called sins were *errors in calculation* - when it was found that the constellation was no longer reliable as a true indicator of time. The Great Bear commenced giving false readings (in terms of her astronomical coordinates) because of the process of precession. Precession causes Ursa Major as well as all other constellations to shift positions over time, so that the logs used by the astronomers to denote planetary movements and cosmic cycles become obsolete and must be updated in order to maintain accuracy. But originally when the ancients first started charting the heavens, they did not factor in precession – they thought the stars were hanging stationary in space – they did not know that the stars were moving. Hence, when the Great Bear commenced giving false readings, they became upset and in their picturesque language, under the guise of the deity, condemned her to total annihilation.

In the biblical verses above, the editors used the analogy for the destruction of mythical Babylon, of a millstone being cast into the sea. This is very appropriate because Ursa Major and the other circumpolar constellations were viewed by the ancients as being perched upon an island, centered at the celestial pole, in the midst of the cosmic sea. Precession caused the Great Bear to drift downward to lower declinations, over the millennia, so that her coordinate signals became altered. She was cast off the heavenly plateau of the celestial circumpolar heaven and cast into the surrounding cosmic sea, in the mythical vernacular. Of course Ursa Major is still a circumpolar constellation but her declination is lower than it was centuries and millennia ago, therefore her astronomical indicators are not correct when based on those outdated cosmic calculations.

Later in Revelations, and elsewhere also, we find verses that refer to numbers that are used in tracking precession:

Revelation 11:3

3And I will give *power* unto my two witnesses, and they shall prophesy a thousand two hundred *and* threescore days, clothed in sackcloth.

Revelation 14:3

3And they sung as it were a new song before the throne, and before the

CHAPTER THREE

four beasts, and the elders: and no man could learn that song but the hundred *and* forty *and* four thousand, which were redeemed from the earth.

Revelation 20:1 through Revelation 20:3

¹And I saw an angel come down from heaven, having the key of the bottomless pit and a great chain in his hand. ²And he laid hold on the dragon, that old serpent, which is the Devil, and Satan, and bound him a thousand years, ³And cast him into the bottomless pit, and shut him up, and set a seal upon him, that he should deceive the nations no more, till the thousand years should be fulfilled: and after that he must be loosed a little season.

These number values (1260, 144, 1000) send signals to the initiated while the uninitiated are sent further astray into dream land with expectations of apocalyptic events that will *never* come to pass – not in a million years, in the way that the religious adherents expect.

I explained in the first chapter of this book how these numbers values are incorporated into *formulas* that were devised for the tracking of precession. The predictions of the apocalyptic events in Revelations are pure fancy – the impending doom threatened by certain biblical verses were written 2000 years ago – and the benighted masses of that era were duped into thinking that the end of the world was at hand way back then. I am amazed at how people of this era can read those prophesies of doom, that never took place in the time of the generation to whom the writings were addressed - and apply those ridiculous prognostications to this era, as if the writings were just penned a few days ago. Take note of the following:

Luke 21:32 through Luke 21:33

³²Verily I say unto you, This generation shall not pass away, till all be fulfilled. ³³Heaven and earth shall pass away: but my words shall not pass away.

Revelation 3:11 through Revelation 3:13

¹¹Behold, I come quickly: hold that fast which thou hast, that no man take thy crown. ¹²Him that overcometh will I make a pillar in the temple of my God, and he shall go no more out: and I will write upon him the name of

CHAPTER THREE

my God, and the name of the city of my God, *which is* new Jerusalem, which cometh down out of heaven from my God: and *I will write upon him* my new name. [13]He that hath an ear, let him hear what the Spirit saith unto the churches.
Revelation 22:20
[20]He which testifieth these things saith, Surely I come quickly. Amen. Even so, come, Lord Jesus.

Now according to these and many, many other passages within the New Testament – doomsday was scheduled 2000 years ago, within *that generation* - so how can the same text (warning of impending doom) apply today. This fear tactic was and is a method used by organizers to get people indoctrinated into a new religious movement – it instills a sense of urgency into the neophytes. As the years go by and the apocalypse remains on hold, some of the people will realize that they have been mislead, though they may never admit it openly. But by that time they will have become acclimated to a new social structure and environment and will generally stay the course out of tradition and a lack of options. This is one of the ways that new religious movements are founded – by instilling fear of an impending (god ordained) tragedy or punishment in the minds of the potential converts.
As I noted earlier in this chapter, there are three primary categories of cosmic symbolisms on which we are focused, namely *Circumpolar, Equinoctial and Diurnal/Nocturnal* symbolisms. The nature of the universe is dualism i.e. natural eternal conflict between the positive and negative forces of the cosmos. From an earthly perspective, the line of demarcation between the positive and negative regions of the universe is the celestial equator, in regards to the equinoctial symbolism. Religiously this contention, between the cosmic polarities, is penned as conflict between god and the Satan, good spirits and evil spirits, light and darkness, morality and immorality etc. The title universally applied to the negative opponent forces is the term, dragon. The mythological definition of the dragon varies, according to the focus of the symbolism – under the

CHAPTER THREE

Circumpolar symbolism the dragon refers to the constellation of *Draconis*, under the *Equinoctial symbolism* the dragon refers to the *Underworld*, the region below the equinoxes, the cosmic southern hemisphere and under the *Diurnal/Nocturnal symbolism* the dragon refers to *Darkness*, the night, the region below the daytime horizons. The book of Revelation makes much to do about the evil Dragon – but the key to correctly deciphering the mythology concerned, is to *remember these three categories that I have just listed* and to focus on the category of the dragon that fits most neatly or has the best application to the content of the particular verses. The positive *counterforce* to the dragon is most often the sun but may also be the light of the moon or stars or groups of stars or perhaps other cosmic entities –but this can only be correctly determined by careful and thoughtful analysis, in accordance with the gnosis.

The Dragon And The Two Beasts
Revelation 13:1 through Revelation 13:5

¹And I stood upon the sand of the sea, and saw a beast rise up out of the sea, having seven heads and ten horns, and upon his horns ten crowns, and upon his heads the name of blasphemy. ²And the beast which I saw was like unto a leopard, and his feet were as *the feet* of a bear, and his mouth as the mouth of a lion: and the dragon gave him his power, and his seat, and great authority. ³And I saw one of his heads as it were wounded to death; and his deadly wound was healed: and all the world wondered after the beast. ⁴And they worshipped the dragon which gave power unto the beast: and they worshipped the beast, saying, Who *is* like unto the beast? who is able to make war with him? ⁵And there was given unto him a mouth speaking great things and blasphemies; and power was given unto him to continue forty *and* two months.

Revelation 13:11 through Revelation 13:15

¹¹And I beheld another beast coming up out of the earth; and he had two horns like a lamb, and he spake as a dragon. ¹²And he exerciseth all the power of the first beast before him, and causeth the earth and them which dwell therein to worship the first beast, whose deadly wound was healed.

CHAPTER THREE

[13]And he doeth great wonders, so that he maketh fire come down from heaven on the earth in the sight of men, [14]And deceiveth them that dwell on the earth by *the means of* those miracles which he had power to do in the sight of the beast; saying to them that dwell on the earth, that they should make an image to the beast, which had the wound by a sword, and did live. [15]And he had power to give life unto the image of the beast, that the image of the beast should both speak, and cause that as many as would not worship the image of the beast should be killed.

NOW THIS IS REALLY A FANCIFUL AND CONVOLUTED TALE, at the exoteric level, but nevertheless we shall untangle it. We are told of a beast with 7 heads and 10 horns whose appearance was a composite of a leopard, bear and lion. The beast possessed power that was bequeathed by a dragon – the beast was wounded in one of his 7 heads but recovered - he exercised unrivaled power and authority for a period of 42 months. A 2nd beast followed the 1st beast, had powers comparable to the 1st beast and advocated that homage be paid to its predecessor. The interpretations of this allegory are expansive and wide ranging through multiple categories of decipherment. I shall focus on that which I consider primary.

First off the dragon represented by this tale is the dragon of the equinoctial symbolism, that is, of the underworld, the region below the equinoxes. This is made evident by the symbolism of the 7 heads and 10 horns. As I indicated above in this chapter, the heads indicate months and the horns, in this case, indicate days of the month. The designated period is the 7th month and the 10th day of the month, which indicates the time of the Hebrew ceremonies (festivals) marking the suns crossing of the vernal equinox. The dragon is the cosmic Underworld, the opponent of the two beasts that are challenging its cosmic rule. The beasts are twin (associated) constellations that define and measure the time line that marks the *passage of the sun from captivity* to preeminence at the point of the vernal equinox. I have indicated several times in my writings that

CHAPTER THREE

when the sun or other cosmic entities fall below the equinoxes, they may be considered captives of the Underworld region.

Revelation 13:10

¹⁰He that leadeth into captivity shall go into captivity: he that killeth with the sword must be killed with the sword. Here is the patience and the faith of the saints.

The King James version of the bible gives the impression that the dragon is the sponsor of the beast, that supports and backs the position and authority of the beast, but this is not accurate. In truth, the dragon *relinquished* (gave) his authority to the beast – see the following from The New Revised Standard Version of the Bible

Revelation 13:1 through Revelation 13:4

13.1And I saw a beast rising out of the sea, having ten horns and seven heads; and on its horns were ten diadems, and on its heads were blasphemous names. ²And the beast that I saw was like a leopard, its feet were like a bear's, and its mouth was like a lion's mouth. And the dragon gave it his power and his throne and great authority. ³One of its heads seemed to have received a death-blow, but its mortal wound£ had been healed. In amazement the whole earth followed the beast. ⁴They worshiped the dragon, for he had given his authority to the beast, and they worshiped the beast, saying, "Who is like the beast, and who can fight against it?"

The *New Revised Standard Version* of the bible makes it clearer that the episode between the dragon and the beast was a *transition of powers*, and this is key to the correct esoteric interpretation. The dragon of the Underworld was forced to *surrender his power and authority to the beast*, at the time of the suns entrance into the Upper World. The positive cosmic forces of Spring and Summer (time frame signified by the coordinates of the beasts constellations) against and overpowering the negative forces of Fall and Winter (the dragon of the Underworld) is the true significance of the transition. The first beast that arises out of the sea and attacks and overpowers the forces of the Underworld is the constellation of *Ursa Minor* – Ursa Minor lays within the sector of Aries, which is the Spring constellation for the astrological era of the Lamb, Aries. This beast

CHAPTER THREE

was described as a composite of a *leopard, bear and lion*. Of course the bear attribute is self-evident in regards to the bear constellation, Ursa Minor. The constellation was also known anciently as a leopard, or I should say the leopard was one of its popular symbols. Note the following from Richard Allen's book *Star Names*: under the heading for Ursa Minor - *"Jensen sees here the Leopard of Babylonia, an emblem of darkness which this shared, there and in Egypt..."*

The beast was described as wounded *but healed* from his wounds – this is in line with the symbolism. The wounding of the beast occurs in the Fall of the year, when the Positive forces of the Upper World are attacked and wounded by the Dragon of the Underworld, of winter. The wound is in the first head (month) of the Jewish calendar at the autumnal equinox when the sun and its companions fall below the equinoxes wounded by the spear in the *side* (in one phase of the symbolism) and in the *head* as indicated by Revelation and some other secret teachings. As the ancients saw it, this mythical wounding caused blood to flow from the bear (or sun as the case may be) and this blood dripped from the heavens onto the earth and turned the green foliage of nature to crimsoned or brown, stained by the blood of the wounded beast or god – and producing the natural brownish colors of autumn. In the picturesque language of the ancients, the bear or sun was healed at the coming of Spring – at this time of the sun crossing the vernal equinox, *his wound was healed* as was evidenced by the fresh budding of the flowers of spring, indicative of a healed nature (earthly landscape), that was returning to verdant life. Note these quotes of reference that show the general acceptance of the wounding of the nature gods in autumn as a symbolical means by which the ancients expressed the coming of the Fall season:

In the Introduction to the book Adonis Attis Osirus by James Frazer, Introduction by Sidney Waldron, published by University Books in 1961 - *"Every year, in the belief of his worshippers, Adonis was wounded to death on the mountains, and every year the face of nature itself was dyed with his sacred blood"*

In the same book, an interesting reference is made to the wounding

CHAPTER THREE

of the nature god *Odin*, in the chapter *The Hanged God* – "*The human victims dedicated to Odin were regularly put to death by hanging or by a combination of hanging and stabbing, the man being strung up to a tree or a gallows and then wounded with a spear*" I actually referenced this quote because of its similarity to a bible passage in regards to the death of Jesus, who was, of course a counterpart to the mythical Odin of the Norse people. The biblical quote indicates that Jesus was killed by being hung on a tree -

Acts 10:39 through Acts 10:40

[39]And we are witnesses of all things which he did both in the land of the Jews, and in Jerusalem; whom they slew and hanged on a tree: [40]Him God raised up the third day, and showed him openly;

This is a clear cross referencing of Jesus as a nature god that was wounded in the autumn and healed with the coming of Spring, as well as being a cosmic sun god that was wounded/killed and revived. Also in the book *Star Names*, by Richard Allen under the heading for Ursa Major – "*The Housatonic Indian, ...said that this chase of the stellar bear lasted from the spring till autumn, when the animal was wounded and its blood plainly seen in the foliage of the forest*" The biblical verses state further that the beast was granted power to rule for 42 months. As I indicated in chapter one, 42 months is the base cycle for a system of time measurement that optimizes at 25,200 years. Please review for your edification. The editors have noted this Time cycle (of 42 months) so as to indicate to the initiated the formulas that should be used in this phase of time measurement.

In verse 11, we are told of a 2nd beast that ascends from the earth and exercises the same powers as the 1st beast and directs praise and homage to the 1st beast. The 2nd beast is Ursa Major – Ursa Major is located in the sector of Virgo. In regards to the equinoctial symbolism, the earth is normally the region above the celestial equator and the sea refers to the region below the celestial equator. Ursa Major and Ursa Minor are associate constellations – Ursa Major

CHAPTER THREE

points the way to Ursa Minor. The Great Bear (Ursa Major) which includes the famous Big Dipper, is arguably the most noticeable constellation in the sky – the lesser bear, Ursa Minor is much fainter than its associate and very difficult to find without help from its mother or associate constellation, Ursa Major. We are able to locate the Little Dipper and its North Star by way of the Big Dipper – two stars in the square of the Big Dipper, Merak and Dubhe point directly to the North Star in the handle of the lesser constellation. Ursa Major is the patron of the lesser bear that directs the stargazers and travelers in the direction of the fainter constellation. Ursa Major causes the lesser bear to be noticed, to come alive in terms of visibility, to speak to us. This, in a sense, is paying homage to the lesser bear in the allegorical format.

During the cycle of precession the Great Bear does not reach the apex of the earth's axis – it is Ursa Minor that is heir to the throne of the celestial polar axis, and this is the point that is emphasized in the inflated, verbose language of the biblical editors that shows greater glory directed toward the lesser bear – *that is made known and usable because of the directive lights of the Great Bear.* The constellations of the celestial polar hub, especially the Greater Bear are the Pillars Of Fire of mythical and biblical Lore that have directed the travelers in darkness throughout the ages.

The two bears are prominent in the equinoctial symbolism as well as the circumpolar symbolism, in fact the bears are the major timekeepers within the diurnal/nocturnal symbolism also. The movement of the bears around the polar hub at night is like a clock movement and indicates the passage of time according to the degrees of arc that are transited. The bears are ever present within the symbolism is the indication. The biblical editors have gone overboard in their efforts of obfuscation within Revelation of the bible, and there is much intertwining of the various levels of symbolism, as I see it – but the truth is there for the initiated and clear when properly defined.

As I have already indicated, *in regards to the stellar circumpolar symbolism,* the conflict between Satan (the dragon) and the Mother

CHAPTER THREE

with the savior child, born to rule – is definitely Ursa Major as the mother and Ursa Minor as the child savior. The battleground is the polar hub, as indicated in the graphics under the section above labeled *Transition Of Celestial Powers* and the devil is clearly the dragon constellation of Draconis. Ursa Minor was the child savior that came to celestial prominence in the era of Pisces and successfully challenged and defeated Satan (Draconis) for possession of the throne of heaven (circumpolar hub). The virgin mother of the child savior was Ursa Major.

See poetic Quote form the book, *Star Names Their Lore and Meaning by Richard Allen* under the Heading for Ursa Major:

> *That every day by Helice [Great Bear] is covered*
> *Revolving with her son whom she delights in*

Anciently, the celestial Polar Hub was seen a the stable *Center* of the *World* because of its constancy. The axis of the *Celestial Pole* was the center of the *Circle of Perpetual Apparition*, it was always visible at night. IT WAS A CALENDAR that measured the seasons, as indicated by the varying positions or attitudes of the *revolving* Great Bear. IT WAS ALSO A CLOCK that tracked the time of the evening, likewise, as indicated by the *ever circling* Great Bear. AND IT WAS THE BATTLEGROUND of the six constellational giants that, in turn, took possession of the Celestial Mount during the cycle of precession over a period of 25,920 years - those constellations being *Cepheus, Cygnus, Lyra, Hercules, Draconis*, and finally *Ursa Minor*, the cosmic savior that ushers in the era or Age of Aquarius.

CHAPTER THREE

Insights on Mystical-Religious Symbolism

The Mystical-Religious aspect of the astrotheological symbolism is very potent and enlightening when properly understood. MYSTICAL-RELIGIOUS SYMBOLISM performs a direct and palpable connection between *astronomically based allegories* and the vaunted *promise of salvation* so prominently expounded by popular religion. *Promised salvation* lays at the *core* of religion; the spiritual core of religion is, and has always been, a covenant of *salvation* to all true believers. The ultimate promise of all religions is salvation, along with eventual spiritual union with god, in whatever form that a denomination or faction may view the sublime essence of god. Usually religious salvation requires the belief in a human *soul*, that is to say, an essentially divine spiritual element or *spiritual self* within the human body. The soul, according to doctrine, holds the potential for eternal spiritual life, apart from the physical body after our earthly deaths. Of course, alternatively, the soul may face eternal damnation if it fails the tests of its final judgment before god. According to the proponents of spiritual salvation, our *saved souls* shall be glorified in heaven, a realm somewhere far beyond the scope of our physical eyes, and likewise, even beyond the most penetrating probes that our rational human minds can muster or imagine.

Anciently, heaven was conceptualized in varying forms by diverse cultures throughout the ancient world; however the most enduring concept of heaven, by far, is the celestial one - even today we call our skies *the heavens above*. The most widely held concept of heaven, anciently, was that it existed out beyond the heavenly dome, out beyond the stars. To the ancients, heaven was a heavenly oasis, a paradise, the home of the gods, a Garden of heavenly delights held in reserve for god's beloved and chosen ones; we might describe it as a biblical Garden of Eden, such as that allegedly inhabited by Adam and Eve before their fall from heavenly grace, resultant from their defiance or failure to follow god's command.

CHAPTER THREE

The struggles of the soul to find its salvation is the nexus; it (the struggles, failures, and challenges of the soul) is the fundamental spiritual message conveyed within the themes of mystical-religious symbolism. Mystical-religious symbolisms and allegories highlight and emphasize the *odyssey* of the soul to find its way to salvation or back to its original home with god, to the promised land, to a heavenly abode, to paradise, to Zion, to its final salvation in the bosom of the god. WITHIN THE SYMBOLISM, the soul, *under its various metaphors*, is often described as having lost its way, as having fallen away from god, *or* being cast away from god because of its transgressions. THE SOUL, within the symbolism, may also be described, *under its various metaphors*, as being drunken, lost, captive, as torn between loyalties to god and to the chthonic or earthly world or Satan.

The ancient Egyptians, Greeks, Hindustanis, Mesopotamians, *as well as the Hebrews* and others wrote great *epic poems* describing various momentous battles, struggles, journeys, and conflicts of the gods, and mortals also, in their mythological legends. Often hidden within the folds of these allegorical tales is the cryptic message pertaining to the *soul's struggle* to redeem itself, to break the chains of slavery to life within the world of gross matter, to return to its spiritual home, to find its salvation, to defeat Satan, to gain god's mercy and forgiveness, to find final salvation and peace. The bible is full of allegories of the type that I have just described. THE TASK THAT CONFRONTS US, as we proceed, is to unmask certain biblical allegories of the bible relevant to the destined *odyssey* of the soul, and its perilous journey back to god. We must unravel major symbolisms relevant to the quest of the beleaguered human soul to find salvation.

Many of the writers of the ancient scriptures or poetic verses, we could say, saw the human race as *fallen souls*, that is to say, *spiritual beings* that were temporarily encased in matter, subject to the temptations and challenges of the flesh. Some wrote that we, as spiritual beings, had fallen from grace into the wilderness of sinful

CHAPTER THREE

matter; others wrote that we had been cast out of heaven because of our failings. This message is replete throughout the bible.

The place of hell and the struggles of the soul to escape hell

The popular monotheistic concept of hell as a place of torment somewhere in the depths of the Earth or further beyond does not accurately reflect the ancient and enlightened Gnostic dogma which prevailed before the theological distortions that took sway or gained dominance at the opening of the Pisces Era or thereabouts. Under the Gnostic form, heaven was out beyond the stars, just as with the Christians, but Hell was not in the distant unseen realms, Hell was conceptualized as the Underworld that laid under the Heavens above; Hell was, indeed, the gross world of Matter into which our forlorned souls have fallen. Our human bodies do not represent who we truly are according to those wise ones, but rather the souls within us, the inner being, the inner spiritual being is who we truly are. We, as inner spiritual beings, are captives within this world of Matter, or so they taught. This world of Matter is the true Hades, the Pit, the Underworld, the Grave, the Prison, the place of Torment espoused so fervently within scriptural lore was their teachings.

According to the ancient wisdom, Hell does not await the body-person after it passes into physical death - the *body* is not divine anyway according to their theology. It is the soul that is of divine essence and *that soul has already suffered death in hell* by the fact of its captivity within the bowels of Satan, that is to say the world of Matter. This Earth, the world of Matter is considered the pit of Satan, a place of trials, temptations, sin, and waywardness; and this condition or circumstance was described as *death* for the soul (inner spiritual being) that abides trapped within the body and world, according to the Gnostics and other wise ones. THE HELL OF THE SOUL IS IN THE HERE AND NOW, in this earthly life that the soul is presently living. It doesn't matter whether the body-person is rich or poor, happy or sad; *for the spiritual soul* that is encased in Matter this life is death, it is a living hell. Accordingly, the spiritualists taught that

CHAPTER THREE

our souls must resist Satan, and vigilantly strive to overcome the temptations of this world, and then, when death overtakes the body-person, an avenue of escape is opened for the spiritual soul, captive within the body-person, to return to paradise. If the soul was faithful and true, its passage back to its spiritual homeland in the heavens would be attained, but if not, the soul was doomed to repeat its life within the bowels of Satan - the soul would be reincarnated back into another body-person (or even body-animal according to some cultures) to repeat the ordeal of captivity in hell. The above is the *original* ancient definition of reincarnation, that is to say the sentencing of the soul to repeated suffering within the world of matter. The original definition of reincarnation was a bad thing and *not*, at all, a good thing as proclaimed by so many of us in this day and time. The modern concept of reincarnation is the attainment of a new lease on earthly life in a new body. There's a lot that we could explore on the subject of reincarnation, but that pursuit would be off focus to our present inquiry.

THE ODYSSEY of the once heavenly soul is that it was cast out of heaven's paradise or garden because of some infraction; however this garden paradise was ethereal, *not earthly*, according to the Gnosis. The soul was cast into the wilderness, into the nether regions of matter as punishment for its sins. The spiritual soul cannot return to its ethereal homeland till due expiation for its sins has been rendered and judged acceptable by the divine. The soul is considered dead, lost, and exiled by reason of its imprisonment within the lower world of Satan, that is to say Hades or Earth. The symbolism is made much clearer in the Quran than in the Bible - witness this quote from my book, *The Biggest Lie Ever Told, Fourth Edition*:

"There were those of old who suggested that the Garden Of Eden was not actually an earthly location, but rather a heavenly domain, ethereal, of the spirits; it was our souls' domain and not of this material world. They teach that our (souls') rebellion or disobedience in the Garden was in the spirit, and our punishment was the sentencing to death, *death in matter*, that our condition of life on this planet is the death sentence that god warned Adam of in the bible; that this planet is actually hell, and our toils and sufferings are the wages of our sins that we

CHAPTER THREE

committed in heaven, *when in our prior spiritual existences*. This concept is actually confirmed in the **Quran** of the Muslims: Witness quote from **Sura 2, Verses 35-36**: "[35]We said: *O Adam! Dwell thou and thy wife in the Garden; and eat of the bountiful things therein as ye will; but approach not this tree, or ye run into harm and transgression* [36]***Then did Satan make them slip from the (garden), and get them out of the state (of felicity) in which they had been. We said: "Get ye down,** all (ye people), with enmity between yourselves. **On earth** will be your dwelling-place and your means of livelihood - for a time."* "

IN THE MYSTIC-RELIGIOUS SYMBOLISM, the soul is the counterpart of the cosmic sun, so when analyzing the odyssey or struggles of the soul in its metaphorical context, we simply substitute the *soul* for the *sun* in the literature, and hence we are in sync with the *spiritual symbolism* of the fallen soul that seeks redemption. So consequently the death of the sun in the pit of the underworld, within the devil sign of Capricorn, is likened to the death of the fallen soul into the pit of the sublunar underworld of matter on Earth.

The fall or casting out of the sun from the upper hemisphere into the lower hemisphere of the dragon of darkness becomes, when in the context of the mystical symbolism, the fall or casting out of the soul from the heavenly domain out beyond the stars; and this is an exact replica of the casting out of Adam and Eve from the heavenly garden (not an Earthly garden) of an ethereal paradise, typed as the Garden of Eden within the Bible and Quran.

Before we can accurately analyze the struggles of the soul in its biblical allegorical context, we must have a proper understanding of the opposing *earthly* forces to which the soul has fallen prey. In the bible the soul is described, in varying degrees, as being enslaved, deceived, captured, and oppressed, as well as being wayward, sinful, profligate, and unfaithful. Witness some verses that help to exemplify these dynamics:

Biblical Verses Relevant to the Beleaguered Soul

Take note of these verses that indicate that the body is a form of death for the soul, which is exactly in accordance with the Gnostic symbolism:

CHAPTER THREE

Romans 7:17 Now then it is no more I that do it, but <u>sin that dwelleth in me.</u> For I know that <u>in me (that is, in my flesh,)</u> dwelleth *no good* thing: **Romans 7:21-24** I find then a law, that, when I would do good, evil is present with me. <u>For I delight in the law of God after the inward man:</u> But *I see another law in my members,* warring against the law of my mind, and <u>bringing me into captivity to the law of sin</u> which is in my members. O wretched man that I am! *who shall deliver me from the body of this death?*

Take note of this biblical passage that highlights the adversarial relationship between the *spiritual soul*, which is of god and the *natural body* which is of Satan, according to the Gnostic theology within the bible:

Romans 8:4-8 That the righteousness of the law might be fulfilled in us, who walk not after the flesh, but after the Spirit. For they that are after the flesh do mind the things of the flesh; but they that are after the Spirit the things of the Spirit. <u>For to be carnally minded is *death*;</u> but to be spiritually minded is life and peace. Because the *carnal mind is enmity against God;* <u>for it is not subject to the law of God,</u> neither indeed can be. *So then they that are in the flesh cannot please God.*

The Biblical Israeli Saga is a Legendary Epic Tale

As regards the Old Testament of the bible, the entire book is focused on the redemption of the Nation of Israel - this is the pervasive motif throughout the books of the Old Testament. The constant recurring theme in nearly every part of the book stresses the overriding goal of liberation and nationhood for the Israeli people. The establishment of a national home centered in Jerusalem of Judea is viewed as the redemption of the Israelites, and a fulfillment of god's covenant with the Hebrew people.

The bible purports that the Israelites have formed a pact (covenant) with god, that if they serve and obey their god, and perform numerous rituals and traditions, that god in return will grant them liberation from their oppressors and victory over their rivals, also bless them with an independent nation of their own, and ultimately, Yahweh will bestow world supremacy and domination to the Hebrews.

CHAPTER THREE

Exodus 19:5-6 Now therefore, if ye will obey my voice indeed, and keep my covenant, then ye shall be a peculiar treasure unto me above all people: for all the earth is mine: And ye shall be unto me a kingdom of priests, and an holy nation. These are the words which thou shalt speak unto the children of Israel.

The odyssey of the Hebrew people begins with the father of their race, Abraham, a nomadic tribesman, who left his home at Ur in Mesopotamia, and along with his family journeyed *down* toward Canaan and Egypt. This trek of Abram or Abraham, as the Father of Israel, marks the beginning odyssey of the Hebrew or Israeli people. Abraham and eventually his progeny traveled and temporarily settled in various places, there were highs and lows in their circumstances. Eventually they came to Egypt and after a span of time, and a turn of events, the Israelites became slaves of the Egyptians, as the story goes.

The nexus or central theme of the biblical Old Testament is focused on salvation for the Hebrew tribes; a conglomeration of ragtag vagabonds, wandering about the Near East, with no settled homeland for themselves or for the Temple which they desire to build for their god's residence. For many generations, all that they truly have is their covenant with their god, a covenant that promises, if they keep faith and obey his commandments that he, Yahweh, will bring them to Zion, a blessed homeland of safety and security, and oneness with Yahweh, their god and deliverer. UNDENIABLY, this is what the Old Testament is all about - the search for the *salvation* of the Israeli people, from Genesis to Malachi the salvation theme lays at the core of the biblical texts. *And it's all a big tale!* It is a legendary epic or composition comparable to many similar epics of various cultures throughout the world, such as the Greek epics. It is well known and taught by multiple scholars, historians, and archeologists worldwide that the biblical history of the Israeli people is a palpable fiction on the face of it. THE BIBLE IS *literature*, not history, the bible is a compilation of epic tales, poems, oral traditions converted to writings, ancient rituals and superstitions; *but it is also symbolism*, and that (symbolism) is the focus of our present exploration.

CHAPTER THREE

The epic tales of the Jews (Israelites) carry no more literal credence than the ancient epics of the Greeks, the Hindustanis, the Egyptians, the Incas, the Irish, and many, many others. But with the Jewish mythology, as with some others, there exist multiple streams or currents of symbolism, discernable at multiple levels of parallel interpretations. We are now focused on the Mystical-Religious cryptology of the Hebrew epic, that of a lost, oppressed, wandering people engaged in a seemingly endless odyssey of national salvation. The odyssey of the biblical Israelis, in terms of spiritual symbolism, represents the *Lost Numinous Souls* that were exiled or fell from the heavenly grace of god's ethereal paradise, and now desire to return home to that spiritual realm - but can't seem to find the way. These forlorned souls were cast out of, rebelled against, or willingly departed from god's paradisiacal garden but are now repentant and want to find mercy, relief, and homage with the divine, however the path back to Zion is fraught with difficulties. Even though the souls are repentant and sincere, the forces rallied against them are as great as their determination to find oneness with god. This theme is epitomized in the odyssey of the biblical Hebrews, *but this human spiritual plight is universal*, that is to say, the universal yearning of the forsakened human soul to escape this earthly milieu in search for something better and *more meaningful* and more *soothing to* and *caressing of* the forlorned and wretched human soul, here suffering and tormented inside the bowels of earthly matter.

THE HEBREW ODYSSEY IS A METAPHOR for the struggles of the forlorned numinous souls that have been separated from heaven, and their (the spiritual souls) quest to return their heavenly Zion. The enduring Jewish odyssey is closely encapsulated in a biblical story known as the *Prodigal Son* - the story is attributed to the Christ, or perhaps I should say Jesus. I have posted the verses below - read this idealized version of the perils of the lost soul, but take no thought of the son himself, rather think of the Prodigal Son as a metaphor for those lost spiritual souls that want earnestly to return to the Father God. The whole Israeli saga , or perhaps I should say *Tale of Lost*

CHAPTER THREE

Souls typed as Israel, is summarized, from an idealized perspective, in this one tale of the *Prodigal Son*.

Prodigal Son:

Luke 15:11-24 And he said, A certain man had two sons: And the younger of them said to his father, Father, give me the portion of goods that falleth to me. And he divided unto them his living. And not many days after the younger son gathered all together, and took his journey into a far country, and there wasted his substance with riotous living. And when he had spent all, there arose a mighty famine in that land; and he began to be in want. And he went and joined himself to a citizen of that country; and he sent him into his fields to feed swine. And he would fain have filled his belly with the husks that the swine did eat: and no man gave unto him. And when he came to himself, he said, How many hired servants of my father's have bread enough and to spare, and I perish with hunger! I will arise and go to my father, and will say unto him, Father, I have sinned against heaven, and before thee, And am no more worthy to be called thy son: make me as one of thy hired servants. And he arose, and came to his father. But when he was yet a great way off, his father saw him, and had compassion, and ran, and fell on his neck, and kissed him. And the son said unto him, Father, I have sinned against heaven, and in thy sight, and am no more worthy to be called thy son. But the father said to his servants, Bring forth the best robe, and put it on him; and put a ring on his hand, and shoes on his feet: And bring hither the fatted calf, and kill it; and let us eat, and be merry: <u>For this my son was dead, and is alive again;</u> he was lost, and is found. And they began to be merry.

CHAPTER THREE

Intra-Cultural Transference Within Religion

Before closing out this chapter, there is one more category of mythological symbolism that I think we should explore, that being myths and legends born out of the fantasizing and or spiritualizing of a tribes engrained cultural traditions, customs, and standards - I call this category *Intra-Cultural Transference*. Many of the biblical myths, which seem grossly absurd on the face of it, actually have sprung forth from rather practical and sometimes rational elements of early Semitic culture. IT IS IMPORTANT to remember that *Semitic culture predates the religion of Judaism.* Judaism was spawned out of Semitic culture, not the other way around. WHEN THE HEBREWS INVENTED their religions, that is to say, both Judaism and Early Christianity, they used the traditions, systems, and standards of their Semitic culture as source material - which is only practical when you think of it. They also, perhaps with near equal importance, desired to persuade the masses that their social systems were divinely ordained hence not subject to challenge by their subjects - this linking of god to the government was common in the ancient world. I have covered this subject of Intra-Cultural Transference, somewhat extensively, in my book *The Secret Origins of Judaism* - I will offer a couple of examples of this category of mythology here so as to acquaint my readers with the basics of how Intra-Cultural Transference into religious dogma usually evolves from within a given culture - in this case Semitic culture.

ALL RELIGIONS ARE MAN-MADE, we can be rationally certain that god has never communicated a religious preference to anyone, regardless of what the religionists claim. All religions are the results of cultural evolution, hence the sources of a religion's tenets are always discoverable within the underlying culture - this includes the language, traditions, legends, social systems, ecology, economy, and also regional influences and societal proclivities of neighboring nations that effect the collective psyche of the community or culture. JUDAISM IS THE CHILD OF SEMITIC CULTURE, which is essentially *nomadic* in many respects. Much of Semitic *religious* culture has

CHAPTER THREE

been derived from the *migration* and *merging* of Semitic societal customs into the rituals, traditions, and doctrine of their religion; this, of course, applies also to Christianity and Islam which are offshoots of Semitic Judaism.

LET US NOW EXEMPLIFY *INTRA-CULTURAL TRANSFERENCE* with reference to a few biblical verses:

God personally guides the Exodus of the Israelites

We have been taught that god, himself, intervened so as to emancipate the Hebrew people from their alleged bondage to the Egyptians, that god persecuted the Egyptians till they agreed to free the Israelites. After the Israelites were freed, it is alleged that god himself, shielded in the *Pillar of a Cloud*, by day; and shielded in a *Pillar of Fire* by night *guided* the Israelites through the desert wilderness in search for a new *Promised Land* in which they would establish their nationhood, under the aegis of their god, Yahweh, conveniently resident in the local Temple. This is a very bizarre story, and I doubt that you can form a rational picture of such an event having ever literally occurred in history. This, on the face of it, is an absurd myth, but nevertheless, in truth, this puzzling tale contains a *germ* of truth which is reflective of its cultural underpinnings. Our task is to expose that *germ* of truth from which this fanciful tale was *germinated*, and utilized by the Jewish Priesthood as they composed this particular fictional episode of the alleged Hebrew exodus from Egypt.

Exodus 13:18 But God led the people about, through the way of the wilderness of the Red sea: and the children of Israel went up harnessed out of the land of Egypt.

Exodus 13:21-22 And the LORD went before them by day in a pillar of a cloud, to lead them the way; and by night in a pillar of fire, to give them light; to go by day and night: He took not away the pillar of the cloud by day, nor the pillar of fire by night, from before the people.

The above verses are unambiguous; according to the bible the Israelites were lost in a desert that, of course, had no roads or travel

CHAPTER THREE

signs to mark the way to wherever they were going - so god himself took charge to guide them through the desert wilderness. Since it is profane to look upon the the divine deity or even to mention his sacred name, god clothed himself in a Pillar formed of a cloud during the day, and he, Yahweh, clothed himself in a Fire Pillar during darkness. This is truly a whale of a tale, however the key to discovering the *germ* of secular truth within this yarn lies in the Semitic *nomadic culture*. THE HEBREWS WERE NOMADIC PEOPLE, and nomads never, or hardly ever, stay in one place more than a season. Nomads are constantly on the move so as to provide pasture for their animals, so these travelers and wanderers were *very adapt at using the dynamics of the natural environment to map their courses* through uncharted lands.

ACCORDING TO THE BIBLE, GOD WAS THEIR **GUIDE**, and god wrote or allegedly Moses wrote how he, god, managed to guide the Israelites through the wilderness. Of course we know that god did not write this fiction - *it was written by a nomadic Hebrew!* And I would add, the tale was written by a nomad that was intimately familiar with systems of mapping a course through uncharted territory by reading *nature's signs of direction* as indicated by the natural environment.

THE CONTENT OF THIS FABLE CLEARLY INDICATES THE MINDSET OF A DESERT NOMAD - so the question that we should ask so as to ascertain the real *germ* of truth, is *how did the nomads actually navigate the deserts* and is there a possible relationship to *clouds* and *pillars of fire* that can explain this navigation. As I have noted above, our path to understanding religious fantasies can often be extrapolated from the underlying culture from which the theological fantasy has evolved, thus indicating *Intra-Cultural Transference*.

The greatest asset for navigating the desert wilderness as well as the open seas are the *guiding* cosmic lights - this has been true since time immemorial. Navigators have always used the celestial North Pole as their guide for determining their position and course of direction on the *open seas* and the *sprawling deserts*. It is not just the Pole Star

CHAPTER THREE

alone that serves as the guide *but the whole region of circumpolar constellations* that circuit the Celestial Pole - these circling circumpolar constellations are *indicators of time and direction* to the trained observer. Chief among all of the polar constellations are the Bear Constellations, commonly called **Ursa Major** and **Ursa Minor**. It is easy to conceive the North Star itself i.e. Polaris as a Pillar of Light, but actually I suggest, and navigational history confirms, that it is the entire circumpolar region that serves as a navigational guide for those who traverse uncharted geographical regions, whether at land or sea. Take note of this quote from the book, *Star Names and Their Meaning by Richard Allen,* under the heading for the constellation **Ursa Major** wherein various historical references to this star-group are explained, the <u>underlining</u> is my own:

"Its well-known use by the early Greeks in <u>navigation</u> was <u>paralleled in the deserts of Arabia</u>, through which, according to Diodorus the Sicilian, <u>travelers</u> **direct their course** by the Bears, in the same manner as is done at sea. They serve this same purpose to the Badawiyy [Bedouin] of today, as Mrs. Sigourney describes in **The Stars**, writing of Polaris:
> *The weary caravan, with chiming bells,*
> *Making strange music mid the desert sand,*
> *Guides by the **pillar d fires** its <u>nightly march</u>*"

THE BIBLICAL PILLAR OF FIRES is a clear reference to the constellations of the circumpolar region which the ancients have used for ascertaining their compass directions since time immemorial. Actually the seven lights (fires) of the Big Dipper were commonly referred to as *Pillars of Fire* as it is the most notable of the circumpolar groupings, and two of its stars, Dubhe and Merak, point directly to the North Star.

NOW AS REGARDS THE USE OF A PILLAR OF A CLOUD to guide the way during the daytime - the *germ* of truth for this assertion is found also within pre-Judaic Semitic or Bedouin culture. Clouds do not flow helter skelter, but rather flow in specific directions depending on the

CHAPTER THREE

type clouds, their elevation, upper atmospheric air flows and other factors. The flow of the various clouds are consistent to conditions prevalent at their elevation, except in cases of weather disturbances. The effect of all this is that the nomads, when starting out on their desert treks could relate their compass directions to the flow of the clouds, and thereby map and maintain their course direction by simply referencing the flow of the clouds as they proceeded.

In the above, *I think that the link to Intra-Cultural Transference is clear* and vivid. It is claimed by the religionists that this absurd tale of god guiding the Israelites through the desert wilderness by means of pillars of fire and clouds was done by god in person, and written into the scriptures by the prophet Moses, but the real truth is too obvious to ignore - THE ACTUAL COMPOSER OF THIS FAIRYTALE WAS CLEARLY A NOMADIC SHEPHERD that wrote a story that clearly reflects his own experiences and culture as a Semitic nomad. The Semitic nomads customarily used the circumpolar constellations and the flow of the clouds to navigate the deserts, and lo and behold, when composing this myth about the Israelite exodus they superimposed their own experiences onto their tribal god with the ludicrous claim that Yahweh led the Hebrews through the wilderness by the same methods that the nomads have used from time immemorial.

The Sacred Blood of Passover

According to the Jews, the celebration of Passover was initiated in commemoration of god's liberation of the Hebrews from bondage in Egypt. Actually Passover, by whatever name, is an old *Semitic tradition* that predates the advent of Judaism. The celebration could not have started to celebrate Jewish liberation from Egypt because the Jews/Hebrews were never in bondage to the Egyptians - this so-called bondage cannot be found in secular history - *only* the Bible and Quran tout this myth as historical fact rather than cultural mythology or literature. Read the following biblical verses concerning the religious meaning of Passover according to Judaic theology.

CHAPTER THREE

Exodus 12:21-23 Then Moses called for all the elders of Israel, and said unto them, Draw out and take you a lamb according to your families, and kill the passover. <u>And ye shall take a bunch of hyssop, and dip it in the blood that is in the bason, and strike the lintel and the two side posts with the blood</u> that is in the bason; and none of you shall go out at the door of his house until the morning. For the LORD will pass through to smite the Egyptians; and <u>when he seeth the blood upon the lintel, and on the two side posts, the LORD will pass over the door,</u> and will not suffer the destroyer to come in unto your houses to smite you.

Exodus 12:24-27 And ye shall observe this thing for an ordinance to thee and to thy sons for ever. And it shall come to pass, when ye be come to the land which the LORD will give you, according as he hath promised, that ye shall keep this service. And it shall come to pass, when your children shall say unto you, What mean ye by this service? That ye shall say, <u>It is the sacrifice of the LORD'S passover, who passed over the houses of the children of Israel in Egypt, when he smote the Egyptians,</u> and delivered our houses. And the people bowed the head and worshipped.

Exodus 12:29-30 And it came to pass, that at midnight the LORD smote all the firstborn in the land of Egypt, from the firstborn of Pharaoh that sat on his throne unto the firstborn of the captive that was in the dungeon; and all the firstborn of cattle. And Pharaoh rose up in the night, he, and all his servants, and all the Egyptians; and there was a great cry in Egypt; for there was not a house where there was not one dead.

So the biblical verses above give recitation to the Jewish basis for commemorating the Passover festival. The gist of this fairytale as given in Exodus of the bible, is that Yahweh, the tribal god of the Hebrews, had to pressure Pharaoh into releasing the Hebrews from slavery; hence the Hebrew god sent ten plagues, in succession, upon the Egyptians. The final plague or punishment that caused Pharaoh to relent and allow the enslaved Israelites (Hebrews) to leave Egypt was the death decree to all the firstborn of Egypt; whereas the god, at the stroke of midnight, *passed-over* i.e. through the land, in misty form we assume, and struck to death the firstborn in every habitat that did not have the *Blood of the Lamb* smeared at the entrance to the place.

CHAPTER THREE

Of course, being that we are rational human beings, we realize that this is clearly a fictional tale; but what actually concerns us, or should concern us, is the *mindset* of the individual (or group) that had the gall to pen this blatantly farcical story as a true and historical event.

I mentioned in the previous explanation above, concerning the farcical Jewish rendition of Yahweh clothing himself in a Cloud by day and Fire by night so as to lead the Israelites through the desert wilderness, that the key to the *real* truth is found by focusing on the *mindset of the writer* of these ludicrous tales. And we have shown and proven, definitively I believe, that the writer was a *Semitic Nomad* who pulled upon his own culture and experiences in the formulation of these mythical stories. These stories were not just pulled out of nowhere or from baseless imagination; these stories are a modified *reflection of the underlying culture*, even though significantly altered and extremely fantasized. *These myths are the offshoot of Intra-Cultural Transference*,without doubt.

According to the biblical verses that we just cited, god instructed the Hebrews to smear sacrificial blood at the entrances to their houses so as to <u>render</u> <u>the</u> <u>home</u> <u>miraculously</u> <u>protected</u> by the *sacrificial blood of the lamb*. This is the gist of it - god said that he would glide through the land bringing death to all of the firstborn, but that those dwellings that were smeared with the blood of the sacrificial lamb, they would be spared or *saved* from the death sentence.

BUT WHEN WE PERUSE THE HISTORY of the Semitic people, which includes, among others, the Phoenicians and Canaanites, as well as the Judaeans - that is to say, *a history that predates* the advent of the Biblical Passover observances; we find, intact, the *germ* from which this vacuous fairytale was generated. THE SMEARING OF SACRIFICIAL BLOOD upon *things* and *people* as a means of *transferring gods protection* to those things and people *touched by the Lamb,s blood* was a <u>commonplace superstition</u> among the Pre-Jewish Semitic communities of the Near East. ALSO, a type of Passover festival, under whatever name, was observed amongst the Semitic peoples of

CHAPTER THREE

the Near East regions long before the evolution of the Semitic Hebrews into a viable national group within Judaea. History shows the Habiru (Hebrews) as roving bandits that terrorized the Canaanite region long before finally attempting to establish a permanent homeland. The New Year festival of the Semites predates the biblical rendition by a significant but unknown period of years, as far as I can tell.

IT WAS THE CUSTOM of the pre-Judaic Semites to celebrate their New Year (Passover) in ways very similar to those described in the bible. The festival was observed during the period of the sun's transiting the vernal equinox. It was the custom of the Semites to slaughter a lamb as a Sacrifice, this was done by the head of the household. *The head of the house (Tent) would daub the* **blood** *of the slaughtered animal and smear it on the main* **tent post** *at the entrance to the tent, thereby conferring* **protection** *to the household*, so graced by the sacrificial blood of the lamb. This ritual was done throughout the Near East Semitic world *long before* the bible was produced,and the Hebrews spuriously claimed that the practice was initiated by godly decree. So in this we see the *germ* from which the Jewish myth of Passover was *germinated*, that is, from within the folds of the underlying Semitic culture, through a system of *Intra-Cultural Transference* of the pre-Judaic Semitic traditions into the new and unfolding made-up religion of Judaism.

The Semitic superstition about the sacredness and saving-power of the blood of the Sacrificial Lamb was also carried over into the theology of the Early Christians - see the following bible verses:

Revelation 7:14 And I said unto him, Sir, thou knowest. And he said to me, These are they which came out of great tribulation, and have washed their robes, and made them white in the blood of the Lamb.

Revelation 12:11 And they overcame him by the blood of the Lamb, and by the word of their testimony; and they loved not their lives unto the death.

CHAPTER THREE

The key factor of the alleged Passover miracle was the belief of the acolytes in the divine healing and *protective* power of the Sacrificial Blood of the Lamb. It was the blood of the lamb smeared at the house entrances that protected the inhabitants from the wrath of god - this goes back to an old pagan belief in the protective powers of sacrificial blood that prevailed in the Near East region and in other lands. The adherents practiced certain ritualistic rites whereas they drenched themselves in Sacrificial Blood with the belief that the blood would purify their souls, and also as a symbol of rebirth, that is to say *being Born again* by virtue of being anointed (drenched) with the sacrificial blood of the lamb. These pagan rites are documented in history.

THERE IS A WEALTH OF INFORMATION to be gained on this subject of the protective and healing powers of blood, as believed by the Semites and others by researching the terms **Taurobolium** and **Criobolium** - these were two forms of ancient blood sacrifice with the use of bulls and/or lambs.

The Passover festival, under whatever name, goes back to times preceding the advent of the Hebrew religious observation which they have named Passover (Pesach). Among the nomadic Semites there was an observance every Spring that had all the trappings of the Jewish Passover. During the springtime *Lambing Season* of the Semites which coincided with their *New Year* as indicated by the crossing of the sun over the Vernal Equinox, it was the Semitic custom to daub the blood of the sacrificed lambs on their tent-post as a propitiation to ward off evil for the coming year; and concomitant with this practice, the agricultural Semites would celebrate the Spring Harvest with the consumption of unleavened bread. The Jews have incorporated both of these ancient customs into their invented religion under the false guise of an absurdly fictional tale that asserts that these traditions are observed in remembrance of god's special deliverance of the Hebrew people from bondage.

CHAPTER FOUR

Chapter four

An examination of biblical allegories relevant to Agricultural deities symbolized as Seed and Harvest gods

Biblical Interpretations Relevant To Agricultural Symbolism

Much of the biblical symbolism is actually a reflection of the Hebrew planting and harvest festivals. As I noted in the Introduction, the original purpose of the holiday (agricultural) festivals was to keep track of the pivotal sowing and harvest seasons by interweaving these occasions into the fabric of the early societies, by making these agricultural dates celebratory. The starry signpost served as signals for when to plant and when to harvest, along with the phases of the moon and declination of the sun and other factors. The Priesthood created feasts (festivals) to correspond to the *appointed times* that the star deities were scheduled to appear, as signals to the populations to look for the stellar signposts and for the commencement of the agricultural activities sanctioned by a particular star or star group. The word *feast* as defined under Hebrew biblical usage means *appointed times* according to the various biblical dictionaries and this definition fits the esoteric symbolism perfectly. The festivals or perhaps I should say celebrations at *appointed times* preceded the religious association is my take, even if only by a short span.

The New Revised Standard Version of the Bible Leviticus 23:4

4These are the appointed festivals of the LORD, the holy convocations, which you shall celebrate at the time appointed for them.

The original purpose of the Feasts (appointed days) was to track time so as to plant and harvest within the constraints of the seasons and this practice was governed by the early star watchers, as we noted in the Introduction. The religious association to the agricultural signal dates was a natural evolutionary process, over

CHAPTER FOUR

time, as the societies developed religiously. Spirits based on physics is the basis of religious evolution, from ancient times to the present.

The Hebrews observed seven biblical Feasts – they are *Passover* (Pesach) on Nisan 14, *Unleavened Bread* (Hag Hamatzah) on Nisan 15 - 21, *First Fruits* (Bikkurim) On Nisan 17, *Pentecost* (Shavuot) on Sivan 6, *New Years* (Rosh Hashanah) on Tishri 1, *Atonement* (Yom Kippur) on Tishri 10 and *Tabernacles* (Sukkoth) on Tishri 15 - 21. Three of these are considered *Pilgrim Festivals* whereas the participants congregate (pilgrimage to Jerusalem), namely Pesach, Shavuot and Sukkoth.

I am providing basic information on these Jewish festivals in the following. **I assure you** - this data will prove invaluable as we pursue our efforts of biblical decipherment. As I indicated earlier in this book – cultural and linguistic input into the symbolism tends to make it somewhat more convoluted and intricate, and such is the case with the Hebrew cultural associations within scriptural esoteric symbolism.

The Jewish Feasts

The observance of these festivals is as follows:

1 - Passover: This festival is alleged to commemorate the exodus of Israel from Egypt, their birth as a free people, after enduring centuries of slavery under the Pharaohs. It is observed on Nisan 14, the first full moon after the vernal equinox. The edict enjoining that the Hebrews commemorate Passover is found in Exodus:

Exodus 12:21 through Exodus 12:28

[21]Then Moses called for all the elders of Israel, and said unto them, Draw out and take you a lamb according to your families, and kill the passover. [22]And ye shall take a bunch of hyssop, and dip *it* in the blood that *is* in the basin, and strike the lintel and the two side posts with the blood that *is* in the basin; and none of you shall go out at the door of his house until the morning. [23]For the LORD will pass through to smite the Egyptians; and when he seeth the blood upon the lintel, and on the two side posts, the LORD will pass over the door, and will not suffer the destroyer to

CHAPTER FOUR

come in unto your houses to smite *you*. 24And ye shall observe this thing for an ordinance to thee and to thy sons for ever. 25And it shall come to pass, when ye be come to the land which the LORD will give you, according as he hath promised, that ye shall keep this service. 26And it shall come to pass, when your children shall say unto you, What mean ye by this service? 27That ye shall say, It *is* the sacrifice of the LORD'S passover, who passed over the houses of the children of Israel in Egypt, when he smote the Egyptians, and delivered our houses. And the people bowed the head and worshipped. 28And the children of Israel went away, and did as the LORD had commanded Moses and Aaron, so did they.

The Passover tradition embraces some intriguing customs – one of which is called the *Seder* observance – for this ceremonial meal, the father dresses in a long white robe (*Kittel*) and white headpiece. Special foodstuffs are prepared and served in keeping with Passover requirements. The Seder table includes three Matzos placed so that one is in the middle of the stack – this middle Matzos is traditionally broken and wrapped in linen and hidden from the eyesight of the guest. The children in due course are sent to search for the missing Matzo which is called the *Afikomen*. When found the Afikomen is shared by all the guest at the Seder Table.

2 - Feast Of Unleavened Bread: The requirements of this festival are that for seven days the faithful must not eat any Leavened bread or allow any form of Leaven whatsoever within their homes. Violation of this ordinance will invoke banishment from the Jewish community. The Old Testament god seems to have an acute dislike for Leaven during the middle part of the month of Nisan, but any other time of the year its consumption is heartily welcomed. Of course the faithful attribute this custom as symbolically reflective of the haste under which the Hebrews exited Egypt, claiming that they did not have time to leaven their bread. Since the Hebrews were never actually in slavery in Egypt, the custom must have another truer

CHAPTER FOUR

meaning. The instructions for this strange ceremony are found in Exodus of the bible.

Exodus 12:17 through Exodus 12:20

[17]And ye shall observe *the feast of* unleavened bread; for in this selfsame day have I brought your armies out of the land of Egypt: therefore shall ye observe this day in your generations by an ordinance for ever. [18]In the first *month*, on the fourteenth day of the month at even, ye shall eat unleavened bread, until the one and twentieth day of the month at even. [19]Seven days shall there be no leaven found in your houses: for whosoever eateth that which is leavened, even that soul shall be cut off from the congregation of Israel, whether he be a stranger, or born in the land. [20]Ye shall eat nothing leavened; in all your habitations shall ye eat unleavened bread.

3 - First Fruits: This festival is observed on Nisan 17 – indicates the Barley harvest, and the concurrent start of Spring, The First Fruit (sheaf of barley) is dedicated, brought to the Temple and waved before the deity. This event is after the Passover. The festival begins the count down to the wheat harvest i.e. Shavuot that takes place 50 days or 7 weeks later. *This is the date (Nisan 17) of the resurrection of the biblical Christ.*

Leviticus 23:10 through Leviticus 23:12

[10]Speak unto the children of Israel, and say unto them, When ye be come into the land which I give unto you, and shall reap the harvest thereof, then ye shall bring a sheaf of the firstfruits of your harvest unto the priest: [11]And he shall wave the sheaf before the LORD, to be accepted for you: on the morrow after the sabbath the priest shall wave it. [12]And ye shall offer that day when ye wave the sheaf an he lamb without blemish of the first year for a burnt offering unto the LORD.

Leviticus 23:15

[15]And ye shall count unto you from the morrow after the sabbath, from the day that ye brought the sheaf of the wave offering; seven sabbaths shall be complete:

CHAPTER FOUR

4 - Shavuot: This is the feast of weeks that comes 50 days after the festival of First Fruits, the barley harvest. The 10 commandments were given on this feast day, according to Jewish tradition. This festival is observed on Sivan 6. This festival commences the Wheat harvest period. This corresponds to the Pentecost of the Christians – the commemoration of the alleged descent of the holy spirit upon the apostles.

Leviticus 23:15 through Leviticus 23:16

15And ye shall count unto you from the morrow after the sabbath, from the day that ye brought the sheaf of the wave offering; seven sabbaths shall be complete: 16Even unto the morrow after the seventh sabbath shall ye number fifty days; and ye shall offer a new meat offering unto the LORD.

5 - Rosh Hashanah: This is the Hebrew New Year, also referred to as Judgment Day (Yom Hadin), as trumpets are blown to recognize this month of destiny. It is the 7th month and 1st day of the Religious year that commences in the month of Nisan and/or it is the 1st month and 1st day of the Jewish civil year i.e. Tishri 1.

Leviticus 23:23 through Leviticus 23:25

23And the LORD spake unto Moses, saying, 24Speak unto the children of Israel, saying, In the seventh month, in the first *day* of the month, shall ye have a sabbath, a memorial of blowing of trumpets, an holy convocation.

25Ye shall do no servile work *therein:* but ye shall offer an offering made by fire unto the LORD.

Some interesting characteristics of *Rosh Hashanah* include the blowing of the *Shofar horn*, as a warning or announcement that Judgment Day (Rosh Hashanah) has arrived. Jewish tradition dictates that Rosh Hashanah is annually the Judgment Day – that on this day god judges his subjects and enters their names into a book that is called *The Book Of Life.* Rosh Hashanah commences ten days of penitence wherein the devout are obligated to seek forgiveness for their sins of the previous year and even ask forgiveness of those whom they may have wronged. After the ten

CHAPTER FOUR

days have passed, on the evening of Yom Kippur, the *Book Of Life is sealed* and the fate of the subjects is destined. The Shofar horn is then blown to announce the sealing of the *Book Of Life* and the closing of the *Days Of Awe*, which is the term that collectively describes Rosh Hashanah and Yom Kippur.

6 - Yom Kippur: This is the Day Of Atonement, a day of prayer and repentance to the Jewish deity. It falls on the 10th day after the Jewish New Year. *Rosh Hashanah* commences 10 days of Penitence which climaxes on Tishri 10 on the day of Yom Kippur i.e. the Day Of Atonement. The Shofar (Ram's Horn) is associated with Yom Kippur. *Rosh Hashanah* also known as *Yom Hadin,* which means Day Of Judgment. Rosh Hashanah means *Head* of the year.
Leviticus 23:27 through Leviticus 23:28

27Also on the tenth *day* of this seventh month *there shall be* a day of atonement: it shall be an holy convocation unto you; and ye shall afflict your souls, and offer an offering made by fire unto the LORD. 28And ye shall do no work in that same day: for it *is* a day of atonement, to make an atonement for you before the LORD your God.

7 - Sukkoth: This is the Feast Of Tabernacles, a harvest festival commemorating the booths (temporary dwellings) in which the Israelites allegedly resided during their wandering in the wilderness, according to the myth.
Leviticus 23:33 through Leviticus 23:36

33And the LORD spake unto Moses, saying, 34Speak unto the children of Israel, saying, The fifteenth day of this seventh month *shall be* the feast of tabernacles *for* seven days unto the LORD. 35On the first day *shall be* an holy convocation: ye shall do no servile work *therein.* 36Seven days ye shall offer an offering made by fire unto the LORD: on the eighth day shall be an holy convocation unto you; and ye shall offer an offering made by fire unto the LORD: it *is* a solemn assembly; *and* ye shall do no servile work *therein.*

Simchat Torah: The closing of the Jewish festival season is the

CHAPTER FOUR

Simchat Torah, which means *rejoicing in the Torah*. This is observed at the closing of the 7-8 day Sukkoth festivities. Jewish tradition calls for the weekly reading of the Torah in the synagogue throughout the year. The readings are proportioned so as to complete simultaneously with the end of Sukkoth. Simchat Torah is the reading of the last verses of the Torah for the year and the immediate commencement of the first reading of the new yearly cycle. The cycle of Torah readings begins with Genesis and runs through Deuteronomy by the end of the annual cycle of readings; thus completing the so-called five books of Moses - Genesis, Exodus, Leviticus, Numbers and Deuteronomy. Originally the book (Torah) was in the form of a scroll and this fact provides nuances that will prove very intriguing as we pursue our biblical interpretations later in this chapter.

Bride Of Judgment: Torah scrolls are called *Kallah (Callah),* which means Bride. The person that reads the closing verses of Deuteronomy is called *Chatan Torah* which means Bridegroom of the Law. The person that reads the 1st verses of Genesis For the New Year is called *Chatan Bereshit* which means Bridegroom Of The Beginning

Shemini Atzeret: this is observed in conjunction with Simchat Torah on the last day of Sukkoth. The term Shemini means 8 and Atzeret means holding back. This is observed to seal the last day of the Sukkoth festival - special prayers for rain are prayed

It is important to note, in terms of the symbolism, that the Sukkoth or Tabernacle is a link between god and his community, that is as a place of worship or communion with the deity. Note these biblical passages:

Exodus 25:8 through Exodus 25:9

8And let them make me a sanctuary; that I may dwell among them.

9According to all that I show thee, *after* the pattern of the tabernacle, and the pattern of all the instruments thereof, even so shall ye make *it.*

Exodus 29:42 through Exodus 29:43

42*This shall be* a continual burnt offering throughout your generations *at*

CHAPTER FOUR

the door of the tabernacle of the congregation before the LORD: where I will meet you, to speak there unto thee. 43And there I will meet with the children of Israel, and *the tabernacle* shall be sanctified by my glory.

We will refer back to the information above (on Jewish Feasts) when we commence our interpretations of biblical verses related thereto. At this point, it behooves us to briefly explore the Christ connection with agricultural symbolism, since Jesus was, in fact, symbolized as a Crop/Seed deity as well as a cosmic deity. Much of the biblical mythology concerning Jesus is most clearly illuminated under agricultural symbolism.

Jesus Christ Was An Agricultural Deity

First off, according to the bible Jesus was born in Bethlehem – this term Bethlehem means House of Bread. This indicates his connection to wheat, as a Crop god. As I noted in my book *"The Biggest Lie Ever Told"* the Madonna and Child is fashioned after the astrological image of Virgo holding forth a sheaf of wheat. The wheat is a symbol of the child god (crop god) born to bring salvation to the world by the sacrifice of his life. The symbolism of the death sacrifice (by the Seed god) is embodied most vividly in the agricultural symbolism, and has been observed over many millennia by various cultures the world over.

It's very difficult to make any sense out of sacrificial death except under the banner of agricultural symbolism – within the crop mythology the answer rings with resounding clarity.

Note the following biblical verses:

I Corinthians 15:35 through I Corinthians 15:36

35But some *man* will say, How are the dead raised up? and with what body do they come? 36 *Thou* fool, that which thou sowest is not quickened, except it die:

John 12:23 through John 12:24

23And Jesus answered them, saying, The hour is come, that the Son of man should be glorified. 24Verily, verily, I say unto you, Except a corn of

CHAPTER FOUR

wheat fall into the ground and die, it abideth alone: but if it die, it bringeth forth much fruit.
Matthew 26:26
26And as they were eating, Jesus took bread, and blessed *it*, and brake *it*, and gave *it* to the disciples, and said, Take, eat; this is my body.

These biblical verses announce correlations between the Christ and Seed Crop, which is exactly as it should be because Jesus symbolized the crop in its planting and harvesting stages. It is not the Seed that symbolizes the Christ but rather the mythical Christ that symbolizes the *seed of life*. The cycle of natural life requires death in order that some form of life be preserved, is the message given here among others. That the Christ had to die in order to save us symbolized the fact that the crop seed, in death, is the fountain of life. This is the miracle of nature – that life comes from death in the agricultural realm – dead lifeless seed, when planted in the bosom of the Mother Earth, bring forth new life and abundant new life, exponentially.

In the agricultural symbolism of the savior god, the Earth itself is viewed as the mother and the sun is the father. I have reviewed some instances whereas water symbolized the father but it's more consistent, I think, when we focus on the sun as the father. But in some allegorical tales water in the form of rain or a river may fit as well or better than the sun (as father) in the symbolism. The sun (and/or water) brings life to the barren earth that is made barren during the Fall-Winter seasons when the sun falls below the equinoxes into the nether regions and is weakened because of the lower declinations (of the sun). When in the Spring the sun meets the vernal equinox and is again potent, it impregnates or enlivens the mother earth that becomes fertile again and produces new life (crops) – children of the mother earth and father sun. This is reflective of the agricultural symbolism which is present in much of the bible along side of the Stellar, Lunar and Solar symbolism. Note the following verses:

CHAPTER FOUR

Genesis 11:30

[30]But Sarai was barren; she *had* no child.

Genesis 25:21

[21]And Isaac entreated the LORD for his wife, because she *was* barren: and the LORD was entreated of him, and Rebekah his wife conceived.

Luke 1:7

[7]And they had no child, because that Elisabeth was barren, and they both were *now* well stricken in years.

The biblical verses above refer to the mythical wives Sarai, Rebekah and Elizabeth. These women were respectively the wives of mythical biblical personalities, Abraham (Abram), Isaac and Zacharius. Actually, within the solar symbolism these wives (who were also the mothers, in turn, of the biblical prophets Isaac, Jacob and Esau, and John the Baptist) symbolized the autumnal equinox (and/or nether regions). They were called barren because the autumnal equinox represents the entrance into the winter season which indicates loss of fertility and productivity. This loss of vitality affects the atmosphere and the land, so agriculturally the land is considered barren during the Fall-Winter season. It is also considered barren during the dry season, hence water may be considered as a father symbol when it revitalizes the dried land.

New Testament Revised Version Of Old Testament

Our contention is that the Hebrews have fashioned their *religious traditions* in association and in *reflection* of their *mundane* agricultural festivals, of planting and harvesting i.e. intra-cultural transference – Spirits based on Physics and in this case, agricultural physics. Much of the New Testament scripture as well as the Old Testament scripture is allegory reflective of crop cycles. These biblical scriptures are a *Registry of sowing and planting cycles written in a mythological format*, as well as being reflective of astronomical phenomena at another level of interpretation.

CHAPTER FOUR

THE NEW TESTAMENT IS A REVISED and enhanced version of the Old Testament. The model after which the biblical editors fashioned the New Testament dogma was the Old Testament. THEY HAD THE OLD TESTAMENT SCROLLS spread out before them and as they composed this fanciful tale about Jesus and his disciples, they used the literature at hand as a *guide* and *pattern* by which they built their storyline. In this way the integrity of the symbolism was maintained and kept consistent – the players of the parts were changed and the stage settings were altered, but the basic plot and theme remained the same. As we have noted over and over again, the underlying purpose of religious scriptures and customs is Time Tracking – i.e. time tracking as it relates to natural cycles of time such as *the precession cycle, the annual cycles of the sun, the lunar monthly and yearly cycles and the daily solar cycle – and also planting and harvesting cycles*. There are also other natural cycles (e.g. eclipse cycles, planetary conjunctions etc.) and artificial cycles (weekly cycles, Metonic cycles, Paschal cycles, etc.) that are used and designed to aid mathematically in the measurement of the *prominent cycles* that I have just noted.

Much of the New Testament is a rehashing of the Old Testament, with an apocalyptic flavor. The primary gauge for *time measurement* used by the ancients was geared to the *transits of the sun* through the equinoxes. The equinoxes are the gateways to apposing polarities i.e. the positive northern polarity entered by way of the vernal equinox and the negative polarity of the southern hemisphere entered by way of the autumnal equinox. The natural polarizing reality that exist between the northern and southern cosmic regions is reflected allegorically as conflict between good and evil or god and the devil, that is, in the mythological religious context.

The Old Testament refers *directly* to the Hebrew Feasts as *core events* around which Judaism is based. This is undeniable – we need not insert several biblical passages to prove this point – a casual reading of the Old Testament reveals this. The New Testament is focused on the same Feasts (appointed times) *as its core*; but the founding Jewish-Christians veiled the Old Form under a New Guise called

CHAPTER FOUR

Jesus of Nazareth, and the apocalyptic renditions in Revelations. The editors that revised the Ancient biblical literature into what came to be known as the New Testament undertook their endeavors with one major objective in mind – the establishment of a new faith targeted toward Hellenic Jews and gentiles, but linked to traditional Judaism as its foundation. In this way their (Jewish) elite status was maintained. The integrity of the symbolism was preserved because they didn't alter the numbers but rather altered the titles. They changed the chosen (son) Israel to the chosen (son) Jesus, they changed the 12 sons (tribes) of Israel (who were destined to lead the world) to the 12 disciples of Jesus (who were destined to spread the gospel throughout the world) – the liberation of Israel from slavery at the time of the Passover was converted to the resurrection of Jesus from death at the time of the Passover, and so forth. Biblical Judaism is an exclusive faith – it is *not* a proselytizing faith – the Jews view their Nation as a Priest Nation, as leaders and guides and rulers of all other humanity (Gentiles).

Exodus 19:5 through Exodus 19:6

5Now therefore, if ye will obey my voice indeed, and keep my covenant, then ye shall be a peculiar treasure unto me above all people: for all the earth *is* mine: 6And ye shall be unto me a kingdom of priests, and an holy nation. These *are* the words which thou shalt speak unto the children of Israel.

Converts from amongst the Gentiles are not sought by traditional Jews, because their society is an exclusive one. They see themselves as gods ordained leaders to the world that are held to a higher standard.

There is no truth in the concept of revealed religion i.e. religion as a revelation from the creator god. This being so, religion was originated by man for man, and we have examined its evolution as part of the topic of this book. We are now focused on the evolution of Christian theology from out of the matrix of Judaic theology; both Christianity and Islam are derived from Judaism. We call these three religions the Abrahamic religions because of their common

CHAPTER FOUR

theological ancestry, in that they all recognize Abraham as the founder or beginning of worship or devotion to one true god. Under Abrahamic style monotheism the Jews are set aside as a special godly chosen people elevated above all other nations. Judaism, at its origin, was a nationalistic religion, not an egalitarian religion that promotes freedom and equality for all people regardless of their diversities. The fantasy of Jewish specialness or godly ordained eminence has been continued and maintained within the scriptures of the Christians and the Muslims. By way of Christianity and Islam, *non-Jews have been brought into the Abrahamic theological fold, as believers in Jewish preeminence* with god, but at the same time the Jews have maintained their separate and exclusive status as a distinct people.

Under this framework, monotheism has misguided billions[1] of the worlds' population into accepting the Hebrews as gods chosen people. Of course some say that they have lost their special status, but nevertheless it remains regrettably true that billions of victims (monotheists) of the greatest confidence scheme or religious scam in history have tenets within their scriptures that stipulate that the Israelites/Hebrews/Jews are or were the chosen nation of god, elevated above all others.

So we have now laid the groundwork whereas we may examine some portions of the New Testament that indicate clearly that the New Testament Christian doctrine is no less than a modified copy of Judaism, *purposely fashioned and engineered as a fit for the Gentile populations and others* by religious revisionists of the Hellenic, Judaic persuasion. Our avenue toward proving that Christianity, at its core, is actually a *spiritualized replication* of *biblical* Judaism rather than a genuinely distinct faith is by proving that the mythical history of Christ et al is metaphorical, it is symbolic, in certain respects, of transitions between the agricultural cycles. *In other words, Jews wrote the Christ myth and used their cultural*

---

[1] This refers to the combined world population of the Christians and Muslims

CHAPTER FOUR

traditions embodied within the Old Testament literature, that was in hand, as guide and Outline for the basic storyline of the New Testament.

First, let us compare the Jewish and Christian calendars for evidence that Christianity is the *calculated* appendage of Judaism, not a new faith but a continuation of the old in a egalitarian and catholic phase rather than the old tribal and nationalistic phase expounded in the Old Testament. The Hebrew era commenced in 3761 B.C. and the Christian era began in 1 A.D.. The Hebrew era is marked by the so-called creation of the world and the Christian era is marked by the alleged birth year of Jesus Christ. We know that the Jewish calendar is measured by Metonic cycles of 19 years – their calendar renews itself every 19 years (235 lunations, 6939.688 days). The Metonic cycle contains 7 Leap years that occur in the 3rd, 6th, 8th, 11th, 14th, 17th and 19th year of the cycle. The Christian era commenced 3763 years after the Jewish era (that's 3761 plus the year zero plus the year one A.D. makes 3763 years). 3762 years contain 198 Metonic cycles exactly i.e. 3762 divided by 19 equals 198. This means that the 3763rd year of the Jewish era and the year one of the Christian era are synonymous. That is to say that the year one A.D. is synonymous with year one of the 199th Jewish Metonic cycle. This of course could only have happened by the design (or extreme coincidence) of the Priesthood (Jewish Founding Fathers) because Jesus Christ was a myth and never lived in actual history. The year one A.D. is clearly a continuation of the Jewish system of time tracking within the Christian era. I view this as evidence that Christianity is a planned appendage of Judaism, under a catholic (universal) guise, not a departure from the rudiments of the old form.

There is a marked discrepancy when theologians try to fit the mythical Jesus into actual history. According to historians, King Herod died in 4 BC and the Census taken when Qurinius (Cyrenius) was governor of Syria was in 6 AD. Of course we know that *Jesus was allegedly born during the census and while Herod was alive* so here we have a gap of 10 years (from 4 B.C. to 6 A.D.) that can't be intelligently explained.

CHAPTER FOUR

Matthew 2:1

[1]Now when Jesus was born in Bethlehem of Judaea in the days of Herod the king, behold, there came wise men from the east to Jerusalem,

Luke 2:1 through Luke 2:5

[1]And it came to pass in those days, that there went out a decree from Caesar Augustus, that all the world should be taxed. [2](*And* this taxing was first made when Cyrenius was governor of Syria.) [3]And all went to be taxed, every one into his own city. [4]And Joseph also went up from Galilee, out of the city of Nazareth, into Judaea, unto the city of David, which is called Bethlehem; (because he was of the house and lineage of David:) [5]To be taxed with Mary his espoused wife, being great with child.

Correlation Of New Testament Compositions With Judaic Traditions And Dogma

The key point to remember concerning biblical scripture is that Jesus Christ of the New Testament is the symbolical counterpart to the chosen tribe of Israel of the Old Testament. This is the key that will help to unlock manifold doors to the hidden wisdom. The biblical symbolism as it applies to Jesus and Israel is identical. This is because when the Hebrews authored the New Testament 2000 or so years ago, they substituted the title Jesus for that of Israel, in their New Testament writings that they fashioned for the then unfolding age of Pisces. The gospels are simply a continuation of the old esoteric wisdom under a new semblance namely the mythical Jesus Christ.

The Passover Plot

The primary components of the Passover story of the Old Testament are the following: It took place near the time of the vernal equinox at the commencement of the full moon, Nisan (Abib) 14, a lamb was sacrificed and its blood smeared upon lintels and doorpost and this action saved the Hebrews from the *death watch* of god. On the 17th of Nisan, 3 days after the sacrificial death of the lamb, the Hebrews crossed the Red Sea thus being liberated (resurrected) from Egypt.

CHAPTER FOUR

This commenced the count down to the next festival (Feast Of Weeks) 7 weeks or 50 days later when the Hebrew god appeared to Moses on Mount Sinai and dispensed unto him the Ten Commandments.

This story of the mythical Passover saga was the prototype for the mythical story that the early Hebrew-Christians composed depicting the sacrificial death of Jesus. They transformed the sacrificial lamb of the Passover into the Lamb of god that had to be sacrificed in order to save humanity, as an expiation for the sins of humanity. This was an exact copy of the sacrificial lamb of the Hebrews under Moses – now in human form and called the Christ. They transformed the son of god under the type of Israel into the son of god under the type of the Christ -

Exodus 4:22 22And thou shalt say unto Pharaoh, Thus saith the LORD, Israel *is* my son, *even* my firstborn:

They wrote that Jesus was resurrected on the 17th of Nisan (Abib), and this corresponds to Israel crossing the Red Sea, whereas liberation is equated with resurrection. Seven weeks later Jesus (the holy spirit) appeared unto the disciples at Pentecost. This is an exact copy of the appearance of god to Moses on Mt. Sinai seven weeks after their liberation from Egypt.

In regards to the above, it is given that Jesus was the Passover and that *Pentecost* (descent of the Holy Spirit) and *Shavuot* (dispensation of the Ten Commandments) correspond. It should be noted that the *peculiar request* of Moses to Pharaoh was actually that the Hebrews be granted the right to journey three days and give sacrifice to their deity. This was the freedom they requested **Exodus 3:18**

18And they shall hearken to thy voice: and thou shalt come, thou and the elders of Israel, unto the king of Egypt, and ye shall say unto him, The LORD God of the Hebrews hath met with us: and now let us go, we beseech thee, three days' journey into the wilderness, that we may sacrifice to the LORD our God.
Exodus 5:3

CHAPTER FOUR

3And they said, The God of the Hebrews hath met with us: let us go, we pray thee, three days' journey into the desert, and sacrifice unto the LORD our God; lest he fall upon us with pestilence, or with the sword.

This, of course, is referring to the three days between Nisan 14 (the commencement of Passover) and Nisan 17 (the offering of the First Fruits i.e. sheaf of wheat to the deity within the Temple). It is in this agricultural and traditional phase of the Jewish mythology that we find the three days elapsing between the sacrificial death of Christ and his resurrection, as the First Fruits (sheaf of wheat) pledged to the deity at the Temple. The three days cannot be found under normal chronology, from a Friday crucifixion to a resurrection on Sunday morning.

After journeying three days into the wilderness, they encamped before the Red Sea where they were overtaken by the pursuing Egyptians

Exodus 14:9

9But the Egyptians pursued after them, all the horses *and* chariots of Pharaoh, and his horsemen, and his army, and overtook them encamping by the sea,...

At this point god intervened miraculously and Moses divided the Red Sea thus providing escape (liberation/resurrection) for the Israelites and Destruction for the Egyptians.

The correlations that I have just provided take us through the first four feasts of the Jewish year, the Spring Feasts or Feasts relevant to the vernal equinox i.e. *Passover, Feast of Unleavened Bread, First Fruits and Shavuot/Pentecost.* You may review these Feasts by turning back a few pages to the heading - The Jewish Feasts.

The Day of Judgment

Let us review another correlation that encompasses the Feasts of the Fall season or the autumnal equinox. The book of Revelations is full of ominous portent. Revelations is an apocalyptic rendition of the symbolism – one reason for this is that much of Revelations pertains

CHAPTER FOUR

to the symbolism of the autumnal equinox. The Fall festivals are the feasts of Judgment within the Jewish culture. The first feast of the Fall season (the 5ᵗʰ of the 7 yearly Feasts), *Rosh Hashanah* i.e. New Years is called *Judgment Day* by the Jews. The astrological sign of Libra (the 7ᵗʰ zodiacal sign) is the zodiacal symbol of justice – the scales represent the weighing of deeds and actions and the determination of justice as a result. Agriculturally Libra symbolizes the weighing and measuring of the harvest and the proper payment in accord with just portions. This transfers, in the mythology, into the judgment of humanity and the measuring and weighing of the actions and thoughts on the scales of justice.

Within the Jewish religious culture the cycle of creation and destruction is broken into seven parts (stations) and is repeated annually. The time span does not cover the entire year actually, that is in terms of the relevant symbolism - by relevant symbolism, I am referring to allegory that is reflective of the Jewish Feasts, which are the center points of much biblical symbolism, penned under the Hebrew influence and other similar influences. The symbolic time span *from creation to destruction* covers the seven months from *Passover to Sukkoth –* Passover is the beginning of time and Sukkoth is the ending of time within this particular symbolism. Note the following:

Exodus 23:14 through Exodus 23:16

¹⁴Three times thou shalt keep a feast unto me in the year. ¹⁵Thou shalt keep the feast of unleavened bread: (thou shalt eat unleavened bread seven days, as I commanded thee, in the time appointed of the month Abib; for in it thou camest out from Egypt: and none shall appear before me empty:) ¹⁶And the feast of harvest, the firstfruits of thy labours, which thou hast sown in the field: and the feast of ingathering, *which is* in the end of the year, when thou hast gathered in thy labours out of the field.

The Jewish holidays (biblical feasts) run from Passover to Sukkoth – note the *End of the Year* is referred to as the *Feast of the Ingathering*, which is *Sukkoth*. These verses refer to the three primary

CHAPTER FOUR

biblical feasts or the three feasts wherein the participants are required to journey to Jerusalem, according to tradition – at the times of Passover, Shavuot and Sukkoth. *The agricultural year is seven months in duration* and this is reflected in much symbolism. All symbolisms and rituals can be traced to a physical or rationally explainable base or origin, as I have repeated countless times – *spirits based on physics* is the key to correctly deciphering biblical and other mythology.

Under the Jewish/Christian mythological culture the autumnal equinox and the agricultural harvest, that occurs in the Fall of the year, is equated with gods Judgment – note the following:

Revelation 14:6 through Revelation 14:7 6And I saw another angel fly in the midst of heaven, having the everlasting gospel to preach unto them that dwell on the earth, and to every nation, and kindred, and tongue, and people, 7Saying with a loud voice, Fear God, and give glory to him; for the hour of his judgment is come: and worship him that made heaven, and earth, and the sea, and the fountains of waters.

Revelation 14:15 through Revelation 14:16 15And another angel came out of the temple, crying with a loud voice to him that sat on the cloud, Thrust in thy sickle, and reap: for the time is come for thee to reap; for the harvest of the earth is ripe. 16And he that sat on the cloud thrust in his sickle on the earth; and the earth was reaped.

Revelation 14:19 19And the angel thrust in his sickle into the earth, and gathered the vine of the earth, and cast *it* into the great winepress of the wrath of God.

We must constantly remind ourselves that the underlying purpose of biblical scriptures is the tracking of time – if we keep this point in mind, we are able to make practical sense out of the parallels that the biblical editors have drawn between mundane agricultural activities and the final judgment of the world. The *end of the world* that's referred to in much of Revelations is actually the end (the harvest) of the crop season. That may be hard to swallow but that is the bitter truth.

CHAPTER FOUR

Chapters Twenty and twenty-one of Revelations warns of the coming Judgment as seen by Saint John The Divine, whoever that was. The book (Revelations) is so puzzling to most that it has spawned the most insane, inane, fantastic and delusional speculations capable of being conjured up by the human mind, in my opinion. I think that the mathematical interpretations that I rendered in earlier portions of this book and that which is to follow should hopefully help remedy a dangerous theological quagmire that has developed in this day and time, due to the gross misunderstandings of the book of Revelations and similar scriptures of various faiths. This is an era when a single religious fanatic can bring devastating horrors upon the general public. There is no greater threat to our safety and peace than those who accept all religious jargon as the literal truth and desire within themselves to commit an act that highlights and proves their faith. The following biblical verses offer some very dynamic insight into symbolism relevant to the agricultural phase. These verses should be read *thoroughly* – they describe the final judgment.

Revelation 20:12 through Revelation 20:13

12And I saw the dead, small and great, stand before God; and the books were opened: and another book was opened, which is *the book* of life: and the dead were judged out of those things which were written in the books, according to their works. 13And the sea gave up the dead which were in it; and death and hell delivered up the dead which were in them: and they were judged every man according to their works.

Revelation 20:15

15And whosoever was not found written in the book of life was cast into the lake of fire.

Revelation 21:1 through Revelation 21:6

1   And I saw a new heaven and a new earth: for the first heaven and the first earth were passed away; and there was no more sea. 2And I John saw the holy city, new Jerusalem, coming down from God out of heaven, prepared as a bride adorned for her husband. 3And I heard a great voice out of heaven saying, Behold, the tabernacle of God *is* with men, and he will

CHAPTER FOUR

dwell with them, and they shall be his people, and God himself shall be with them, *and be* their God. 4And God shall wipe away all tears from their eyes; and there shall be no more death, neither sorrow, nor crying, neither shall there be any more pain: for the former things are passed away. 5And he that sat upon the throne said, Behold, I make all things new. And he said unto me, Write: for these words are true and faithful. 6And he said unto me, It is done. I am Alpha and Omega, the beginning and the end. I will give unto him that is athirst of the fountain of the water of life freely.

Revelation 21:9 through Revelation 21:10

9And there came unto me one of the seven angels which had the seven vials full of the seven last plagues, and talked with me, saying, Come hither, I will show thee the bride, the Lamb's wife. 10And he carried me away in the spirit to a great and high mountain, and showed me that great city, the holy Jerusalem, descending out of heaven from God,

Revelation 21:21 through Revelation 21:27

21And the twelve gates *were* twelve pearls; every several gate was of one pearl: and the street of the city *was* pure gold, as it were transparent glass. 22And I saw no temple therein: for the Lord God Almighty and the Lamb are the temple of it. 23And the city had no need of the sun, neither of the moon, to shine in it: for the glory of God did lighten it, and the Lamb *is* the light thereof. 24And the nations of them which are saved shall walk in the light of it: and the kings of the earth do bring their glory and honour into it. 25And the gates of it shall not be shut at all by day: for there shall be no night there. 26And they shall bring the glory and honour of the nations into it. 27And there shall in no wise enter into it any thing that defileth, neither *whatsoever* worketh abomination, or *maketh* a lie: but they which are written in the Lamb's book of life

I TRUST THAT YOU HAVE READ THE FORGOING BIBLICAL VERSES WITH DUE DILIGENCE – the cardinal factors are these: The *End Of Time* is being described by these verses, that is the *Final Judgment of mankind*, the so-called *apocalypse*. The verses describe the procedures by which the subjects are brought to final judgment

CHAPTER FOUR

before the throne of god. We have the resurrection of the Dead who are paraded before the throne – their names are looked for in a Book that is called *The Book Of Life*. If their name is not found in the *Book Of Life* then the Dead are killed all over again but in a very gruesome way that bespeaks of heinous punishment for their sins.

The old Heaven and Earth is destroyed so as to be replaced with a new Heaven and Earth. The new Heaven and Earth is described as New Jerusalem and also described as a *Bride* adorned for her husband – the groom in this case is the god himself, the Lamb, The Christ. In the end, all those that are found in the *Book Of Life* are blessed with eternal Life and a *Fellowship* with god almighty – the *Christ and his subjects are projected to live together in this New Jerusalem* and shall reign eternally, immune from defilement and inequity. This is what the bible says and millions seem to accept this as the literal truth. I am amazed and bewildered at how religion causes some people to abandon all reality and logic in the name of faith.

YOU SHOULD HAVE NOTICED the EERIE SIMILARITIES between the biblical account of the judgment depicted in the forgoing verses of Revelations and the description I provided of Jewish traditions in regards to the Fall Feasts of *Rosh Hashanah, Atonement and Sukkoth*. If perchance you did not notice the *striking similarities*, please take the time now, to review my description of these *Autumn Feasts*:. THE SUGGESTED REVIEW IS IMPORTANT.

5 - Rosh Hashanah: This is the Hebrew New Year, also referred to as <u>Judgment Day</u>, as trumpets are blown to recognize this month of destiny. It is the 7th month and 1st day of the Religious year that commences in the month of Nisan and/or it is the 1st month and 1st day of the Jewish civil year i.e. Tishri 1.

Leviticus 23:23 through Leviticus 23:25

23And the LORD spake unto Moses, saying, 24Speak unto the children of Israel, saying, In the seventh month, in the first day of the month, shall ye have a sabbath, a memorial of blowing of trumpets, an holy convocation. 25Ye shall do no servile work therein: but ye shall offer an offering made by

CHAPTER FOUR

fire unto the LORD.

Some interesting characteristics of Rosh Hashanah include the blowing of the Shofar horn, as a warning or announcement that Judgment Day (Rosh Hashanah) has arrived. Jewish tradition dictates that <u>Rosh Hashanah is annually the</u> **Judgment Day** – that on this day god judges his subjects and enters their names into a book that is called <u>The Book Of Life</u>. Rosh Hashanah commences ten days of penitence wherein the devout are obligated to seek forgiveness for their sins of the previous year and even ask forgiveness of those whom they may have wronged. <u>After the ten days have passed, on the evening of Yom Kippur, the Book Of Life is sealed and the fate of the subjects is destined.</u> The Shofar horn is then blown to announce the sealing of the Book Of Life and the closing of the *Days Of Awe*, which is the term that collectively describes Rosh Hashanah and Yom Kippur.

6 - Yom Kippur: This is the *Day Of Atonement*, a day of prayer and repentance to the Jewish deity. It falls on the 10th day after the Jewish New Year. Rosh Hashanah commences 10 days of Penitence which climaxes on Tishri 10 on the day of Yom Kippur i.e. the Day Of Atonement. The Shofar (Ram's Horn) is associated with Yom Kippur. Rosh Hashanah also known as <u>Yom Hadin, which means</u> **Day Of Judgment**. Rosh Hashanah means Head of the year.

Leviticus 23:27 through Leviticus 23:28

27Also on the tenth day of this seventh month there shall be a day of atonement: it shall be an holy convocation unto you; and ye shall afflict your souls, and offer an offering made by fire unto the LORD. 28And ye shall do no work in that same day: for it is a day of atonement, to make an atonement for you before the LORD your God.

7 - Sukkoth: This is the Feast Of Tabernacles, a harvest festival commemorating the booths (temporary dwellings) in which the Israelites resided during their wandering in the wilderness,

CHAPTER FOUR

according to the myth.

Leviticus 23:33 through Leviticus 23:36

33And the LORD spake unto Moses, saying, 34Speak unto the children of Israel, saying, The fifteenth day of this seventh month shall be the feast of tabernacles for seven days unto the LORD. 35On the first day shall be an holy convocation: ye shall do no servile work therein. 36Seven days ye shall offer an offering made by fire unto the LORD: on the eighth day shall be an holy convocation unto you; and ye shall offer an offering made by fire unto the LORD: it is a solemn assembly; and ye shall do no servile work therein.

Simchat Torah: The closing of the Jewish festival season is the Simchat Torah, which means rejoicing in the Torah. This is observed at the closing of the 7-8 day Sukkoth festivities. Jewish tradition calls for the weekly reading of the Torah in the synagogue throughout the year. The readings are proportioned so as to complete simultaneously with the end of Sukkoth. Simchat Torah is the reading of the last verses of the Torah for the year and the immediate commencement of the first reading of the new yearly cycle. The cycle of Torah readings begins with Genesis and runs through Deuteronomy by the end of the annual cycle of readings; thus completing the so-called five books of Moses - Genesis, Exodus, Leviticus, Numbers and Deuteronomy. Originally the book (Torah) was in the form of a scroll and this fact provides nuances that will prove very intriguing as we pursue our biblical interpretations later in this chapter.

Bride Of Judgment: <u>Torah scrolls are called Kallah (Callah), which means Bride</u>. The person that reads the closing verses of Deut. Is called Chatan Torah which means <u>Bridegroom</u> of the Law.

The person that reads the 1st verses of Gen. For the New Year is called Chatan Bereshit which means <u>Bridegroom</u> Of The Beginning

Shemini Atzeret: this is observed in conjunction with Simchat Torah on the last day of Sukkoth. The term Shemini means 8 and Atzeret means holding back. This is observed to seal the last day of

CHAPTER FOUR

the Sukkoth festival - special prayers for rain are prayed

It is important to note, in terms of the symbolism, that the Sukkoth or Tabernacle is a link between god and his community, that is as a place of worship or communion with the deity. Note these biblical passages:

Exodus 25:8 through Exodus 25:9

8 And let them make me a sanctuary; that I may dwell among them.

9 According to all that I show thee, after the pattern of the tabernacle, and the pattern of all the instruments thereof, even so shall ye make it.

Exodus 29:42 through Exodus 29:43

42 This shall be a continual burnt offering throughout your generations at the door of the tabernacle of the congregation before the LORD: where I will meet you, to speak there unto thee. 43 And there I will meet with the children of Israel, and the tabernacle shall be sanctified by my glory.

Now that your review is completed, we can continue our decipherment. Actually there is very little more that I need to note, in view of the comprehensive information provided under the subject – The Jewish Feasts. The premise that I offered early on in this chapter was that the *New Testament* was written by Jewish-Christian Priest and that they used the scriptural text in hand, that is to say, the *Old Testament* and their own *cultural traditions* as a guide and outline by which they composed the New testament portions of the bible. It is very important that we remember that the Early Christians did not have written scriptures of their own - they had only the Old Testament of the Jews. The Early Christians did not compose their own *New Testament* literature until several years after the Christian movement had started. The biblical account of the Judgment is clearly an inflated apocalyptic account of Jewish cultural activities that take place during their harvest Feasts observations in the Fall of the year. The prophecy of **Judgment Day** found in Revelation of the bible is clearly a metaphorical rendition of the **Jewish New Year Festivals** ranging from **Rosh Hashanah, Yom Kippur,** and

CHAPTER FOUR

Sukkoth - Think! how sinister and pernicious the mindset of those who committed such a scam! Clearly their intent was not to save souls but rather to enslave souls; they deliberately set out to enslave unsuspecting, sincerely religious people to an abject lie! THIS VERSION OF THE END DAYS WAS CONTRIVED by the Jewish-Christian Priest and foisted on the Hellenic Jews,who were dissenters from traditional Temple based Judaism; and likewise this distortion was proffered to the non-Jews of 2000 years ago, and must be considered as spiritually reprehensible. Their actions were venomous and uncaring and unfortunately very successful – because millions today accept this New Testament fairytale as historical and/or divinely inspired, and likewise millions look upon the Hebrews as god's chosen.

IN SUMMATION, the Holy Days and rituals of the Jewish Autumn holidays are as follows: the festivities start off on **Tishri 1** or Rosh Hashanah which is celebrated as New Years Day - they call **Rosh Hashanah** *Yam Hadin* which is to say **Judgment Day**. By tradition they have a period of repentance and Atonement during the first ten days of Judgment which is climaxed by the **Day of Atonement** which is observed on Tishri 10; during this interlude the faithful repentants strive to have their names entered into **The Book of Life** which certifies their Salvation - by Jewish tradition The Book of Life is sealed after the 10th day. The last Jewish festival of the Autumn season is called **Sukkoth** otherwise called the Feasts of Tabernacles - the **Tabernacle** or Sukkoth represents the **House of God**, the holy dwelling place that is built for god in person wherein god will take communion with the faithful, and wherein both god and the blessed will sojourn together in union.

It should, I think, be abundantly clear to all after reviewing and comparing *this summation* and the *apocalyptic verses* from the **Book of Revelation** that I have supplied for references; that indeed the apocalyptic writers, of 2000 or so years ago, fashioned that biblical tale as a cryptic copy of their Jewish end-of-the-year traditions, and then labeled it an *apocalypse* portending the prophetic events

CHAPTER FOUR

attendant to an actual ending of the world, and god's final coming. By comparison the link between the Jewish Autumn end-of-the-year holidays and the biblical narrative that describes the End-Times is clear and certain. As a side note, I would imagine also, that the Jewish-Christian Priests (early Church Fathers) that completed this wily yarn way back then were probably grinning, laughing and wildly congratulatory of each other after completing such a pernicious, unique and deceptive literary farce.

Note These Interpretations - The *Book Of Life* of Revelations is synonymous to the *Book Of Life* of *Rosh Hashanah* – the Judgment of Revelations is the Judgment of Rosh Hashanah also called by the Jews, Yom Hadin. New Jerusalem is the Torah, the Bride of the Jewish Judgment. *The old world that is destroyed refers to the completion of the readings of the Torah and the New World is the commencement of the New Readings of the Torah* by the Chatan Bereshit (Bridegroom of the Beginning). The coming of god to dwell in fellowship with his chosen at the End Of Days is reflective of the Feast Of Tabernacles, Sukkoth – the end of the Feasts when god enters the Jewish tabernacles or booths as described in their traditions. *This is vivid.*

Judgment Day Under The Astronomical Symbolism

Judgment Day, as interpreted under the astronomical symbolism is much different than that represented by the Jewish harvest festivals. The occurrence is not in the Fall but rather in the Spring, at the vernal equinox. *In terms of the annual cycle of the sun*, the vernal equinox is symbolized as a bride and the sun is the bridegroom. The marriage of the bride and bridegroom occurs when the sun, on its annual path, meets and crosses the vernal equinox in the spring on March 21. Of course the vernal equinox is the intersection of the celestial equator and the ecliptic of the sun – so when the sun enters that point of intersection, it has under the annual solar symbolism entered into the bridal chambers of marriage. This intersection point also represents

CHAPTER FOUR

the consummation of the marriage that commences the gestation of the *son* of the sun that will be born 280 days later when the sun enters the winter solstice of December 22 and is reborn, under the solar mythology, on December 25, as Jesus, Mithra, Krishna, Buddha, Horus and the various other solar deities throughout mythological history that were said to have been born on December 25.

The vernal equinox is the Gateway to the upper region of spirits, the celestial northern hemisphere – it stands as the border between heaven and hell i.e. the upper and lower regions of the cosmos as demarcated by the celestial equator. The sun and the other celestial entities are judged and subsequently resurrected as they rise above the equinox in their annual apparent cyclical journeys around the universe, from an earthly perspective. THE WAR OR CONFLICT that occurs at the *End Of Days* in some symbolisms refers to the conflict between the positive and negative forces of the upper and lower regions of the cosmos. This is the war that ensues when the positive redeeming forces of summer conquer the oppressive forces of winter, at the sun's crossing of the vernal equinox. The sun always wins this conflict, after a wilderness battle or trial or struggle that lasts for 40 days – please see the previous books of this series for expanded explanations of this point.

One of the ancient symbols that was used to signify the equinoxes, both the vernal and autumnal, was the crocodile as can be noted on ancient graphics. Oaanes was an ancient symbol of the sun as a god that was half fish and half human – this enabled the deity to traverse the upper regions upright and to swim the lower regions beneath the equinoxes as a fish. So when the sun, in the form of Oaanes reached the vernal equinox, he was coupled in marriage with the crocodile, which stood as a symbol of the equinox positions as previously noted. I perceive that the symbolism of the god Oaanes and his crocodile bride is displayed in our marriage ceremonies. The long traditional train of the modern bridal gown is clearly a copy of the *wagging tail* of the crocodile and the formal (tuxedo) attire of the groom, with *tail fins*, signifies the *fish* god Oaanes. It seems clear that some wise sage (sages) of the past sought to send us a clue as to esoteric truths.

CHAPTER FOUR

It must be remembered that the bible, especially Revelations, is a mix of various phases of mythology, including Stellar, Lunar, Solar, Environmental and some other intricate categories that we need not discuss at this point of our investigation. There is not one formula that works in deciphering all the various categories

CHAPTER FIVE

Chapter Five

An inquiry into the origins and underlying objectives of monotheism

The Scourge Of Monotheism

The scourge of monotheism is the arrogant and repressive doctrine of Jews, Christians and Muslims which postulates that the god of their faith (faiths) is the only true god and that spiritual salvation can only be obtained from within their ranks or through them, as the bona fide agents of the only true god. This elitist tyrannical conception was spawned by Jewish style monotheism, and is absolutely deplorable in my opinion; this dogmatic attitude, expounded by the monotheists, is a manifestation of religious bigotry to the highest degree. And this religious bigotry has engendered and continues to sow the seeds of political, social, financial and racial bigotry within every fabric of monotheistic society and tends to contaminate other social structures that ordinarily would not share these biases.

Any society founded on monotheism is by its very nature a meddlesome community, intent on interfering in the affairs of others and seeking to subvert or override the social/political systems of others, pursuant to the ostensibly high-minded goals of help and improvement. This is the clarion call of monotheism, that is to bring all others into the one so-called true path (faith) – and that translates into subversion, aggression, and interference into the social structures of nonbelievers, with a godly edict to do so.

Mark 16:15 through Mark 16:16

15And he said unto them, Go ye into all the world, and preach the gospel to every creature. 16He that believeth and is baptized shall be saved; but he that believeth not shall be damned.

Matthew 28:19

19Go ye therefore, and teach all nations, baptizing them in the name of the Father, and of the Son, and of the Holy Ghost:

CHAPTER FIVE

Matthew 24:14

14And this gospel of the kingdom shall be preached in all the world for a witness unto all nations; and then shall the end come.

Monotheists seemingly have thoughtful and admiral concepts concerning the equitable application of law, respect for individual freedom and liberty and property rights etc. Their moral precepts are laudable for the most part, in my opinion, but rarely lived up to. Their sense of justice is widely proclaimed (as if those within their ranks are the only true proponents of justice) but not universally applied, actually it is favored for those of faith. This is reflective, perhaps subliminally, of their religious doctrine that states clearly god's final condemnation of all disbelievers on that great Judgment Day. This attitude, that people of different religious persuasions are actually in rebellion against the true faith or are somehow victims of the wiles of Satan, and thereby servants of the devil, opens the door to any manner of injustices and oppression toward non-monotheist.

WITNESS A PARAPHRASE FROM MY BOOK, *The Biggest Lie Ever Told:*

"The religious *doctrine* of the monotheist (i.e. the *doctrine* that they are the only correct worshippers of the only *true* god) tends to infuse itself into the political and social fabric of their societies. It follows in their thinking (whether openly acknowledged or not) that since their doctrine is the only true faith, that likewise their political and social systems must also be superior to all others.

Consequently, they are implicitly justified by their deity in imposing their doctrines (political, financial and religious) upon the lost (non-believers) of the world. The Muslims and Christians tend to impose their doctrines by direct attack and the Jews act by methods of subversion. So this religious attitude of the monotheists indeed makes them the greatest menace to world peace, and I think that history verifies this. Of course the laity within the monotheistic systems are for the most part sincere and loving believers, who firmly believe that they are doing god's will by spreading his doctrine. My focus here is on the *underlying effect of the monotheistic doctrine*, and the attitude it engenders in those that adhere to this doctrine; which sounds so benevolent at the first hearing, but when thoughtfully analyzed is found

CHAPTER FIVE

to bear the seeds of religious and political tyranny. The indications are that our Founding Fathers realized this and therefore sought to limit the powers of the monotheists within our government, but the menace is ever-present.

Monotheism is a natural fit for political union, because monotheism helps bring cultural sameness to a given society which is of obvious benefit to governmental leaders. It was common anciently for governments to have a State Religion. Christianity grew exponentially when it became the State religion of the Roman Empire. The precepts of monotheism seem to have flourished in the era of Aries which commenced about 4000 years ago; the Hebrews have obviously copied that precept of State god and State religion, and have benefited from it greatly. The world has shifted from those times of religious tolerance that marked the ancient eras, to the religious aggression that has followed in the wake of monotheistic preeminence. It was common for the various villages and tribes to have their own tutelary deities and totem symbols in those bygone days – with mutual respect and tolerance[1].

The monotheistic creed was further augmented under the astrological sign of Pisces (manifested by the sect of the Christians and later under Islam), which commenced about 2000 years ago. The nature of the monotheists is to wipe out all opposition to their domination by demanding that the populations submit entirely to one omnipotent god (under one religious system) and concurrently to one world theocratic government (under one type of political system). The ultimate aim of the monotheists is to obliterate all political and financial independence worldwide by making them interdependent. Of course, political unity is greatly facilitated by cultural unity; hence the monotheists tend to use their religious dogma as a tool pursuant to cultural fusion.

The monotheists tend to demean and belittle the religious beliefs of others outside their own ranks, privately if not publicly – they tend to have an elitist and superior attitude. They label disbelievers as heathens and pagans who are doomed to total annihilation on the great Day of Judgment. Hence history shows that the monotheists are capable of unspeakable cruelty toward various populations, and all in the name of one omnipotent god"

IF AND WHEN the monotheists adhere faithfully to their religious concepts, which encourage them to spread their doctrine to the far

---

[1] This attitude of religious tolerance is defined as *Henotheism* whereas a tribe , community, or nation may have their own patron deity but nevertheless have respect and honor for the deities of other groups.

CHAPTER FIVE

reaches of the world, they in affect become a menace to all cultures that would like to be left alone to worship or not worship according to their own customs. This proselytizing of culture and faith is a certain formula for world unrest and contention, so long as it is pursued. The ancients knew this and consequently, practiced a system of henotheism, that gave tolerance and respect to diverse philosophical and religious views - but monotheism (a useful tool of imperialist) broke the cycle, and now it (monotheism) must be broken before peace and stability can be restored, in my opinion. All religious dogma is reflective of a material base, a foundation anchored in matter (the physics of nature). *Spirits based on Physics* is my trademark phrase in reference to this premise of dualism, i.e. all spiritual concepts have a counterpart in physical nature; and we could also say that all religious concepts have mundane counterparts within the core of the underlying culture from which the religious precepts have emerged. The physical counterpart of monotheism is the all-conquering light of the sun. The sun does not allow any other heavenly light to exist within its domain. The sun not only destroys darkness with the dawn of its day, but it also blots out all of the night lights (lesser gods) - the starry and planetary lights of darkness are destroyed, without mercy, by the sun at its dawning.

WITNESS ANOTHER QUOTE from my book, *The Biggest Lie Ever Told:* "All of the monotheistic religions, which primarily include Islam, Christianity and Judaism are mythological representations of the natural environment. The ancients fashioned their spiritual concepts as mythical copies of natural phenomena, the environment and its interactions. They pictured the sun as the ruler of the universe, the life giver, the conqueror of darkness and cold, the scorcher with its *intense* fire, the compassionate with its *soothing* heat. When the sun triumphantly appeared on the eastern horizon at the dawning of the day, the whole universe (from our earthly perspective) was seen bowing in submission to the greatest of all lights. All the stars and planets of the higher and lower heavens were vanquished without trace at the downing of the great sun god. This physical reality is the true seminal generator of our religious rituals in reference to an omnipotent conquering god, evolved from the customs of the ancients".

CHAPTER FIVE

All of our religious concepts are engendered by physical nature or are reflective of physical nature— it can be no other way, because we are physical creatures ourselves and are molded by our environment. We are forced to live within the limitations set by our natural environment and if we explore beyond these confines, we must carry a portion of our earthly universe with us, in order to sustain ourselves. Our base is physical and our spiritual concepts are built upon this material base, hence the nature of dualism is revealed in this aspect of spirit and matter. Of course this is debatable as there are many that insist the Spirit is the first creation or bases of creation that preceded Matter, and that god is spirit. I don't know which came first, and will never *Know*. I*t is my belief however, that spirit and matter are interdependent and have always coexisted* and will forever be joined or associated. I wholeheartedly accept the vaunted axiom of the Ancients that the universe is eternal - there never was a time when the universe was not. I do know, that you and I are *physical beings* and are only capable of conceiving spiritual things because *we in the first instance physically exist* as physical beings, and can think (spiritualize) – this is reality. We can investigate matter, analyze matter and scrutinize matter – everything that is physical is subject to our intelligent evaluation, but *that which is spiritual can only be conjectured upon* and will forever prove theoretical, regardless of how much faith one may have in his or her conclusions. A basis does not exist in the physical universe for proving or dispassionately evaluating religious concepts that are alleged to have sprung from a spiritual base, because the spiritual is not subject to natural laws of proof but rather is considered supernatural.

The dualistic approach, as I see it, stipulates that all spiritual concepts, in order to be valid, must have a physical counterpart. This dualistic concept proposes that this physical universe is a material copy of the presumed spiritual universe or vice versa. The spiritual is not subject to natural laws of proof but rather is considered supernatural (i.e. beyond physical/natural laws of proof), so without a physical reference by which to analyze the spiritual we tend to wonder into wild imaginary, ungrounded speculations, and this leads

CHAPTER FIVE

to irrationality. However the ancients, in their wisdom, when discerning and molding that which was spiritual, used the physics of nature, as their guide and model, is my contention – and hence all religious dogma is reflective of a physical basis, according to the gnosis.

WITNESS THIS QUOTE CONCERNING MONOTHEISM, from the late **James Frazer**, in his book <u>Adonis, Attis Osiris, chapter 7, Osiris And The Sun</u> - which echoes my sentiments or we may say that my expressions are an echo of his prior inputs:

"For the religion of ancient Egypt may be described as a confederacy of local cults which, while maintaining against each other a certain measure of jealous and even hostile independence, were yet constantly subjected to the fusing and amalgamating influence of political centralization and philosophic thought. The history of religion appears to have largely consisted of a struggle between these opposite forces or tendencies. On the one side there was the conservative tendency to preserve the local cults with all their distinctive features, fresh, sharp, and crisp as they had been handed down from an immemorial past. On the other side there was the progressive tendency, favoured by the gradual fusion of the people under a powerful central government, first to dull the edge of these provincial distinctions, and finally to break them down completely and merge them in a single national religion".

Monotheism is inherently intertwined with nationalism from its conception to this day. Monotheism is the child of centralized political systems, a means toward cultural fusion and national unity, with a single god as the tutelary deity and unifying spirit of the nation.

AS I HAVE NOTED REPEATEDLY, monotheism is mythically derived from the symbolism of the sun as the all-powerful god, greater than all other heavenly gods (lights). This was the physical base, potentially, on which this religious concept of monotheism was founded. The primary origin of this monotheistic concept is traceable

CHAPTER FIVE

to ancient Egypt. The ancient Egyptians elevated the god *Amen-Ra* (sun-god) to supremacy over all other deities. The Hebrews copied the concept by elevating their tribal deity *Yahweh* to the status of the only true god.

WITNESS THIS QUOTE from the late Egyptologist **E. A. Wallis Budge** in his book, <u>The Gods Of The Egyptians Volume Two:</u>
"Thus by these means the priests of Amen succeeded in making their god, both theologically and politically, the greatest of the gods in the country...And when his royal devotees...carried war and conquest into Palestine and founded Egyptian cities there, the power and glory of Amen their god, who had enabled them to carry out this difficult work of successful invasion, became extraordinarily great...but the priests of Amen were not content with claiming that their god was one of the greatest of the deities of Egypt, for they proceeded to declare that there was no other god like him, and that he was the greatest of them all."

It's clear that monotheism and nationalism are joined at the hip, especially when the nationalistic culture is expansive and imperialistic. As the monotheists expand their territories, they always claim their successes are bequeathed by their deities. Such has been the case with the biblical Jews, the Christians and the Muslims – all claim that their aggressions (proselytizing) carry the blessings and sanctions of their omnipotent god (gods).

The eternal quest of humanity is the search for our father (creator) who seemingly abandoned us at birth. We are orphaned and our father is unknown – our mother is considered as the earth, because it is evident that we were created from the essence of this physical planet – but he/it (i.e. the Intelligence) that molded us and breathed the breath of life into us is unknown, and may always remain unknown. But our eternal quest is to search, to the ends of the universe, if necessary, for the father (creative intelligence) that abandoned or otherwise obscured itself from our physical eyes. But

CHAPTER FIVE

the claim of the monotheist is that our father (creator) is not unknown – they claim that the creator left a message for us in the form of revealed religion i.e. religion as a product of divine revelation to so-called prophets, and further that we shall be joined with our spiritual father in a spiritual world, to be entered into upon our departure from this physical existence. However we must submit to the rituals and customs dictated by monotheistic dogma in order to qualify for admittance into this spiritual afterlife. The net result of this form of belief is that our physical lives are controlled and managed by the proponents of this doctrine, and our spiritual lives are in question – based totally on faith, with no factual (provable) basis or support.

The terror of monotheism is that it is political as well as religious – it is a joint cultural force with an edict and command from their god to go forth to conquer and subdue. The Jewish god of the bible is clearly a tribal deity, a war god that advocates for his chosen, without compassion or just regards for the other members of the human family. And when the Jews follow faithfully behind the biblical edicts of their deity – they can only be that which many claim they are - a menace and impediment to the peace and stability of the world.

Hebrews Allegedly Destined To Rule

The biblical commands to the Jewish people (monotheist) are clear and unambiguous – their tribal god says obey me and I will give you the world. This philosophy of world domination lies at the core of Jewish monotheism, a message to the Hebrew people that they are the chosen of god and are destined to rule and control this planet. Let us review some biblical passages that reinforces this point:

Exodus 19:5 through Exodus 19:6

5Now therefore, if ye will obey my voice indeed, and keep my covenant, then ye shall be a peculiar treasure unto me above all people: for all the earth *is* mine: 6And ye shall be unto me a kingdom of priests, and an holy nation. These *are* the words which thou shalt speak unto the children of Israel.

CHAPTER FIVE

Exodus 23:30 through Exodus 23:33

[30]By little and little I will drive them out from before thee, until thou be increased, and inherit the land. [31]And I will set thy bounds from the Red sea even unto the sea of the Philistines, and from the desert unto the river: for I will deliver the inhabitants of the land into your hand; and thou shalt drive them out before thee. [32]Thou shalt make no covenant with them, nor with their gods. [33]They shall not dwell in thy land, lest they make thee sin against me: for if thou serve their gods, it will surely be a snare unto thee.

There can be no doubt, the god depicted by the biblical verse above, is a tribal god, *that becomes a universal god by means of political/military conquest.* The crux, the central point of the covenant, as expressed above is that god promises territory and political sovereignty to the Hebrews if they will worship and obey him. The tribal gods prove their worth or superiority by bringing earthly success and domination to their subjects is the clear indication. The Jewish god admits the existence of other gods, according to these and other biblical verses, but declares that he Yahweh is the true and greater god. This is clearly a reflection of ancient tribal culture when primitive tribes sought protection and guidance from their tutelary deities and touted them in times of war or conflict. And hence the political/military successes of a tribe tended to vindicate the worthiness and power of their god and likewise expanded the theological presence of their deity concurrent with the political territorial expansion of the adherents to the tribal deity.

Aggression is inherent to monotheism - political, social, military and financial hostility and interference into the affairs of non-believers is central to this belief system - and the bible is adamant on this point. According to the bible non-believers should be killed and oppressed without mercy in this life by the true believers and are doomed to total annihilation or perhaps eternal suffering in the next life. Take note of these verses from the bible that verify my contention:

CHAPTER FIVE

Deuteronomy 13:1 through Deuteronomy 13:3

1If there arise among you a prophet, or a dreamer of dreams, and giveth thee a sign or a wonder, 2And the sign or the wonder come to pass, whereof he spake unto thee, saying, Let us go after other gods, which thou hast not known, and let us serve them; 3Thou shalt not hearken unto the words of that prophet, or that dreamer of dreams...

Deuteronomy 13:5 through Deuteronomy 13:9

5And that prophet, or that dreamer of dreams, <u>shall be put to death</u>; because he hath spoken to turn *you* away from the LORD your God...

6If thy brother, the son of thy mother, or thy son, or thy daughter, or the wife of thy bosom, or thy friend, which *is* as thine own soul, entice thee secretly, saying, Let us go and serve other gods, which thou hast not known, thou, nor thy fathers; 7*Namely*, of the gods of the people which *are* round about you, nigh unto thee, or far off from thee, from the *one* end of the earth even unto the *other* end of the earth; 8Thou shalt not consent unto him, nor hearken unto him; neither shall thine eye pity him, neither shalt thou spare, neither shalt thou conceal him: 9<u>But thou shalt surely kill him;</u> thine hand shall <u>be first upon him to put him to death</u>, and afterwards the hand of all the people.

Deuteronomy 13:12 through Deuteronomy 13:15

12If thou shalt hear *say* in one of thy cities, which the LORD thy God hath given thee to dwell there, saying, 13... Let us go and serve other gods, which ye have not known; 14<u>Then shalt thou inquire, and make search,</u> and ask diligently; and, behold, *if it be* truth, *and* the thing certain, *that* such abomination is wrought among you; 15Thou shalt surely <u>smite the inhabitants of that city with the edge of the sword, destroying it utterly,</u> and all that *is* therein, and the cattle thereof, with the edge of the sword.

According to our preachers and ministers, the bible is a direct revelation from god – and in his book (bible, torah, Quran) we are ordered by god almighty to murder those that do not share our belief. And not only are we ordered by this monotheistic god to kill non-believers, which is horror enough actually - but also, as indicated

CHAPTER FIVE

by verses 12 through 15, we are told to search out those that disbelieve, to make *inquisitions* into the affairs of the citizenry and to execute those that are proven wayward.

This, I contend, is the Terror Of Monotheism – intolerance, aggression and merciless hostility toward those that choose not to accept this primitive doctrine. **You must read further** on what god, according to the bible directs his servants to render unto non-believers:

Deuteronomy 7:2

²And when the LORD thy God shall deliver them before thee; <u>thou shalt smite them, *and* utterly destroy them; thou shalt make no covenant with them, nor show mercy unto them</u>:

Deuteronomy 7:5 through Deuteronomy 7:6

⁵But thus shall ye deal with them; ye shall destroy their altars, and break down their images, and cut down their groves, and burn their graven images with fire. ⁶For thou *art* an holy people unto the LORD thy God: the LORD thy <u>God hath chosen thee to be a special people unto himself, above all people that *are* upon the face of the earth.</u>

Deuteronomy 7:16

¹⁶And thou shalt consume all the people which the LORD thy God shall deliver thee; thine eye shall have no pity upon them: neither shalt thou serve their gods; for that *will be* a snare unto thee.

Deuteronomy 7:22 through Deuteronomy 7:25

²²And the LORD thy God will put out those nations before thee by little and little: thou mayest not consume them at once, lest the beasts of the field increase upon thee. ²³But the LORD thy God shall deliver them unto thee, and shall destroy them with a mighty destruction, until they be destroyed. ²⁴And he shall deliver their kings into thine hand, and <u>thou shalt destroy their name from under heaven: there shall no man be able to stand before thee, until thou have destroyed them.</u> ²⁵The graven images of their gods shall ye burn with fire: thou shalt not desire the silver or gold *that is* on them, nor take *it* unto thee, lest thou be snared therein: for it *is* an abomination to the LORD thy God.

CHAPTER FIVE

These verses are definite and unambiguous – the biblical god clearly directs his adherents to exact a scorched earth campaign against those that reject the doctrine of monotheism and would rather worship or not worship in accordance with their own individual consciousness. This war-god of monotheism even promises and urges his flock to consume and decimate the worlds disbelievers with planned precision, that is in degrees, step by malicious step, little by treacherous little is the biblical instruction. This, I contend is the terror of monotheism, the scourge of monotheism, that it is, at its religious core, a political (theocratic) system of forced indoctrination. It (monotheism) is fundamentally a form of imperialism or at the least an adjunct to imperialism, defined as a system of territorial expansion, nation building or the expansion of national influence – whether through direct control or through coercion. Sovereignty (legal government) gives the monotheists control of the body - and monotheistic doctrine itself gives them control of the mind and serves as a unifying national spirit. This is the hard truth that we must contend with, and place in proper perspective. And this, historically, has been a function of monotheistic doctrine, that is the enhancing of national and regional cohesion through cultural assimilation.

True biblical monotheism does not allow for peaceful coexistence with people or societies of different philosophical or religious persuasions. God's command to the monotheists, according to the bible, is to overcome them by stratagem or by direct aggression. This is the message of the biblical verses that I have submitted for your perusal, and this message rings with resounding clarity throughout the so-called Holy Scriptures of the Jews, Christians and Muslims. The Jews are certainly in compliance with this biblical godly directive. They (Hebrews) most certainly have a stratagem by which they have and are consuming the world of the gentiles, little by little as their god directs. The Christians and Muslims are also in compliance, as both have as cardinal tenets within their doctrines the advocacy of proselytization.

CHAPTER FIVE

In Conclusion

My overriding motivation in writing this series of books on the origin and evolution of religion has been to aid those that have perhaps languished in the same or similar quagmire of doubt and confusion that enwrapped me several years ago. About forty-five years ago, I began to have serious doubts about the veracity of religion. I noticed that traditional religion could not withstand probing intellectual analysis and I wondered why, if it is true and ordained by god.

It is psychologically jolting and traumatic to discover that the cherished beliefs and hopes of the masses of this planet are based on lies and deceit – illusions.

Even in this intellectual age of science and technological progress, most human beings are just as superstitious and irrational as our progenitors may have been at the dawn of civilization. It's amazing that even those that appear to be most intellectual are incapable of coming to grips with the truth of religion on a rational basis. They seem to fear the truth and look upon we who seek to analyze and evaluate religion scientifically as enemies of the faith. Some say that we researchers and analysts are inspired by the devil and are possessed by evil demonic spirits – and this is the 21st century! It seems unreasonable to me that religion should be exempt from critical analysis, but this seems to be the opinion of the vast majority. I have been told that I must allow my faith to overcome reason, that this is the test of true belief and submission to god's will. Such a course is incomprehensible to me, but in fact the majority chooses to live by faith rather than reason and perhaps that is their fate as well as their choice. **I don't believe that the majority of humanity will ever understand**, accept or come to grips with divine truth – my definition of divine truth is *that* which does not attempt to defy nature. Nature tends to weed out and destroy all that defies it or counteracts its purposes – only truth (compliance with natural law) can successfully advance from stage to stage under the tests of nature. This is my guide, I can see no other way.

After all this time of research and investigation and evaluation of religious symbolism and allegory, I stand convinced of one reality

CHAPTER FIVE

– that we are indeed the children of Providence, not chance. We humans are the product of a Creative Intelligence that we shall never fathom – but our natural and eternal quest must forever be for knowledge of the Creative Intelligence that spawned us. The Ancients have preserved much truth for us under the veil of myth and fable. It is very interesting that the search for truth aims backward and not forward. I have covered much in this series of four books and *this is the final of the series*. Much has been written and much remains unwritten.

EPILOGUE

Epilogue

The Dawn of Intellectual Consciousness

We have covered most of what I wanted to cover in this 2nd Edition of this book; a continuation of the subject matter can be found in my book, *Lifting The Gnostic Veil*. However there are some comments that I would like to add, exegetically, on the subject of *Creation*, which we covered in Chapter 3. I would like to take us to *another level* on this very important subject. We have been taught by our cultures that CREATION MARKS THE BEGINNING OF TIME, the bringing of the world into existence - but according to some of the ancient wise ones, the world is actually eternal, without beginning or end. Just as god has no beginning, likewise the universe has no beginning. The universe is likened to the body of god, or a material reflection of the numinous dynamics of god; of course by the term *god*, we mean source, generator, spark, spirit or the like, *not a personal god* that can be identified by name or religion.

We find in one of the seven Principles of Hermes that the universe is structured in repetitive *Patterns*, that throughout the universe (above and below) the same Patterns, at infinite levels of manifestations, are repeated throughout - some translations may use the term *Correspondences*, or *Parallelism*, or something similar - I prefer the term *Patterns*. In line with our focus on *repetitive patterns*, I also wrote in my book, *The Biggest Lie Ever Told 4th Edition*, the following: *"I should mention at this juncture that Natural Truth (that is truth governed and in accord with divine and natural law, i.e.. God's creative law) is as a Spiral ascending from a Divinely perfected core. Each level of the spiral, expanding to infinity, represents a different Level of Truth."* …

WE ALSO FIND amongst the Hermetic Principles that the universe is actually *Mental*, a mental reality, a reality or perception of reality

EPILOGUE

existing within the Mind of the *All;* some may use the term *Mentalism* to describe this perception. *The All* is often described as God or the *Mind of God* - that sounds very profound, but actually takes us nowhere, except into a bigger mystery than we started out with; I think that the theory that we are *living in the Mind of god* produces more questions than answers for the rational individual. I think we need to break this truth down to a degree whereas our rational minds can logically comprehend it - what good is truth, if it's too mysterious to be understood?

Let's review some tangential remarks that I wrote in Chapter 3 concerning Creation: "THERE NEVER WAS A TIME WHEN THE WORLD WAS NOT - this is a difficult concept for the human brain to handle, but in reality it is no more difficult to conceive. than the concept of the world popping into existence from out of nowhere by reason of deified proclamation. Truthfully, not even the bible declares that the universe was created ex nihilo - the bible presupposes the preexistence of Matter, how be it, this Matter was unformed and seemingly ungoverned. "

I HAVE UNDERLINED the sentence above that expresses a very important and salient factor concerning the Egyptian and biblical renditions of Creation, both versions acknowledge the preexistence of Matter and/or Water before the Creation took place. The circumstance that preceded Creation was an Abyss of Darkness and Chaos according to Egyptian and biblical literature. Witness also this following snippet from Chapter 3, "The underlying occult truth of much of Genesis reflects an abyss of seemingly chaotic cosmic disorder or lack in human psychic perception that stunned and prevailed before the birth or evolution of intellectual Man (Mind), a disorder or chaos that was *transformed* into psychic order or form by the *emergence* of human *consciousness,* into the abstract, emerged from out of the depths of the unknown or unconscious, the symbolic Nu" ... Now, from the information that I have offered above, I believe that we are ready to extrapolate some profound, cogent and rational conclusions a priori.

EPILOGUE

First off, I should repeat the premise of the Ancients that the Universe is eternal, that it has always existed, that there is no beginning. The universe is alleged to be eternal, an eternal fire that feeds on its own waste, or self, or by-product as symbolized by the *Serpent Uroboros* shown in a cycle (circle) of feeding on its own tail. The universe is the divine *Matrix* itself, the Eternal Fire fueled by innumerable flames of burning gaseous fire-balls (Suns or Stars) that burn and rekindle themselves throughout eternity, without beginning or end. The individual fire-balls (stars) may wither or explode, or go super-nova thus dying and initiating fuel cycles for the births of new stars, but nevertheless the whole flaming universal conglomeration is constant, endless, infinite, and eternal.

OF PRIMARY IMPORTANCE to our analysis is the root meaning of the word *Man*. It is the Creation of Man that capped off the creation of the world in the sixth day according to the bible, so the root or fundamental definition of the term Man is vital. The term *Man* is etymologically linked to the Sanskrit term *Manu* which carries the attribute *To Think*. According to Hindu mythology MANU WAS THE FIRST MAN, the first human created and the progenitor of mankind. The etymology of the word Man takes us to Thinker, Mind, Spirit and the like; but more importantly the word *Man* (Man = Mind) points the way to *abstract thinking* - this is the category of thinking that separates Man from all other beings on Earth and even from the compulsive geotic brutes that coexist with and among the numinous human beings. Some animals *think* (at the functional level) but only relative to their survival and pleasure - nothing else; this is indicative of animal or geotic nature, wherein the numinous element is not detectable but suppressed, or underdeveloped; however it is *abstract thinking* that causes Man to look to the heavens and wonder why! This level of self-conscious abstract thinking sets Man into a class of his own, by endowing Man with intellectual curiosity of everything; this includes the spiritual as well as the mundane. The elevated Man is not enslaved to the passions of the flesh, he believes in the unseen as well as the seen, he *senses* a need for spiritual

EPILOGUE

nutrition as well as physical nutrition. Numinous Man is not mesmerized by materialism to the point whereas he can't get enough - he understands that it is he, for the sake of his true self, that must subdue the world, and not fall victim to the wiles of Satan[1] (Nature).

However Man has not always been the advanced thinker that he is today, he was, once upon a time, no more than a smart animal, an ape-man that thought only of survival and pleasures as do all other lower animals. Some say that it took the *earthly environment* and the *numinous teleological forces* millions of years to evolve Man to the status of Wise Man or Homo Sapiens. Before his intellectual ascension, Man (Mind) gestated or was bound in the abyss of darkness and chaos of the unconscious, and was *indistinct from the unconscious*[2], and was driven by the instinctive impulses of the unconscious as are all other animals.

Some of the ancient Gnostic writers say that God looked from afar(in heaven) at the plight of Man, suffering at the whims of Yaltabaoth, his original creator, and had mercy on Man; and hence, God sent his essence or numen (light), which embedded itself into the psyche of Man, therefore functioning as a savior or saving force so as to enlighten the Man - of course, such a scenario is mythology[3], even though it rings with very potent symbolism, which we shall explore in due course. Be that as it may, our focus at the present is *Creation*

---

[1] The root meaning of the term Satan is *adversary*- the eternal adversary of Man is Nature itself. Realistically and Esoterically it is Nature that eternally opposes the rise and survival of Man (Intellectual Mind). Satan (Nature) is the blind god of Matter that instinctively seeks to destroy or harness any force within its domain that it detects as deviant or nonconforming. I give further explanation of this issue in my book *Lifting The Gnostic Veil.*

[2] The unconscious is that aspect of the human psyche that controls and instigates all actions of the body, in the background so to speak, below the awareness of the conscious.

[3] This message of God transferring his essence into Man, as a saving force, can be found, *in very Arcane form*, in Gnostic literature such as the Apocryphon of John

EPILOGUE

and the seminal connection that Creation has with the intellectual advancement of Man to the point of *Abstract Consciousness*, that is to say, the type of Consciousness that envisions *beyond* the natural norms of human biology and its interactions within its habitat. Abstract Consciousness causes Man, enwrapped with boundless curiosity, to question his place in the universe; to look deeply into the marvels of his universe, with wonderment of how and why it developed, and to question who or what was its creator. Before the dawn of intellectual consciousness mankind had no such thoughts as I have just described. Before the *emergence* of Abstract Consciousness into the *psychic complex*, the geotic man's thinking was limited to earthly pursuits revolving around survival and pleasure, as with all other animals.

With the *emergence* of the intellectual Man (Mind) from out of the *unconscious Nun*, Man, that is to say the *ego-self*, became a new creation, but not only a creation, the Man became also a *Creator*, a new sovereign within his earthly domain. Man,as earthly sovereign, was granted the authority to Create a whole new world, a world totally *structured as a reflection of his Conscious Perceptions*. This truth is reflected at the lower exoteric level of myth within Genesis of the bible: note the following:

Genesis 1:26-28 <u>And God said, Let us make man in our image, after our likeness: and let them have dominion</u> over the fish of the sea, and over the fowl of the air, and over the cattle, and <u>over all the earth</u>, and over every creeping thing that creepeth upon the earth. So God created man in his own image, in the image of God created he him; male and female created he them. And God blessed them, and God said unto them, Be fruitful, and multiply, and replenish the earth, <u>and subdue it:</u> and have dominion over the fish of the sea, and over the fowl of the air, and over every living thing that moveth upon the earth.

IN THE ABOVE biblical verses, Man is made *vicegerent* of the Earth and is given the *authority* to *rule* it and also to *subdue* it to his service - this is momentous! Man (Mind) is, according to the biblical

EPILOGUE

text, made in the image of God, and *bestowed with the power of a god* as it concerns the sublunary world. LET ME REITERATE what I wrote earlier in the book: "One significant hint as to the sensible interpretation of creation is given in the bible. In Genesis 2 verses 19 and 20, whereas god gives Adam the authority to name the elements of creation i.e. animals, trees etc. The actual first cause or creation that humankind witnessed is the one that man participated in and actually governed, that is *creation born out of discernment*. When mankind came on the scene, so to speak, the world existed as an amorphous mass, and that was chaos. The lack of designations and boundaries and sections and titles engenders social and developmental chaos. When man first gazed upon the starry heavens, witnessing that great mass of billions of undesignated untitled unnamed lights, he was viewing from within the darkness of intellectual chaos. But when he (Man) began to group those lights into constellations and permanently name the constellations and the stars – that action was the first creation. Something that did not exist before had been created out of chaos – that is the discernment and permanent naming of the star groups and stars actually created those elements conceptually. The same goes for all parts of nature – take the forest for example made up of thousands of types of trees – when the types are undesignated chaos ensues. But when Man delves into the forest and examines and discerns the different types of trees – each time he names a tree, it has in intellectual fact been created. Man is the father of creation when we understand its true fundamental and practical meaning. That which accurately defines the world's creation is a very important subject that is grossly misunderstood by most "

NAMES, NUMBERS, AND GEOGRAPHIC CONFIGURATIONS are all abstracts, *not* natural realities; their reality is held only in the mind. It is by these abstracts that Man (Mind) is able to label, organize, and *intellectually produce the semblance of order in an otherwise, apparently, chaotic milieu*. It is through the use of these abstracts

EPILOGUE

that Man has created a world that exist and is sustained only by Man's ability to hold this world concept within the Conscious, within the Collective Conscious. Without Man (Mind) the world that we know and perceive would disintegrate into nothingness, that is to say, become unrecognizable. The world would become unrecognizable because absent the *perceiver* the world would not be *perceived* or *conceptualized* from within the Cosmic Inner Sanctum of Earth. The ancient wise ones have pronounced repeatedly, this world is an illusion - that is exactly right, the world that we know or perceive is a product or reflection of the Mind's conscious projection upon the milieu that enfolds us. The world that we perceive has been crafted or carved into the Mind's own internal reality as the Mind (Man) perceives it. This is exactly in accord with the Hermetic Principle that states unequivocally that the world is Mental, that is to say, the world that we perceive is actually a projection of the Conscious Mind, a mental conceptualized internal reality. I made similar observations in another of my books - See quote from my book, *Lifting The Gnostic Veil*:

"**This world is an illusion,** both physically and spiritually. An illusion is defined as a misconception, a false appearance, an error in perception; a condition of being deceived by a false perception. Indeed, physically this world is an illusion, because our perception of reality is not determined by the *underlying* reality itself but rather by the interpretations that our sensory organs relay to us of this phenomenal world. We are actually not capable of perceiving the *ultimate* physical reality with our five senses, because we are limited by the *interpretive readings* of our senses. Our scientists teach us that some animals, insects, and fishes do not see the world as we see it because in some cases their sensory organs are made differently or calibrated at different frequencies than our own. So what is the *true* appearance of the world, when it is obvious that if nature or god had altered or recalibrated our sensory capabilities to different levels and/or perceptions, the world would appear different without really *being* different? Is the world we perceive a true representation of what is really there, or is it an illusion, an interface that transmits signals and impressions to us in accordance with the calibration and tuning of our senses - without ever revealing its *true self*? "

EPILOGUE

WE ALL HAVE GAZED upon the starry heavens at night, in awe of the spectacle. We fancy and marvel at the sights of the zodiac and the multiple constellations, whose recorded configurations, stretch back into ancient history. Actually, in truth, none of these constellations, as perceived, actually exist - there is no Orion or Big Dipper or any other star group that has an existence outside of our consciousness. Man (Mind) has created these star-groups so as to bring order out of chaos, so that we can navigate the skies. The constellations are all mental concepts, existing only within the Collective Conscious - they are not physical realities. So much of what we call reality, *including our gods*, are only concepts with absolutely no existence outside of the Consciousness of Man - these conjured concepts amount to nothing (no-thing), if not for the consciousness of Man which has evoked them into life or mental substance within the human psyche, the Mind.

WE COUNT the *time* of the day and night, the week, the month, the year, the centuries, the millennia going forward and backward in time. But time itself is an illusion, *our version* of time is suited only to our existence and ours alone. It is Man (Mind) that needed time as a measurement so as to successfully navigate through the abyss of chaos that we, Man, encountered when Man (Conscious Mind) first came on the scene. We tracked the movements of the heavenly lights, the Moon, the Sun, and consequently we, *Man, created Time*; we divided the cycles of the sun into seconds, minutes, hours, days, years, and thousands, millions, and billions of years. We have recorded histories going back thousands of years in time; we project into the future in accordance with time. Again, all of the aforementioned are abstracts that have no existence or utility outside of the human conscious.

Before Man emerged into Abstract Consciousness, our world, from our mental perspective, did not exist in a coherent form; that which existed was chaos and disorder. All of the myriad cosmic and terrestrial interactions that we now witness were dynamically active

EPILOGUE

but seemingly random. Concurrently with the *emergence* of Man and the birth of intellectual consciousness, this abyss of chaos and darkness was destroyed and replaced with a new world of time and order; *this occurred in reflection of the Mind* that projected its consciousness into the worldly abyss and accordingly created and shaped the world as a fit for the consciousness of Man. Before the emergence of Intellectual Consciousness, there was no witness to intellectually record the existence of our world from the inside of the complex, but with the advent of Man, the world was brought into consciousness and hence into Creation or existence, indeed we carry the world upon our shoulders. The universe is eternal, it is not subject to creation or destruction. It, the world, is in a constant state of *Becoming; it is that which it is* - it is dynamic, constantly generating, decaying, and regenerating eternally. The only Creation (recognizable new world) that is possible is the Creation that comes with the birth of Intellectual Consciousness.

For untold years, many have uttered that oft-repeated Hermetic dictum *The World is Mental* without really having a rational understanding of the true potency of that sagacious pronouncement. They have, perhaps, entertained some mystical, *amorphous thoughts* that applaud the profundity of the precept, but amorphous thoughts often have no useful application in the practical world.
In the foregoing I have attempted to convey the rational underpinning of the ancient, esoteric and profound wisdom contained therein, expounding it as *not* mere rhetoric but rather as cogent and enduring truth.

Malik H Jabbar

Closing Remarks

Thus far, over several years, I have written seven books on the subject of *Astro-Theology*; those books being **The Biggest Lie Ever Told**. **The Astrological Foundation Of The Christ Myth** *in 4 volumes*, **Lifting The Gnostic Veil**, and **The Secret Origins Of Judaism**. All of these books are focused on the theological science of astro-theology. IT IS MY INTENTION to offer two more books on the subject so as to complete *this initial phase* of our investigation into the subject, in-line with this new perspective that we have offered.

We are in search of truth, but not an *absolute truth*. Personally I don't accept the notion of an absolute truth or doctrine, because *absolute* indicates that which is *complete* and *final*, and *thought* to be beyond improvement or enhancement. The notion of finality, as I see it, contradicts that which I consider an *eternal truth*, and that is, that *we are eternally in a state of becoming*. Nothing is static, all is dynamic - even the truth. After all, what is truth - other than a *perspective* that satisfies the intellect at a given point and time in our evolution. To be continued…

Book Four Index

A

B

C

D

E

F

G

N

O

P

Q

R

S

T

U

Underworld 74-76, 103, 107, 108, 110, 112, 117, 119, 121, 135-138
Universe   26, 122, 134, 187, 192, 193, 195

V

Vernal Equinox 31, 36, 57, 63, 74, 75, 80, 89-90, 110, 112, 116-118, 120, 136, 138, 161, 168, 170, 174, 176, 186-187
Virgin   20, 113
Virgo   91, 139, 167

W

Water 48, 50, 56, 59-61, 85, 88-90, 116, 119, 127, 129, 168, 169, 178, 180
Week   30, 40, 41
Wilderness 61, 62, 89, 90, 107, 108, 112, 115, 117, 119, 165, 175, 176, 182, 187
Winter Solstice   57, 75, 187
Woman 48, 49, 62, 63, 75-76, 83-85, 107, 108, 111-112, 116, 117, 119
World   209
worship   20, 113, 135, 166, 178, 184, 192, 197, 200

Y

Yahweh   111, 195, 197
Yom Hadin   165, 182, 186
Yom Kippur   161, 165, 182

Z

Zacharius   81, 169
Zeus   130
Zodiac   19, 31, 75, 117, 123, 127, 177